DISCREPANT DISLOCATIONS

DISCREPANT DISLOCATIONS

*Feminism, Theory, and
Postcolonial Histories*

MARY E. JOHN

UNIVERSITY OF CALIFORNIA PRESS
BERKELEY   LOS ANGELES   LONDON

University of California Press
Berkeley and Los Angeles, California

University of California Press, Ltd.
London, England

An earlier version of chapter 1 appeared in "Post-colonial
Feminists in the Western Intellectual Field: Anthropologists
and Native Informants?" in *Inscriptions, Traveling Theories,
Traveling Theorists* 5 (1989): 49–74.

Library of Congress Cataloging-in-Publication Data

John, Mary E., 1956–
    Discrepant dislocations : feminism, theory, and
  postcolonial histories / Mary E. John.
      p. cm.
    Includes bibliographic references (p.   ) and index
    ISBN 0-520-20135-3 (alk. paper). — ISBN 0-520-20136-1
  (pbk. : alk. paper)
    1. Feminist theory.   2. Intercultural communication.
  3. Cross-cultural orientation.   I. Title.
  HQ1190.J62   1996
  305.42'01—dc20   95-12580
                                        CIP

Printed in the United States of America
9 8 7 6 5 4 3 2 1

To my parents,
Juliane H. John
and
E. C. John

Contents

Acknowledgments

It is difficult to find an adequate way to acknowledge all the friends, colleagues and teachers who have helped make this book a reality.

Donna Haraway's intellectual and political commitment to a more accountable and composite feminism has been unforgettable. Crucial also has been James Clifford's sensitivity to the predicaments of cross-cultural academic work. I owe much to the guidance of Carolyn Clark, Teresa de Lauretis, David C. Hoy and David M. Schneider. Without the warmth of Billie Harris, and also of Sheila Peuse, studying at UCSC would have lost much of its special quality.

Nothing made my graduate years in California more meaningful than the friends who, in their different ways, provided support and comradeship: Ronaldo Balderrama, Faith Beckett, Vince Diaz, Ruth Frankenberg, Kathy Hattori, Lata Mani, Brinda Rao, Chela Sandoval, David Scott, Marita Sturken, Ananthram Swami, and Yumi Yang. I owe a unique debt to a special group of students, particularly Claudia Castaneda, Margaret Daniel, Ramona Fernandez, Nanci Luna-Jimenéz, and Kristal Zook, who brought hope of new alliances. Friendships old and new in India, especially with K. Lalita, Janaki Nair, R. Srivatsan, D. Vasantha, Rajeswari Sunder Rajan, and Susie Tharu have been sustaining me and helped me to finish this book. I am particularly grateful to Vivek Dhareshwar for all the intellectual inspiration he has shared at so many moments. Tejaswini Niranjana has been of invaluable help in thinking about our postcolonial trajectories over the years.

To little Apoorv, whose arrival threatened to postpone indefinitely the completion of the manuscript, my gratitude for not having disrupted my working life entirely. But for Satish Deshpande, this book would not have been possible.

Special thanks to Naomi Schneider at the University of California Press and to Ruth Behar, Kamala Visweswaran, and the other anonymous readers of the manuscript for their generosity and encouragement.

Hyderabad
January 1995

Introduction

The conjunctures of the nineties have been critical for a number of political initiatives and intellectual projects, and feminism is clearly among them. Tensions, conflicts, and challenges of all kinds—some would even call them crises—characterize feminist work in many parts of the world. The essays brought together here traverse the contemporary feminist field by charting a passage between India and the United States. Taking their cue from recent debates around colonialism and nationalism, they attempt to interrogate the theoretical and political claims embedded in feminist scholarship in order to broaden the frames of reference within which such claims must be evaluated in a rapidly changing international context.

One of the notions third-world intellectuals have brought into circulation in the wake of their encounter with Western locations and theories (especially poststructuralism) is "the postcolonial." The term has borne varied, even conflicting meanings. It has sometimes been used as a marker underlining the dislocations experienced by third-world intellectuals residing in the first world; at other times, it has functioned as the label for an epoch, referring to the careers and cultures of the ex-colonies after their emergence as independent nations. "Postcolonial" has even been turned into a universalizing description of the contemporary predicaments of the globe as a whole.

This study does not set itself the task of adjudicating between these uses. Instead, it tries to render more productive the constellation of intellectual and political forces that made the notion of the postcolonial possible in the first place. The point is to see what discrepancies become visible when theories are understood as being bound up with historical locations—within the West as much as within the postcolony. The power of the West is manifested, of course, in its ability to project its influence beyond its own geonational borders—to render selectively permeable the boundaries of *other* states and nations. As a consequence, the lives of peoples everywhere have been enmeshed in transformative processes for centuries now. Even emancipatory programs such as the feminist one have not remained immune to this geopolitical configuration.

In this book I trace a series of responses to the experiences of Western domination from personal, political, and theoretical perspectives. Each chapter opens up the West to a different kind of reading in order to prepare the ground for alternate theorizations of the divergences and connections between feminists in the United States and India. The stage is set in chapter one through a discussion of the subject positions available to third-world feminists in the first world. The anthropological imperative to translate other cultures for the West can turn postcolonial feminists into "third-world women" for first-world agendas. Living in the West, however, has also offered an opportunity: to reverse the flow of information, and to alter its content, by stressing those aspects of U.S. feminist culture that would normally not reach an Indian audience.

Chapter two takes up the institution of "theory," which has been so decisive for feminist and postcolonial scholarship. "Theory"— here shorthand for the broad orientations enabled in part by poststructuralism—is a recent entrant in the Western intellectual field to have been accorded a global identity, cutting across disciplines. I argue, in an effort to make such theory give up its universalistic assumptions, that postcolonial and feminist theorists need to become more aware of the partial and composite characteristics of the theories they depend on. Greater self-reflexivity about the biases, discrepant registers, and different forms of analysis of "theory" will, I believe, enable it to "travel" better into the postcolony. Such considerations could also be a useful corrective to relativistic moves that look upon "East" and "West" as unconnected entities, to be somehow understood in their own indigenous terms.

U.S. feminist theory is the focus of chapter three. Expanding upon arguments and concerns expressed in the previous chapters, I use a historical, genealogical approach to examine the rise of gender as a new category of analysis within the conjunctures of the eighties and nineties in the U.S. academy. The oft-repeated slogan calling for the integration of gender with race, class, and sexuality provides no clues to the often divergent or asymmetrical trajectories of these terms in their relation to feminist scholarship and politics. Given the conflicts around difference that characterize U.S. feminism today, an examination of the conceptual and historical constraints governing the use of such terms is vital. Moreover, because the international circulation of scholarship is directly related to what is dominant in the geographical West, an understanding of the heterogeneous character of U.S. feminism is an indispensable step toward a more far-reaching and critical exchange between feminists in India and the United States than has been possible so far. I have been particularly concerned with questions of race and the demands of women of color, both for what they tell us about Western culture and in the belief that these issues might speak to the impasses besetting contemporary feminist debates in India.

Chapter four makes the transition from the United States to India, as the site from which I write. In chapter one, the metaphor of anthropology is employed to highlight aspects of the multiple subject positions of a third-world feminist in the first world. Anthropology is taken up somewhat differently in chapter four to discuss the largely suppressed issue of national location. Using recent debates in Western feminist ethnography as a wedge, I try to show how inequalities between first- and third-world locations translate into an association of feminism with the West. It would seem from these ethnographic debates that only "women" live in the third world—not the institutions or subjects of feminism. Most of the chapter, therefore, concentrates on some of the crucial dimensions of feminist scholarship that emerged in connection with the present postindependence phase of the women's movement in India. As in chapter three, my perspective is a historical one: starting in the seventies, I trace the shifts in frameworks necessitated in the eighties and especially in the nineties as feminism in India has been responding to—and influencing the course of—profound changes in the country.

This book has been in the making over a historically significant period of time. The first three chapters were written in the United States between 1989 and 1991—between the collapse of the Berlin Wall and the onset of the Gulf War. The final chapter was largely conceived in India a few years later, during a period of unprecedented national transformation. Each of the chapters has its own theme and mode of approach. At the same time, they do not stand alone but are meant to be read together. Indeed, they need one another in order to substantiate a set of interrelated claims about differences, linkages, and power relations in contemporary feminist scholarship.

Questions of location are becoming increasingly elusive today, historically and theoretically. Whether it be the ambivalent meanings embedded in the term "postcolonial" or the contemporary processes of globalization (to which the Indian nation is a latecomer), the present trend seems marked by an unwillingness to recognize nations as places defined by difference and domination. Thus, for instance, the urban middle classes in India today seek to erase their colonial past by claiming to have the same right as anyone else to the images, goods, and lifestyles of "the world." Meanwhile, many of their emigrant sisters and brothers in countries like the United States attempt to compensate for their cultural dislocations by cultivating a variety of fundamentalisms that collude strangely with those of their counterparts at home.

The following chapters do not simply seek to reverse such global currents. The time when national identity could be claimed easily seems to have gone, especially for feminists. In attempting to think through the realities of Western power, and by affirming a politics of location, I have tried to conceive of the beginnings of an alternate internationalism for feminist theorists who wish to be equally accountable to unequal places.

Chapter One

Postcolonial Feminists in the Western Intellectual Field

Anthropologists and Native Informants?

What makes us decide we have to re-educate ourselves,
even those of us with "good" educations?
> Adrienne Rich,
> *Notes toward a Politics of Location*

As for how I came to be in Delhi, these were for reasons
. . . that have more to do with an "unexamined life."
> Gayatri Chakravorty Spivak,
> *The Post-colonial Critic*

In the first world and elsewhere, the tasks of intellectuals are increasingly being questioned. Whether couched in the older terminology of the "universal" intellectual or the claims and potential of "specific" intellectuals, the debate shows few signs of coming to a close. Michel Foucault, from whom I borrow these distinctions, has quite possibly been the latter's most persuasive proponent. He has argued for a mode of critical political activity based on a specific relation to local power through expertise. With uncharacteristic optimism, the particularities of such an intellectual's field of specialization could, he felt, connect up with the general functioning of the production of truth, especially given that the university plays such a privileged role:

[T]ransverse connections have been able to develop between different areas of knowledge, from one focus of politicisation to another: magistrates and psychiatrists, doctors and social workers, laboratory workers and sociologists have been able, each in his own field and through mutual exchange and support, to participate in a global process of politicisation of intellectuals.[1]

5

What "global process" is Foucault referring to? Moreover, what further questions could one raise about the *specificity* of such specific intellectuals? I have in mind not just their social and intellectual history but also their very site of enunciation, their location and audience—issues that in Foucault's scheme of things (for all the attention he once paid to the formation of enunciative modalities) remain unexamined. As a third-world feminist who initiated these reflections while studying "theory" in the first world as a doctoral student, how might I take the following commitment seriously?

[A]t every moment, step by step, one must confront what one is thinking and saying with what one is doing, *with what one is*. . . . I have always been concerned with linking together as tightly as possible the historical and theoretical analysis of power relations, institutions and knowledge, to the movements, critiques, and experiences that call them into question in reality.[2]

In the contexts of U.S. feminist theory and politics as I have come to know them, the call has gone out for quite some time now that the way to engage in such a confrontation is by *positioning* oneself along the "axes of race, class, gender and sexuality." Doing so would yield the following inventory in my case: upper middle class, heterosexual woman, Indian national. Many have highlighted the ritualistic and, therefore, dissatisfying aspects of such exercises; such criticism may help account for the limited number of actual examples available. Also, as Maivân Clech Lâm has recently pointed out, the pressure to mark and locate oneself is far greater on scholars of color than on those who are white. She goes on to add that life's trajectories simply cannot be cast into something as geometric as positionality.[3] In my view, the pointillistic and static connotation of "positions," however multiple and contradictory they may be, elides the need to confront "what one is" through a more extensive questioning of the entanglements of one's history within History.[4] Such questioning must be broached by historicizing the present and one's place within it. The ironies that accompany the following interrogation, initiated in the United States, a country placed at the culmination of History, should not be lost on anyone. But perhaps such a mode of self-location is one way to make a connection between one's claims as a "specific" feminist intellectual and the realization that one's site of enunciation is both a home and a historical choice.

Departure

Let me begin, then, with a sketch of an Indian intellectual's formation and her choice to go westward, to make the West her site of enunciation. Such a decision is, without a doubt, overdetermined by class aspirations. Though the characterization of the economy of a society such as India's has been the subject of exhaustive and unflagging debate (are we semifeudal, capitalist, something else?), the nature of the Indian middle class—the composition of the petty bourgeoisie and intelligentsia—has not been studied with the same zeal. A common point of reference is the peculiar nature of its development as a class under colonial rule, beginning in the eighteenth century. Here is a standard description:

The British attempted as part of their educational policy to create a class comparable to their own, so that it might assist them in the administration of the country and help in the development of its internal resources, necessary for the payment of the increasing imports of British manufacture. . . . These ideas and institutions of a middle class social order . . . were implanted in the country without a comparable development in its economy and social institutions.[5]

The main reason this description is so standard is that it takes the social structure of the West as its norm. Keeping the beginnings of the British middle classes as backdrop—where the rapid expansion in trade and industry threw up a concomitant group of professionals—the dissimilarity of the Indian case stands out in sharp silhouette. Our antecedents emerged within, and were transformed by, an economy that, far from creating an autonomous home market, was subjected to a colonial machinery for the development of empire elsewhere. Of course, it should go without saying that the Indian middle classes were (and are) a heterogeneous group, landed and mercantilist as much as professional and administrative. It is a sign of my own bias that this opening chapter expressly concentrates on the sliver of the middle class we have come to designate as the intelli-

gentsia—indeed, to construe matters more narrowly still, on those
within the intellectual field structured by academic institutions.

At least among the intellectual avant garde, it has become increasingly common to question the notion of development, with its
underlying implication that Western history is the only model of
progress. Yet in listening to a discussion on the self-conceptions of
the Indian intelligentsia—here, between the Indian art critic Geeta
Kapur and the Sri Lankan feminist Laleen Jayamanne—one has to
think carefully about the kind of rupture the intervening centuries and the achievement of political independence have wrought.
Drawing upon a distinction between social and cultural processes of
modernization, the two scholars laud cultural processes as being
"several steps ahead," "not hav[ing] to bear the burden of 'under-
development' or remain backward with regard to the 'developed'
world," a "congenial and hopeful situation for so-called 'developing'
countries."[6] Though the use of scare quotes is meant to question
evaluations of development, these critics end up—no doubt uncon-
sciously—reinscribing them instead, thus enacting a deep schizo-
phrenia. A pious wish that matters were otherwise would be out of
place. We should simply acknowledge the extent to which connections can be drawn between Macaulay's group of "interpreters" in
his famous Minute on Education of 1835,[7] and the contemporary
intelligentsia, a class now investing in a Western education in order
to qualify for membership within the new international cultural
bourgeoisie.

The depth of the ideological creation of "the West" in India's
history, to which a postcolonial feminist such as me is an heir, can
perhaps find no more vivid and ironic depiction than that the
discipline of "English studies" had its very inception and beginnings
in nineteenth-century colonial India, prior to its institutionalization
in Britain itself.[8] In Ashis Nandy's words, therefore, the modern
West is less a geographical or temporal entity than a psychological
space (and surely a social, economic, and cultural space as well):
"The West is now everywhere, within the West and outside: in
structures and in minds."[9] What name, then, might one give to such
a configuration of "the West" as a transnational category, capable of
extending beyond geographical determinations and creating new

and specific loci of power/knowledge through the manifold processes of Westernization?

If the historical formation of the class that effectively came to direct the Indian nation is often alluded to, so is the conspicuous presence of women among its professional ranks. One of the legacies of the Indian nationalist movement is that middle and upper class women have been less invisible within academic and public institutions than their counterparts in the geographical West. To give a particularly striking historical example, two women graduated from Calcutta University in 1883, *before* women in Britain were granted academic credentials. Or think of Toru Dutt (1856–1877), who published her first book of verse translations, *A Sheaf Gleaned from French Fields*, at the age of twenty. This was by no means an uncomplicated process of Westernization—it was precisely such women who were subjected to profoundly modern reinventions of tradition in the battle for a national culture.[10]

In the oft-cited case of Bengal, for example, Partha Chatterjee has referred to the literal domestication of the nationalist project within the home, combined with a general demand for formal education of middle class women:

Formal education became not only acceptable, but in fact a requirement for the new *bhadramahila* (respectable woman), when it was demonstrated that it was possible for a woman to acquire the cultural refinements afforded by modern education without jeopardising her place at home, i.e. without becoming a *memsahib* (Englishwoman).[11]

How might one unravel specifically feminist mobilizations by women such as these in such a complex web of contending forces and scrambled discourses of modernity and tradition? Dealing as we are with a vastly uneven and unequal exchange between patriarchies, it is tempting to conclude, as Kumari Jayawardena has done, that

revolutionary alternatives or radical social changes did not become an essential part of the demands of the nationalist movement at any stage of the long struggle for independence, and a revolutionary feminist consciousness did not arise within the movement for national liberation.[12]

At this preliminary stage in my reflections, my purpose is less to dwell on the need for more careful evaluations of the colonial past

than to recognize moments of continuity between my history and
this obviously oversimplified—to a degree, deliberately so—sketch
of an earlier time. Looking back on my own intellectual formation as
a "daughter of independence," I am struck by the extent to which I
could take the presence of women as peers and teachers for granted,
even as powerful and diverse struggles by women were taking
place, albeit overwhelmingly outside academic walls. There can be
no question that men are still far more likely to know the prestige
and privileges that professional qualifications bring.[13] Even so,
some of the more ambitious among us have pushed for inclusion
within the deceptively unmarked spaces of the new international
class; given the often impossible complexities of our personal identities, we can experience the promise of modernity this class holds
out, its "independence" from gender and culture, as a special lure.
Under the circumstances of the continuing satellite status of third-
world educational systems, the subsequent move to a U.S. academic institution is then but a culmination of processes already in
place at home, where the geographical West represents the obvious
goal in the pursuit of excellence.

Indeed, a closer look at my own generation of academic women,
born well after Indian independence, reveals new twists in the
mixed legacy of modernity and tradition. If earlier generations, still
overwhelmingly formed within the private sphere, wrestled much
more closely with the hub of "tradition" bequeathed by the nineteenth century, marking their subjectivity in terms of degrees of
containment within its frames—the home, religiosity, community,
caste, and so on[14]—"the West" has normed the questions and desires of postindependence women differently. In ways that will be
amplified in chapter four, the imperative to Westernize in postindependence India came coded within the institutions, structures, and
terminologies of modernization, progress, and secularism. These
provided a space for some middle class women to articulate themselves beyond the confines of prior constructs of "tradition" and
especially to take advantage of the mobilities of education. I might
only be arguing for a shift in the complex of forces, a shift that has
been possible partly because of refurbished Western connections in
our educational system since the electronic revolution, especially

after the dwarfing of Britain by the United States as "our" contemporary metropolis. The promises of the new class have never been as fully emblazoned in the languages of English and the sciences as they are today. Formal education is, after all, also a process by which we learn to avow and remember certain knowledges and devalue and forget others. We grow up repudiating the local and the personal in favor of what will get us ahead and away—thus coming of age within an intellectual field that, by no means arbitrarily, creates disinterest and oversight in some areas and directs desire elsewhere. It is within such an interlocking mechanism for the production of knowledges and "sanctioned ignorances"[15] that our subjectivities are forged. This apparatus makes our transition to first-world institutions, especially in the United States, quite possibly among the smoothest within the third-world.

What happens to us after we go West? In her powerful and arresting essay, "Notes toward a Politics of Location," the U.S. feminist Adrienne Rich addresses her Dutch audience with the question of a woman's "struggle for accountability," as she puts it. These "notes" consist of a series of accounts by a feminist who, although deeply disloyal to the civilization that continues to place her in the oppressive position of "woman," finds that she can no longer quote Virginia Woolf's statement, "As a woman I have no country. As a woman I want no country. As a woman my country is the whole world."[16]

Taking my cue from her example, I might have entitled the following reflections "notes toward a politics of arrival." In contrast to Rich's more aphoristic style, these "notes" have been collected within scenarios, in the form of real and imaginary sites of questioning and self-questioning around three plausible subject positions. I call them scenarios to make room for their staged, almost theatrical qualities and to deemphasize their constructedness around my own experiences. As much impositions as inventions, they are uncertain explorations around the possibilities and disturbances living in the United States came to throw up. None of them is complete or consistent, nor could they be. These scenarios also feed off one

another and have been held apart as an enabling device for foregrounding questions that might otherwise get lost. In these next
pages—not unlike what has come before—the problems with the
"I" and "we" slots are obvious. Each of them asserts too much: the
"I" too much authenticity, the political becoming purely personal,
and the "we" too much commonality, when the identity of this "we"
is precisely what needs to be discovered and demonstrated, not
assumed. The strategy of shifting uneasily between them is a poor
one, but perhaps it is indicative of where I/we stand.

Immigrants

Often I have caught myself wondering what it would be like to make
the United States into a permanent home—almost everyone presumes that when one journeys to the first world, one has come to
stay. After all, isn't this the most common scenario for anyone
headed West? Just a brief glance at the history of worldwide immigration into the United States reveals the fact that by 1920, "women
outnumbered men among West Indians, Bohemians and Jews, and
in the decades following World War II the majority of all immigrants
were women."[17] This picture is surprising; it is, however, also a little
misleading, in that the great unevenness in U.S. immigration history remains largely invisible. Because we do not have a good sense
of the contradictory logics operative for different women, it is crucial to hold on to the distinctness among the variety of reasons that
have been offered so far: the creation of a service-oriented labor
market more "attractive" to third-world women; the 1965 change in
immigration laws, giving preference to relatives of communities
that initially had been predominantly male; the reopening of the
United States to immigrants from Asia, after they had been subjected to immigration-exclusion laws in the first decades of this
century; and the desire to escape forms of economic, political, and
religious oppression shared by men and women, as well as those
unique to female experience.

The choice of the term itself is telling—not emigrant, but immigrant. One comes across less about where women have come from,
much more about what they have come to—here the language of

arrival has been truly valorized. Thus, in a collection of oral histories by women who made their way to the United States over the course of this century, barely one-tenth of its three hundred pages have been brought together under the heading "Why They Came." It is rather their modes of survival in the new land that are extensively addressed.[18] Moreover, essays by new arrivals are often to be found mixed with essays by those whose ancestors were brought as slaves centuries ago, those whose lands were taken away, and those who are descendants of immigrants. *This Bridge Called My Back*, for example, intersperses the experiences of newly immigrant women with those of Native Americans, African Americans, Chicanas, and Asian Americans.[19] Surely this overall emphasis on arrival has something to do with America's raison d'etre as an immigrant nation (the extreme difficulty of "keeping faith with the continuity of our journeys,"[20] as Adrienne Rich has it)—its inexorable demand that people reconstitute their identities within its borders alone.

At the same time, however, it has become obvious that the United States is not simply heading toward the "melting pot," if it ever was. With the rise of the "new ethnicities" in the social ferment of the sixties, what has become visible is the enormous complexity of the United States's internally colonized communities, leading to very particular fears and uncertainties. According to the Cuban immigrant Mirtha Quintanales, speaking with reference to the complex hybrid and hyphenated identities emerging among domestic third-world women,

[n]ot all Third World women are "women of color"—if by this concept we mean exclusively "non-white." And not all women of color are really Third World—if this term is used in reference to underdeveloped or developing societies. . . . Yet if we extend the concept of Third World to include internally "colonised" racial and ethnic minority groups in this country, so many different kinds of groups could conceivably be included, that the crucial issue of social and institutional racism and its historic tie to slavery in the U.S. could get *diluted*, lost in the shuffle. . . .

I don't know what to think anymore. Things begin to get even more complicated when I begin to consider that many of us who identify as "Third World" or "Women of Color," have grown up as or are fast becoming "middle class" and highly educated, and therefore more privileged than many of our white, poor, working class sisters.[21]

Quintanales's worry is a powerful expression of the predicament facing a politics of identity among U.S. minority women today, when the multiple axes of oppression themselves resist easy definition. Within such intertwining processes of complexity *and* dilution, it is crucial not to generalize about the reasons and motivations for the kind of dislocation that coming to the United States entails. Although many recent immigrant women, particularly lesbian women of color, may well see themselves, in Cherríe Moraga's phrase, as "refugees of a world on fire,"[22] how might I position myself as an aspiring intellectual, and one, moreover, who shares the "advantages" of heterosexual privilege?

Arguably, most Indian women arrive on U.S. shores as the wives of green card–holding professional men. Only a small percentage come singly; even fewer recognize or question their socialization into "compulsory heterosexuality." Whether married or not, a significant number have educational and professional ambitions of their own. It becomes all the more urgent in such a context, therefore, to examine as sharply as possible just what kind of immigrants postcolonial Indians—neither exiles nor refugees—would be. The contemporary Non-Resident Indian (NRI) in the United States might well pause to locate herself with respect to peoples of Indian origin living elsewhere around the globe—such as the descendants of indentured laborers in Sri Lanka, Fiji, Mauritius, South Africa, Surinam, and the Caribbean; or Indians in Britain who share a more mixed class background, with a visible history of combating the racist legacies of colonialism; or the overwhelmingly working class populations residing in the so-called Gulf countries of Dubai, Kuwait, and Saudi Arabia, by far the most reliable in sending remittances back home. Even "Asian American" hides more than it reveals by conflating the disparate histories of the Chinese, Japanese, Filipino, and Vietnamese in the United States, on the one hand, with those of most South Asians in this country, on the other. The histories of immigrants of East Asian origin, moreover, extend back many generations now and can include the direct effects of U.S. colonialism and interventionist policy.

As recent additions to the present wave of overwhelmingly urban and highly educated graduate students entering the United States, today's NRIs would not even be aware of the battles against racism faced by early Indian labor immigrants after the turn of the century, and not simply because they only numbered a few thousand.[23] As potential academics, we inhabit a different social space, one that also sets us apart from the victims of New Jersey's "dot-busters."[24] One might well be led to believe that the promises of universalism that brought so many of us to the United States will not let us down; we have, moreover, reaped the benefits of the civil rights and feminist movements that preceded us.

Through which routes and at what point does a vastly different sensibility creep in, as I reflect over the uneasy coexistence of confident public identities with a tendency to ethnicize and privatize other aspects of their lives, including gender relations, among Indian immigrants? In his detailed study of Asian immigration, Ronald Takaki has emphasized the danger in perpetuating the myth of the "model minority," the manner in which Asian Americans have been celebrated (and also resented) in the United States. Although there is no doubt in my mind that, as far as the advantages of a first-world educational system and the very real need of financial security are concerned, one could not be better off, the other side of the picture remains to be explored. Takaki refers to "a glass ceiling" in the high-tech job market—"a barrier through which top management positions can only be seen, but not reached, by Asian Americans"[25]—and there is no reason to suppose that academia should turn out to be more benign. At some stage, then, one could discover the deep cracks of marginality in an identity sheathed by the significant, but by no means exclusive, determinations of class privilege. Such realizations have, in fact, led a few Indians to become effective "specific intellectuals," linking up with local struggles both within and outside U.S. university politics. Political issues have ranged all the way from discriminatory practices against third-world students in admissions policies and the prevalence of sexual violence against the wives of NRIs, who have often only recently arrived through "arranged marriages" from India, to the new conflicts around identity, race, and gender faced by a second generation of Indian Americans just coming of age.

It should be obvious by now that in order to be able to insert the contemporary postcolonial intellectual within the larger immigrant scenario, we must mark dislocations and alterities carefully to avoid conflating processes that are discrepant. What need to be held in tension with each other are the general dislocations characteristic of migrating third-world peoples who have been heading Westward before and after decolonization; the specific "brain drain" among the professional classes and intelligentsia which received a new impetus since the sixties, particularly in the United States; and the experiences of dislocation more unique to women. It is my belief that a good many postcolonial women, including self-identified feminists, find themselves gazing and going Westward for reasons that cannot be rendered intelligible in the language of a presumed or proposed international feminism alone.

Discrepant dislocations do, nonetheless, produce unintended effects. For some of us, the dislocation from a sheltered Indian middle class environment, where a consciousness of privilege predominates, to a milieu as highly sexualized and with such intensified and refined "technologies of gender"[26] as the North American one does lead to the espousal of a more explicitly feminist politics. What might earlier have passed as privilege now becomes recognizable as disavowal and "sanctioned ignorance," demanding a reconstitution and renarration of identity all its own. Of course, I do not for a moment mean to imply that it is this particular dislocation from the safety and blindnesses of "home" that is most conducive to feminism. As chapter four will discuss in some detail, feminists in India for over two decades have been waging struggles shaped by and shaping the specificities of India's postindependence context, where questions of women's subordination have a long and complex history. The feelings of "extreme dislocation, 'craziness' and terror," which Rich has linked to the "leap of self-definition needed to create an autonomous feminist analysis,"[27] surely never required that we go so far away—hence my urge to hold dislocations apart.

As immigrant feminists predominantly, though by no means only, in the social sciences and humanities,[28] what kind of political functions in our new locations might we take on? What kind of "specific intellectuals" might we become? At the cost of an apparent digression, let me look briefly at what Foucault's conception of the specific intellectual entails. In Gayatri Chakravorty Spivak's view, the danger lurking in this model—particularly as Foucault articulated it in conversation with Gilles Deleuze[29]—lies in its *unrecognized* specificity. In his constant distancing from questions of representation (Foucault's hope being that the "oppressed" will be able to speak for themselves, with intellectuals ideally only performing a relaying function between groups and struggles), Spivak finds denegation, an abdication of responsibility. For the specificity that is to take the place of an older Western universalistic humanism is no less geopolitically delimited, though it still masquerades as something more: having invoked Maoism, Vietnam, and immigration restrictions, Foucault gives out an impression of globalism and geographical discontinuity but passes over the effects of imperialism and the international division of labor elsewhere. In other words, for Spivak, Foucault's model of an alliance politics between heterogeneous groups, though unwilling to acknowledge as much, has not really taken into account the discrepant differences and discontinuities of "other" places; it remains a form of intellectual politics realizable only within the first world.

If we are to take Spivak's demands for less transparency and more attention to representation seriously, perhaps the best place to start is not by pointing out how easy it is for Western intellectuals to forget the advantages of "hard currency" and a "strong passport"[30] but to turn our gaze upon ourselves. Is she suggesting that the model of an alliance politics works best when we are immigrants and can thus perform representative functions in the first world in our own right? Furthermore, how might we include our third-world status within a first-world location? If our third-world identities are to play a directly representative role—that is, to reflect the demands and needs of a new U.S. domestic minority of Indian-Americans—will we participate, however unintentionally, in the diluting process Quintanales highlighted so well? Alternatively, can one position oneself in such a way as to puncture the construction of a "multiculturalism" that is only too ready to amplify the model minority image and so disavow the growing dimensions of racial inequality?

Anthropology in Reverse

My second scenario is in certain senses an extension of the first. If I have been sketching the pull of the universalist and "unmarked" attractions that bring many of us to the United States, and if I have hinted at the dilemmas around identity and community that immigrant women face, this section contains notes on some of the issues facing U.S. feminist identity politics. In ways I shall elaborate upon in chapter three, U.S. feminists are attempting to contend with a multiple interrogation of the sanctioned ignorances that universalistic assumptions contain. Why have I called it an anthropology in reverse? Chiefly because this scenario of a "politics of arrival," unlike the previous one, has questions of return on its horizon, is fueled by the anticipation of return. For if Rich is right to challenge Woolf's claim that, as a woman, her country could be the whole world, we have a choice to make and to be accountable for. What sort of experiences, what sort of "field notes," would I wish to see carried back to a third-world nation such as India?

As David Scott has pointed out so persuasively,[31] the anthropologist, by definition, must leave home, but only so that s/he can return. It is "there," wherever home is, that the writing, the skilled act of translation from one culture into the idiom of the other, takes place. However, given the fundamental discrepancy between the history of the institution of anthropology (the West leaving home to know the rest) and the relations of power that brought me to the United States, is the notion of a *reverse* anthropology intelligible at all? For one thing, what is this "other culture" into which I might translate the "truths" of the American one? Whereas the Western anthropologist has to undergo specialized training in order to ready herself for fieldwork in a distant place, one that her culture does *not* prepare her for, isn't it clear that, in sharp contrast, everything can collude to bring third-world women westward, and hardly for anthropological reasons? In spite of, or within, these obvious contradictions, let the following scenario on the heterogeneity of first-world feminisms be held within a reverse anthropological frame, fragile and dissembling though it might be. These notes—or, rather, "field notes"—are questions that await their transcription in India.

One of feminism's central demands has been to break out of universalistic assumptions and realize that it takes a very particular perspective, "trained on a determinate and particular field of experience,"[32] to render visible the contradictory statuses of women *and* men. It would, however, be extremely misleading to claim that it is women, and not men, who perceive the effects of patriarchy because they are so directly affected by them, as though knowledge of oppression bore some natural relation to its experience. Being and knowing have never been immediately connected; as Donna Haraway has put it in a related context, "[t]o see from below is neither easily learnt nor unproblematic, even if 'we' 'naturally' inhabit the great underground terrain of subjugated knowledges."[33]. Far from being *a priori*, the connection between women and knowledges about them is a *result*, struggled for, constantly renegotiated and learned anew.

Perhaps another way of posing this is to say simply that feminism is a politics as much as it is an epistemology—where questions of representation must deal with who speaks for whom, along with what is being said. Indeed, from among a host of other descriptions, feminism could be described as a narrative about the discovery of representation itself—from the prior moment, when women's identity as women was either largely accepted or disregarded, to the present, in which we make it our subject, politically and interpretatively. Men need to cultivate the necessary vision "to learn how to see faithfully from another's point of view";[34] this may even be the only way to recognize their own implication and accountability within the gendering process. Such considerations still make men's place within feminism an ambiguous, if not "an impossible one," as Stephen Heath has claimed. "Their voices and actions, not ours. . . . Women are the subjects of feminism, its initiators . . . the move and join from being a woman to being a feminist is the grasp of that subjecthood."[35] Regardless of how men have been responding, "the move and join" between female experience and feminism, where *both* the nature of such experience and its feminist reconstruction are in question, remains the pivot around which feminism turns. Female experience is not simply "there" and whole, waiting to be organized; it is more likely to be contradictory, at once too scrutinized and opaque. And yet, or rather, for precisely these reasons, women must represent themselves.

But which women am I referring to? It probably goes without saying that the "West" arrives on other shores in monochromatic terms; it travels elsewhere considerably whitened. Indian school and college students know of the "discovery of America," but little else about the Conquistadores and their significance within a prior history of peoples native to the American continents. They will learn much more about Abraham Lincoln and George Washington than the American institution of slavery; and the Rev. Martin Luther King Jr. possibly plays the analogous role in India that Gandhi does in the United States. But the histories of oppression of black women and women of color on U.S. soil are nowhere to be found. What would it be like to read Harriet Jacobs, or *This Bridge Called My Back*, in India? There is also another side that the third world does not see—a white woman's attempts to come to terms with her complicities and sanctioned ignorances, of "unlearning her privilege as loss," as Spivak phrased it in a different context. It has been remarkable to discover the degree to which U.S. feminisms are no longer primarily addressing men but *one another*. The problematic position of men in feminism is perhaps a matter of less concern than the relationships between the identity politics of different groups of women, to the point that these questions could be setting the conditions for Western feminism's future.[36]

"Let's face it. I am a marked woman, but not everybody knows my name." So begins Hortense Spillers in an essay that unravels the negativity at the heart of a black woman's identity, an identity buried within the overdeterminations and simplifications wrought by too many names: "In order to speak a truer word concerning myself, I must strip away through layers of attenuated meanings, made in excess in time, over time, assigned by a particular historical order."[37]

Spillers must begin in the present and then work her way backwards. Breaking open the presuppositions embedded in the officially sanctioned truths of the Moynihan Report, she confronts the "pathological" status of the "matriarchal" black family: no father to speak of, and the fault lying squarely on the power of the female

line. Her search for legibility in the history of African Americans—
through the narratives of the first captives, the conditions of "Middle Passage," and subsequent slavery—goes beyond the revelation
of the breakdown of even the semblance of family structures in such
situations to brutalized bodies reduced to "hieroglyphics of the
flesh,"[38] indecipherable in their gendering. Apart from being the
target of rape, the African female was subjected to forms of torture
one would have thought the prerogative among men; as a means for
reproduction, she was more a piece of property than a wife or a
mother. Thus, "the problematizing of gender places her outside the
traditional symbolics of the female . . . [leading to] a radically
different text of female empowerment."[39] Female empowerment
emerges only through a process of re-membering, a necessarily
inventive tracing of the history of African American women within
the violence of colonialism and slavery.

On a very different register, white women in the United States
have had to be interrogated on the extent of racism within the
women's movement, discovering the degree to which their very
choice of listening or remaining deaf to women of color was a part of
their race privilege. It is one thing for Spillers to come to terms with
the imbrication of her history within History, quite another for a
white woman to learn where her location and the best of educations
have brought her. As Biddy Martin and Chandra Talpade Mohanty
have put it, it is not so much a question of whether "white" or
"Western" feminisms are relevant to women of color or third-world
women as one of challenging the assumption that "the terms of a
totalizing feminist discourse are *adequate* to the task of articulating
the situation of white women in the West."[40]

Martin and Mohanty choose to focus on Minnie Bruce Pratt's
autobiographical essay, written in astonishment and pain, as she
tries to unmake an identity so pervasively woven out of the sanctioned ignorances and official knowledges that come from being
middle class, white, and Southern. Over and over again, Pratt questions every truth that she has held, such as her obliviousness to the
history of race, those "old lies and ways of living, habitual, familiar,
comfortable, fitting us like a skin."[41] Like Spillers, she must perform
a stripping away, though from her position of accountability, it goes

right down to the frightening possibility that the culture she was raised in may embody nothing worth saving. Such a mode of self-questioning sometimes runs the danger of implying a desire for an impossible position of innocence. But Martin and Mohanty's fine reading underscores the absence of any simple linear progression in Pratt's narrative, her constant shifting, her refusal to remain with rigid stabilities. As they also continue to point out,

only one aspect of experience is given a unifying and originating function in the text: that is, her lesbianism and love for other women, which has motivated and continues to motivate her efforts to reconceptualise and recreate both her self and her home.[42]

These qualities are striking, as is her ability to avoid the twin pitfalls of high, arid abstraction and guilt-ridden self-absorption. I have been overwhelmed by the relentless quality of the interrogation she undertakes: the weaving of her personal history within History is so fraught with loss precisely because so much of her identity has been bound up with the habit of considering her culture "as the culmination of history, as the logical extension of what has gone before."[43]

On the one hand, we are strongly reminded of the shift in perspective necessary to bring questions of feminism into view, to pull back from the lure of universality and imagine a different dislocation from the fixity of "woman." On the other hand, what could remain subdued in the earlier discussion of feminism and has become so sharply foregrounded here is the question of History itself, showing how women's narratives have been written within and against its delineations. To be a "specific intellectual" in the context of contemporary U.S. feminisms thus goes way beyond what Foucault might have envisaged: one's "local" position within the first world turns out to demand extended levels of accountability, even before more "global" configurations are broached.

Native Informants

It was difficult, from an American vantage point, to picture what a "transference" of these experiences to a different geopolitical location would be like, in the mode of an anthropology gone awry.

While in the United States, I learned to desist from offering ven-
triloquistic fantasies, of speaking from a location where I was not,
even as memories and imaginations took me there. At the same
time, there is an important sense in which the foregoing considerations could reemerge in my third—and final—scenario for a third-
world feminist in the metropolis: "the native informant." Such a
scenario could be inaugurated by the "hunger of memory"[44] or, as in
the example offered by Trinh T. Minh-ha, from being interpellated
by difference:

My [American] audience expects and demands it; otherwise people would
feel as if they have been cheated: We did not come here to hear a Third
World member speak about the First(?) World. We came to listen to that
voice of difference likely to bring us *what we can't have*, and to divert us
from the monotony of sameness.[45]

Contrary to the assumptions that brought some of us to the United
States, we may thus find ourselves forced to contend with our places
of departure, asked to function as native informants from "elsewhere." From what position of authority would we speak? The very
attempt to become such cultural representatives, the falterings of
our memory, must, then, lead to a different realization: the need for
an examination of the historical, institutional, and social relations
that have, in fact, produced subjects also quite unlike "the native
informant" of old.

As is well known, scholarship on distant third-world spaces is by
no means absent from the first world's intellectual field. The discipline of feminist anthropology contains a rich and varied history,
of women—predominantly white—who have brought the lives of
other women—predominantly third-world—to first-world ears.[46]
Feminist anthropology itself is an offshoot of the larger discipline of
anthropology, which in turn has been one of the many modes of
knowledge production by which the "East" was rendered into an
object to be laid bare and understood at every level. This is where,
to my mind, the full paradox of the "sanctioned ignorances" among
postcolonial women can come into view. How might one account for
the discrepancy between the exorbitant writing on other non-Western cultures—sometimes including, sometimes effacing women—

that has been the hallmark of the West, and *our* emergence as postcolonial subjects, produced by the kind of Western-oriented education which I alluded to earlier? It would be deceptive to focus only on the proliferation of discourses while losing sight of the incitements to ignorance that have accompanied them, indeed, that have intrinsically structured the precondition to knowledge.

Let me back up a bit and try to pinpoint the issues as I see them. The West has been witnessing the emergence of third-world feminists like me, eager to delve into archives or engage in fieldwork in order to lay claim to a lost and repudiated history. We also perform indispensable tasks in the critical evaluation of our discursive inheritance of the lives of women who inhabit non-first-world places. Thus, for example, Chandra Mohanty has convincingly demonstrated that too many contemporary accounts are scored through by an "ethnocentric universalism," the tendency of presuming "women" as a category of analysis: "The homogeneity of women as a group is produced not on the basis of biological essentials, but rather on the basis of secondary sociological and anthropological universals."[47]

On the one hand, these analyses tend to assume a universal "woman," both analytically and politically, thus also generating prescriptions on the issues around which *all* women should organize. On the other hand, as Mohanty continues to argue, because what separates the lives of such women from the self-conception of the feminist researcher is equally obvious and glaring, a difference is also supplied—the "third-world difference." In fact, she goes so far as to suggest that the true subjects of these histories are the researchers themselves. From a different perspective, Spivak has urged against acts of obliteration—the insidiousness of conflating the third worldism of the indigenous elite woman abroad with that of the range of women who, whether deeply imbricated in the circuits of capitalism or not, do not speak on a first-world stage.[48]

The need for these critiques is urgent and undeniable. My limited purpose here is to hold on to some of the further implications they open up for postcolonial feminists, implications that tend to get elided or left transparent when the researchers are not Westerners.[49] For, as Mohanty herself has insisted, the feminist scholars in question are not necessarily those born in the West:

[E]ven though I am dealing with feminists who identify themselves as culturally or geographically from the "West," what I say about the[ir] analytical strategies or implicit principles holds for anyone . . . whether third world women *in the West*, or third world women in the third world writing *for the West*.[50]

Mohanty's general indictment of ethnocentric universalism may sound dated to some ears—it is, after all, a problem that has been increasingly acknowledged and genuinely felt, even if the task of producing more differentiated and multicoordinated analyses has been easier to name than to accomplish. In any event, my immediate concern here focuses on the less obvious aspect of her critique. For what she seems to be highlighting in the passage I just quoted is the institutional production and reproduction of the "West" as an effective site of enunciation, and not just in the geographical West alone but also through non-Western subjects who are facing West, if not centrally located within it.

Even in the very attempt to speak our difference from the West, institutions bind us to Western locations. For one thing, only a tiny percentage of crucial archival materials remain in, or have been brought back to, non-first-world centers—knowledges are overwhelmingly stored in Western libraries. (This also effectively prevents those who are unable to gain access to the financial resources and cultural credentials necessary for travel to first-world institutions from believing that they could be undertaking first-rate academic research.) Writing as far back as the seventies about the condition of students from Arab and Islamic nations, Edward Said remarked that although

no Arab or Islamic scholar can afford to ignore what goes on in scholarly journals, institutes, and universities in the United States and Europe; the converse is not true. . . . The predictable result of all this is that [the] Oriental student (and Oriental professor) still want to come and sit at the feet of American Orientalists . . . in his relations with his superiors, the European or American Orientalists, he will remain only a "native informant."[51]

The force of this rendition lies at least partly in that it is not specific to the intellectual relations between the Middle East and the West and that it continues to be true. What I am trying to come to terms with here is the elusive complexity of our relation with the West, a relation that has set "us" up as an object of knowledge and simultaneously rendered us especially susceptible to "disappearing" into universality—i.e. heading Westward—when there is a chance.

It would be easy to conceptualize this relation on a more narrow epistemological plane. As Partha Chatterjee has expressed it, one is quite simply "always a Western anthropologist, modern, enlightened, self-conscious (and it does not matter what his nationality or the colour of his skin happens to be)."[52] Or, to try and rephrase this predicament more accurately, third-world intellectuals would be a peculiar, even impossible, mix of anthropologist and native informant, composed of shuttling identities and locations, in order to claim a history that faces West. But too much is left out of the picture if we remain with the following formulation: "It is the epistemic privilege which has become the last bastion of global supremacy for the cultural values of Western societies . . . while assiduously denying at the same time that it has anything to do with cultural evaluations."[53]

This is where the struggles of Pratt and Spillers in the second scenario may offer a further perspective on our situation: Neither of them could view the negativity at the heart of identity as a purely *philosophical* problem alone. Thus, though they would surely concur with Barbara Johnson that "if identities are lost through acts of negation, they are also acquired thereby, and the restoration of what has been denied cannot be accomplished through simple affirmation,"[54] they would place this more squarely within the terrain of *history*. For Spillers it is a matter of discerning the roles played by white men, white women, and black men in the narratives about and by black women and of the possible redemption of the historically severed relations between fathers, mothers, and daughters in the black community. Through what co-constructed narratives, embedded in which institutions and practices, are Indian feminists retrieving their histories? How are we prompted? What becomes sayable at particular historical conjunctures? It is one thing to acknowledge the intricacy of our relation with the West and its enabling constraints. But I would also like to sharpen this interrogation of "the West" as an institutional site of enunciation, and my own sense of having "disappeared" within it, around concerns that may not only be peculiar to my own subject formation. I have been brought up short, for instance, by my inability to be a specific intellectual and carry out a discussion like this one in an Indian language. Whatever the complexities of India's linguistic heritage, this, to my mind, is sanctioned ignorance. Enunciation, understood as the very possibility of raising such questions, requiring the development of a metalanguage, is ineluctably bound up with the hegemony of English (the cultural capital of German and French notwithstanding) and the extent of my intellectual formation within it, right up to this attempt to present my/our condition.

Having become the bearer of conceptuality and History's language, English is nevertheless a language with which only a section of professional Indian women are conversant. Thus, such a realization comes into play long before the more basic aspect of literacy— writing as a property of the educated classes—is brought into view. The exclusivity of English should not be conflated, therefore, with the following response to Gail Omvedt, an American who has been living and working in parts of the Indian state of Maharashtra since 1974, by Kaminibai, an illiterate agricultural laborer. Omvedt had been interviewing Kaminibai in order to write about political organizations among women in rural areas. When the value of such a study was impressed upon her, Kaminibai replied, "Yes, but will she write to us? She'll write something worth reading and writing, but it will be in thin small letters and we won't be able to read it, not at all, there will be no profit or loss to us."[55]

At the same time, the possible lesson for me is that Kaminibai's cynicism could well be generalized to a much wider group of Indian women, by no means illiterate, for whom these pages' thin, small letters are also neither profit nor loss. Furthermore, what might be the best way to name the irreducibility of the difference between my agency and Omvedt's—the difference between the politics surrounding a white woman's decision to make her home in a postcolonial nation such as India and a politics of return?

These foregoing "notes toward a politics of arrival" with questions of return on their horizon have been introduced in the present chapter because I see them as extending into the book as a whole. But

whereas the multiple subject positions alluded to above—the immigrant, the anthropologist in reverse, and the native informant—
were meant to draw greater attention to the possibilities and limits
of my identity in the United States, they would remain entirely self-
indulgent if I did not go on to specify in some detail just what these
constraints have permitted me to take up by way of ongoing intellectual work. In the subsequent chapters I attempt such a task.

Rey Chow's opening question in the introduction to her book,
Women and Chinese Modernity, resonates with my own when she
says: "We live in an era in which the critique of the West has not only
become possible but mandatory. Where does this critique leave
those ethnic peoples whose entry into culture is, precisely because
of Western imperialism, already "Westernized"?[56]

She continues by warning her reader that the direction she would
advocate cannot be a return to one's pure ethnic origins. It is hard
not to agree, especially considering how unattractive such a line of
reasoning would be for a feminist. My most intimate yearnings for
home are equally constituted and ruptured by the impossibility of
any simple return, by a desire for different dislocations.

What discrepancies then—epistemological, historical, political
—are brought into play when a sense of dislocation is articulated
across disciplines, by feminist subjects differentially constituted
between the West and Westernization? Which meanings are valorized, which ones suppressed? And how does one's location, however provisional or permanent it may be, condition the very form
and direction experiences of dislocation take? This book circulates
among questions such as these. While on the look-out for con-
tinuities and congruences, the following chapters claim that we
stand to benefit by being more sharply vigilant of the discrepancies
such questions open up, discrepancies that have yet to receive their
proper focus and need to be accounted for.

Chapter Two

Partial Theories/ Composite Theories

> We have entered into the "Age of Criticism" which could be defined as a preoccupation with theoretical structures often not internalized: we feel that theory is power.
>
> > Tey Diana Rebolledo,
> > *"Doing" Theory in*
> > *Other Modes of Consciousness*

> The interdisciplinarity that we look toward would attempt to apprehend epistemological constellations as they reciprocally provide themselves with a new delimitation of their objects and a new status for their procedures.
>
> > Michel de Certeau,
> > *The Writing of History*

At least in some disciplines in the humanities and social sciences, people have come to refer in a self-evident manner to "theory." When used in this characteristically unqualified way, the term no longer stands for conventional discipline-based forms (as in, say, "sociological" or "economic" theory) or even the transdisciplinary modes (such as "Marxist" or "positivist" theory) already familiar to us. Today, "theory" has come to denote a combination of some rather specific kinds of theorizing that have acquired a metadisciplinary universal status: poststructuralism, feminism, semiotics, hermeneutics, psychoanalysis, and continental philosophy.

Interestingly enough, if there is any one academic activity that intensifies the enabling and disabling constraints of the subject positions introduced in the previous chapter, it is this very one of "doing theory." Whereas at an earlier point—especially during the sixties and seventies—it looked as though "theory" came from a

delimitable group of people, of which Jacques Derrida, Michel
Foucault, Julia Kristeva, Jacques Lacan, and Luce Irigaray have
been prominent members, the situation today is considerably transformed. Feminists in many more parts of the world, theorists of race
and ethnicity, and postcolonial scholars are becoming equally well-
known for the kinds of "theory"[1] they do.

It is the West that structures the "immigrant," the "anthropolo-
gist-in-reverse," and the "native informant"—notice the extent to
which the "immigrant" can swamp the other two, as if to underline
the power of those Western contours. Theory, too, stands under the
sign of the West. There is surely no better manifestation of this than
that postcolonial intellectuals have felt its compulsion, in some cases
leaving home to take up academic apprenticeship, if not residence,
in Western places. At the same time, such a state of affairs has also
produced deep reactions and resistances to theory. For if theory is so
irreducibly Western, what could it offer to intellectuals who wish to
question the extraordinary influence of the West over their projects?
In fact, wouldn't an engagement with theory be precisely part of the
problem? As Homi K. Bhabha, a prominent postcolonial theorist, is
forced to ask: "Are the interests of 'Western' theory necessarily col-
lusive with the hegemonic role of the West as a power bloc?"[2]

Phrased in just this way, of course, the question leaves little room
for a simple affirmative. It is too well established that some of the
most profound articulations of the "critique of the West" have been
in the very languages of theory. One need only the reminder of the
indispensable force of its terminologies—postmodern, deconstructive, antifoundationalist, antihumanist—and what they have come
to stand for: an unprecedented destabilization of the conditions of
possibility of Western thought. Moreover, it is precisely the dislocating effects of "theory" that have been so attractive to Westernized subjects such as ourselves.

What, then, is the reason for unease? Or, as Bhabha would have
it, "what is at stake in the naming of critical theory as 'Western' "[3]?
Here is a response from Vivek Dhareshwar:

One must recognise the fact that though the new "theory" emerged and
established itself as a critique of Western humanism, it nevertheless occupies the same institutional structures; it may have deconstructed "the
discourse of universality," but its own discourse has now become a norm,

in the sense that it now has the power to determine contexts of research and set the agendas.[4]

As a result, the "others" of the West, those very subjects who most stand to benefit from theory's oppositional impulses, have rediscovered themselves in relations of domination, albeit within the discourses produced by the critical agendas of theory. "[N]ever the active agent of articulation," the "other" has been contained "in its *location* as the 'closure' of grand theories."[5] In the face of such a diagnosis, Bhabha argues for a renewed "commitment to theory," though on "[an]other site," the site of cultural difference manifest in poststructuralist readings of colonial rather than metropolitan texts. Dhareshwar thinks that "the predicament of theory," as he calls it, demands something further, a more "genuinely self-reflexive theory" that also analyses "the political, institutional, and epistemological constraints within which it must operate."[6]

In this chapter I shall attempt a response to the "predicament of theory," a predicament perhaps most acutely felt by those subjects who perceive the discrepancies between the existing bodies of theory and their own concerns. In order to investigate whether theory can play a part in the analysis of postcolonial subjects for whom it was not made—in order, that is, to broach the difficult task of becoming "active agent(s) of articulation"—these pages will explore the *structures* of certain dominant Western theories more closely, both to see where some of the current problems lie and to find constructive avenues beyond them.

I hope to show that, in spite of claims to the contrary, theory can become more pliable in our hands, open to innovation and change. For this to be true, however, we need what we do not yet have—a sufficiently rich and nuanced analytical sense of the *partial* and *composite* structure of theory, of its limits, its multilayered and mixed forms. Part of the problem, particularly in the eyes of critics, has been the adoption by too many practitioners of rather simple if not homogeneous theoretical strategies.

The Authority of Philosophy

What, then, is this entity, "theory," which is evoked, claimed, or repudiated, yet so often remains in itself remarkably underanalyzed? To begin with, such an assertion concerning the outstanding need for an analysis of theory might seem surprising, when one considers how much it is in evidence across such a wide range of disciplines. In fact, there has rather been an excessive preoccupation with theory. But I think Josué Harari has captured part of the difficulty when he says: "[I]t is the very 'advances' of theory . . . that are blurring our present attempts to understand what theory is."[7]

According to another commentator, Quentin Skinner, the most significant and paradoxical effect of contemporary theoretical endeavor has been "a return to Grand Theory [i.e., grand theories of human nature and conduct] in the human sciences."[8] Finding evidence of such a return in moral and political philosophy, or in the philosophy of science, may not seem particularly remarkable. Philosophy is, after all, by virtue of its concept of itself, directly caught up with the production and evaluation of claims to truth that are general and universal in scope. In fact, a majority of the theorists under consideration in Skinner's book would probably identify with, if not actually belong to, the discipline of philosophy. His edited text consists of individual chapters on the following "grand theorists:" Hans-Georg Gadamer, Jacques Derrida, Michel Foucault, Thomas Kuhn, John Rawls, Jürgen Habermas, Louis Althusser, Claude Lévi-Strauss, and the Annales Historians.[9]

But, to my mind, such a strong philosophical presence is exactly what is worth paying attention to, as Skinner is not primarily addressing philosophers, nor is he one himself. Why would a sociologist, historian, literary critic, or, to come closer to home, postcolonial feminist feel called upon to attend to the practitioners of this discipline? Could it be that what has come to characterize the advances of theory in a number of disparate fields is a concern with the kinds of presuppositions and critiques that were considered to be the business of philosophers? In spite of (or is it because of?) theory's critical destabilization of the foundational structures of philosophy—at times resulting in proclamations regarding "the end of philosophy"—theory has been especially prone to that philosophical habit by which a particular subject being studied becomes the *instance* of a general theory, a theory *already* in place, which the subject then serves to exemplify.

A detailed example might make more precise the unease I have with the kind of authority philosophy has come to enjoy, an authority that is now increasingly being taken over by those fields centrally implicated in the production of "theory." What happens when we consider a feminist critic who, though a well-established producer of "theory" as I have been outlining it so far, begins to question some of its presuppositions?

In a remarkable self-critique, Barbara Johnson, equally known as the translator of Jacques Derrida's *Dissemination* and as a deconstructive theorist within the field of literature, framed the introduction to her collection of essays *A World of Difference* as a reevaluation of her own prior work, its theoretical and canonical structures. Notwithstanding the promise contained in her earlier book's title, *The Critical Difference*, difference had, she felt, been effectively erased. For one thing, her unquestioned framework of "linguistic universalism or deconstructive allegory" made it possible to line up "prose and poetry, man and woman, literature and theory, guilt and innocence" as a series of elements in a parenthetical list with no effort given as to how "each pair operates with very different stakes in the world." Furthermore, she continued,

[it] was when I realized that my discussion of such differences was taking place entirely within the sameness of the white male Euro-American literary, philosophical, psychoanalytical, and critical canon that I began to ask myself what differences I was really talking about. To say, for instance, that the difference *between* man and woman is an illusion created by the repression of differences *within* each may to some extent be true, but it does not account for the historical exclusion of women from the canon.[10]

Whatever her discomfort about being "falsely progressivist," the considerations she was now introducing in the new book *A World of Difference* surely represented a necessary step ahead, if questions of difference were to attain fuller shape. The new set of essays contained analyses of writings by Mary Shelley, Dorothy Dinnerstein, Nancy Friday, and Zora Neale Hurston. Her more acute sense of the internal boundaries fostered by the academic institution as a real locus of power also led to hitherto unexplored questions of address and the politics of her own identity as a white woman. Yet it remained unclear to me whether the overall theoretical principles guiding her work didn't come through this autocritique with their authority intact and their logic unquestioned.

For example, one of her main questions in *The Critical Difference* had circled around "the functioning of *what is not known* in literature or theory." Given her subsequent realization, tinged with irony, that "woman" turned out to be one of the things she did not know she did not know and that "it would be no easy task . . . to undertake the effort of reinflection or translation required to retrieve the lost knowledge" (*WD*, p. 41), it is surprising to find Johnson answering this very same question in traditionally philosophical terms in a later chapter. She argues there that Socrates's demand in Plato's *Phaedrus* for a plurality of teachers, along with his more well-known desire to teach his students what they do *not* know, could be construed as a feminization of authority. Certainly we need to confront Socratic ignorance. But however much "the conflicts and contradictions *between* teachers serve as the springboard of learning" (*WD*, p. 85), this in itself hardly amounts to feminism. It simply does not follow in the mode of logical entailment that "just as the existence of more than one sex problematizes . . . universality . . . , so contradiction suspends and questions the centering of Western pedagogical paradigms" (*WD*, p. 85). In order to bring the specificities of sexual knowledge and feminism into perspective, we need considerably *more* than a statement on the nature of contradiction, however suggestive it may be, and I tend to think that the authority and elegance of a philosophical argument has hidden this need from view. In addition, as Johnson herself asks elsewhere (in a discussion of race and gender), how about other contradictions and pluralities, " . . . the nations, the regions, the religions, the classes, the professions" (*WD*, p. 169)—would philosophy alone suffice to realize our ignorances of these?

Reading Zora Neale Hurston, for instance, could take one into questions of method and history, into an institutional encounter between Johnson's "deconstructive allegories" and the legacy of a black woman writer, one that leaves *both* transformed. But it is rather the sense of congruency, however unexpected, between deconstruction and Hurston's writing that remains the high point of the analysis. In other words, the reasons for Johnson's dissatisfaction with her earlier work (the kinds of texts it was focusing on, the institutions it was upholding, the universalisms that remained unnamed) should—but in fact do not—rebound on the theoretical corpus she has inherited and is deploying in advance. If I may put it this way, the processes of deuniversalization and desimplification she unravels with such sensitivity in Hurston's narratives might lead to the realization that the theories one employs cannot simply be confined to a philosophical level of abstraction but must be examined for their own *partial* and *composite* structure. Theories and theoretical strategies are rarely univocal or simple but are themselves composed of heterogeneous elements at differing levels of abstraction, of which the philosophical can be one, though a very specific one.[11]

The term "partial" may require less of an introduction, given the number of theorists who have been making explicit reference to the partial nature of the methodologies they advocate. The German feminist Maria Mies, for one, has called for a method of "conscious partiality" in Women's Studies, namely "a critical and dialectical distance" between the researcher and her subject on the basis of a limited identification.[12] Though Mies is working within a tradition of social science research quite unlike the literary criticism practiced by Barbara Johnson, it is this relation of partiality between one's theoretical presuppositions and one's subject (whether that subject be Hurston's novel *Their Eyes Were Watching God* or Mies's work among women's organizations in Germany and India) that I do not want to lose sight of.

As the titles of their respective essays suggest, James Clifford ("Partial Truths") and Donna Haraway ("Situated Knowledges: The Science Question in Feminism and the Privilege of Partial Perspective") have also claimed strong commitments to partiality. It is the special ambiguity contained in this concept, alluding as it does to a simultaneous sense of one's biases and stakes (i.e., where one is partial rather than impartial or indifferent) along with a recognition of the limited part those biases may be playing (here the contrast terms would be part/whole), that needs to be held in view. Speaking from within the crisis of anthropology, Clifford lays greater emphasis than Haraway on the intrinsically incomplete production of cross-cultural "truths," as "strategies of ellipsis, concealment and partial disclosure determine ethnographic relations."[13] Haraway, located at the intersection of feminism and science, has a somewhat different point to make. Feminist partial perspectives are *more* rather than less objective because, unlike the scientistic "god-trick of seeing everything from nowhere . . . the false vision promising transcendence of all limits and responsibilities," such "situated knowledges" *can* be held to account.[14] The prerequisites for accountability involve naming the double invisibility effected by pre- and antifeminist worldviews, where men disappear into "abstract masculinity,"[15] the transcending norm that goes without saying, and women, saturated by their particularity, drop below the threshold of legitimate knowledge. Within the context of this chapter, how do such concerns impinge more directly upon the structure and scope of theory?

In the spirit of privileging the potential generality of theories, it has, as we know, become commonplace to distinguish between a theory and its context and to evaluate a theory's range of applicability by the degree to which this context has not rendered it provincial, so to speak. There is, no doubt, a good deal of truth to such a view. What follows, however, when we do pay closer attention to the context of a given theory—be it disciplinary (philosophical, linguistic, sociological, psychoanalytic, . . .), a matter of genre (structural, narratival, inter-textual, biographical, "general," "narrow"), or a matter of a theory's *location* in a more geopolitical sense? For contexts, in some of the ways that I have been specifying them, do accrue to theories; and although much fur has been flying around the necessary theory-ladenness of facts, we know considerably less about the possible "data-ladenness" of theories. What difference does it make that deconstruction is data-laden by its context in Western philosophy and U.S. literary theory, that anthropological theories of cultural difference were conceived within the colonial encounter, and that feminism emerged as a theory "from below"? It

is considerations such as these that call for greater theoretical reflex-
ivity than has been forthcoming so far.

Should a theory no longer be defined by just one discipline, a
single analytical register, or a unique location, one may speak of its
composite structure. Perhaps philosophy is less composite than
other fields; it has certainly been more concerned with guarding its
borders and with repressing its context and "apparatus of production."[16] In spite of the newer methodologies of "theory" that hold
onto the contradictory and heterogeneous "repressed" structure of
a text, the need for multiple levels of abstraction and disparate units
of analysis has not been well understood. We need to conceive of
theories as already embodying or, at any rate, as requiring, say,
both rhetorical and historical dimensions, with explanatory powers
at specific as well as more inclusive levels of analysis.

Often enough it is precisely through the kind of dialectical interplay Mies referred to, here understood as taking place between
theory, on the one hand, and the subject one is analyzing, explaining, or reading, on the other, that the theory one began with can be
transformed and recomposed. That is why the interrogations of
theory staged so far become sharpened when a theory "travels," to
use Edward Said's indispensable notion.[17] Moreover, harking back
to my opening remarks at the beginning of this chapter, questions
surrounding the structure of a theory have taken on a special cast
when the theory appears to be indelibly marked by its origins—is
called Western, for instance. This has been one of the more immediate ways in which the partial nature of theory has been acknowledged.

At a time when the intellectual hegemony of the West is rapidly
growing, naming its unmarked theories is crucial. But, unfortunately, such an ascription has also resulted in a misleading relativiz-
ation and reification, producing a "non-West" as some outside to
which Western theories cannot apply. An essential aspect of my
argument will be to show that setting up a theory as either relative
to its context or universal in its applicability is wrongheaded from
the start. At best, I think these are extreme options, perhaps to be
visualized at either end of a complex, many-layered theoretical and

political spectrum. We could then consider relative those theories that are so local and rigid in their purview as to be incapable of meaningful movement and transformation, whereas a theory so general and abstract as to be true at all times and places would qualify for universality. I'm sure we could come up with examples for either category. However, it is the vast space in between—considerably less elegant, no doubt—that interests me; it is one that, moreover, is actively enabling most of our ongoing intellectual work, even as we grant it so little methodological attention.

Hence my preferred choice of terms: partial (not relative), composite (not universal). Even in a restricted context or in cases where a theory is being applied on its own home ground, so to speak, we would be better off being more aware of the biases motivating its use and the institutions that are thereby promoted than to rest content with business as usual. Moreover, instead of getting locked into unproductive debates such as whether or not the existence of the unconscious is universal or whether feminism is indelibly Western and little else, why not think of these bodies of theory as compositely structured—made up of a network of assumptions, disciplinary affiliations, historical sedimentations, and global connections that have never been fixed or uniform but that evolve in an uneven, power-laden flux?

More certainly needs to be said to make these arguments in favor of explicitly partial and composite modes of theorizing plausible. But we also have to be wary of repeating that seductive philosophical gesture yet again by which one's theoretical claims are always already in position, needing only a suitable exemplar. A more persuasive approach might emerge by our continuing to conceptualize these issues within the context of forms of travel that theories have undergone. The trends I explore in the rest of this chapter—in the work of Gayatri Chakravorty Spivak and the legacy of Freudian psychoanalysis—are, therefore, emphatically not illustrations of a theory already in place. On the contrary, I am attempting to open up (in the hope of recomposing) the very theoretical space—with all its "hybrid forms," "tensions and ambivalences"[18]—that makes a negotiation such as this one possible in the first place.

"Traveling Theory"

When has history ever contradicted that
practice norms theory . . . ? In the open-
ended "making-other" . . . of the properly
self-identical . . . lies an allegory of the theo-
rist's relationship to his subject matter.

Gayatri Chakravorty Spivak,
In Other Worlds

When Said proposed his conception of the traveling of theories, their "transplantation, transference, circulation and commerce,"[19] he did not pause to dwell on the fact that "traveling theory" is, after all, a pleonasm—for most theories one might name have a history and are destined for future borrowing and transformation. He was more concerned with the kinds of stages one could plot along a theory's course—from a provisional point of origin, the necessary traversal of distance to conditions of acceptance and change in another time and place.

Gayatri Chakravorty Spivak seems to suggest a similar tack for the significance of "travel" when she considers theory to be an "active transaction" of reading. But where Said poses his explorations in terms of the more or less straightforward relationship between a traveling theory and its changing circumstances (which could be measured and determined by what he called a "critical consciousness"), Spivak operates differently and in ways more conducive to my purposes here.

To begin with, two of her essays I wish to examine are themselves structured by the actual *practice* of travel, becoming sites for transactions between deconstructive methods, strands in Western feminist theories, and texts of Indian subaltern historiography and fiction. Second, and quite unexpectedly, it is by following through the *discrepancies* between these essays—"Subaltern Studies: Deconstructing Historiography" and "A Literary Representation of the Subaltern: A Woman's Text from the Third World"[20]—that the notions of partiality and compositeness I have been trying to make analytical room for can emerge more substantively. Given the complex and continually growing corpus of Spivak's work, there can be no question of doing justice to her scholarship, let alone of assessing the decisive impact she has had on the agendas of theory. My decision to limit myself largely to the two aforementioned essays has to do with their initial publication in India, unlike her other writings, which have been published predominantly in the West, mostly in the United States.

As the title of the first of the two essays makes manifest, a theory—here deconstruction—is made to analyze or "read" the subject of historiography. I do not mean historiography in a general sense but rather a body of work known as "subaltern studies" produced by a collective of scholars who have been making critical interventions in the discipline of Indian colonial history for more than a decade.

It would be impossible to summarize the work of these historians in such a limited space, let alone provide a detailed sense of the theoretical, historiographical, and political trends within and against which this group has been self-consciously writing. Moreover, the range of themes and approaches has diversified over the years.[21] Within the complex presence of colonialist, liberal, Marxist, nationalist, and indigenous writing on India, Marxism—as a paradigm both for politics and for theory—has played a dominant role in the intellectual history and self-understanding of a group such as this one.[22] Indeed, the legacy of Marxism is evident precisely in these historians' attempt to provide themselves with a distinct and distinguishing self-definition. According to an early formulation by Ranajit Guha, they identified themselves by an orientation toward a

domain of Indian politics in which the principal actors were not the dominant groups of the indigenous society or the colonial authorities but the subaltern classes and groups constituting the mass of the laboring population and the intermediate strata in town and country—that is, the people. This was an *autonomous* domain. . . . As modern as indigenous elite politics, it was distinguished by its relatively greater depth in time as well as in structure.[23]

How one might follow up such a notion of autonomy, historically and methodologically, has interested and troubled many reviewers.[24]

But for Spivak, this very focus on the subaltern, sometimes iterated as the desire to gain access to forms of subaltern consciousness, reveals in itself structures of irreducible *failure*. Indeed, the experience of failure is by no means identified as specific to subaltern attempts to become agents of historical change: "If we look at the varieties of activity treated by them [ie., the collective], subaltern, insurgent, nationalist, colonialist, historiographic, it is a general field of failures that we see" (*OW*, p. 200). To take some scattered examples, subaltern movements fail mostly because of the strength of elite and colonial power, the nationalist movement fails to form potential alliances with subaltern struggles, and even elite historiography fails to determine what could count as credible evidence in the archive. But—and this is absolutely crucial—Spivak further implies that we cannot afford to ignore how all these conceptions of failure are tied up with preconceived and dominant criteria of success. She therefore seems to suggest that both because of its *generalizability* and because of its often hidden binary relation with success, the tracking of levels of failure in the texts of the subaltern historians should be conducted via the practice of deconstruction. Thus, although Spivak does not explicitly announce it as such, Derrida's mode of textual analysis is brought into transaction with Indian historiography.

In one of his more well-known interviews, Derrida explained the logic of his deconstructive method as follows. Instead of "simply *neutralizing* the binary oppositions of metaphysics," there was a need, he claimed,

to recognize that in a classical philosophical opposition we are not dealing with the peaceful co-existence of a *vis-a-vis*, but rather of a violent hierarchy. . . . [T]o deconstruct the opposition, first of all, is to overturn the hierarchy at a given moment. . . . [T]he necessity of this phase is structural.

That being said, . . . we must also mark the interval between inversion, which brings low what was high, and an irruptive emergence of a new "concept," a concept that can no longer be, and never could be, included in the previous regime. . . . Henceforth, it has been necessary to analyze, to set to work *within* the text of the history of philosophy, as well as *within* the so-called literary text, certain marks . . . that *by analogy* I have called undecidables. . . . Neither/nor, that is *simultaneously* either *or*.[25]

It is by following through this kind of "theory" of reversal and displacement in the structure of binary oppositions that Spivak seeks out the "failure" lodged within the very "success" of historiographic methodology. Where the text valorizes success, her reading would "overturn the hierarchy" suppressing moments of failure, ultimately revealing the undecidable co-construction of them both. In fact, she points to a more invidious and perhaps intractable version of "sanctioned ignorance" in the form of "success-in-failure": The very belief of having successfully interpreted a historical moment is the strongest barrier against the realization of possible cognitive failure, hence calling for the most stringent efforts of deconstruction. (Consider, for instance, the "success-in-failure" of so much economic historiography on India, which has interpreted levels of subaltern consciousness within a purely "working-class" or "peasant" frame, thus obscuring from view crucial concurrent identities such as those of community, caste, region, and gender.)

Spivak's point seems to be, therefore, that *it does not matter* what the specific type of failure may be—it is ultimately unimportant who is failing or for what reasons. We may be speaking of the failure of peasant insurgency brought about by the specific successes of colonial power, or of Gandhi's success-in-failure in his negotiations with the nationalist bourgeoisie, or even of the ways cognitive failure casts its shadow over the vigilance of the most successful deconstructive critic. The lesson to be learned is that no one is immune from the recursive structure of the sanctioned ignorance that incites us to see success despite the co-presence of failure.

What kind of theory travel are we witnessing here? To an extent, the kinds of questions left unresolved in Barbara Johnson's analyses seem to return again, especially those relating to "theory's" problematic position as the successor to philosophy. For when Derrida was looking for a new "concept" that could never be included "in the previous regime," the regime he explicitly referred to was the history of Western philosophy. Now the structural necessity he reveals to have been governing those philosophical discourses will certainly crop up in the most unlikely places, where one would least expect it, and it is crucial to be reminded of that. Indeed, the most innovative and rewarding aspect of Spivak's scholarship for us today lies precisely in her ability to transact with, and so dislocate, colonial and postcolonial rather than Western contexts.

At the same time, however, the new deconstructive concepts that can emerge by working through texts concerning subaltern struggles in colonial India (texts that are not merely further extensions of a seamless Western philosophical text) should then be marked by the specific context in which the deconstructive reading is performed. In other words, these emergent concepts can*not* be governed by the context—the comparatively homogeneous medium of philosophy—within which questions of undecidability initially took form in Derrida's writing. Therefore, when Spivak claims that "what had seemed the historical predicament of the colonial subaltern [i.e., the irrecoverability of a direct, unmediated subaltern consciousness] can be made to become the predicament of *all* thought, *all* deliberative consciousness" (*OW*, p. 204, emphasis original), I sense an example of all-too-successful travel, leaving too little room for an experience of failure *not* preordained by the theory being deployed.

However, a few pages further on, just when we might have been left with the impression that the differences between historiography, philosophy, and accounts of political struggle were being effectively neutralized, the argument takes a new turn—we are introduced to historiography not as an exemplary model for deconstruction but as *strategy*. The most telling aspect of Spivak's use of this term does not lie for me in the oft-quoted oxymoronic phrase "strategic essentialism." Rather, I am interested in the way her consideration of "historiography as strategy" forces a wedge into the narrowly philosophical and linguistic edifice structuring the essay so far, thus demanding that the historiographical no longer just remain an instance of the philosophical.[26]

It is when a theory recognizes its entrance onto territory for which concepts are not ready at hand, starts to stumble over the new ground, that a theory can be said to be traveling well. Inserting the additional concept of strategy—not determined in advance—is one way of coming to terms with the partial nature of the theory one is working within—in this case, deconstruction's partiality for levels of abstraction that bypass more specific issues.

What meanings can we attach to the notion of strategy? Thinking of one's theory as a strategy is immensely suggestive—it strikes a middle ground between the tendency of viewing theory as the logical application of a preset method, on the one side, or as a practical tool, with no subsequent effects or commitments, on the other. The text unfortunately does not elaborate or refer us to its militaristic and Marxist connotations, where strategy, as de-liberative and careful planning in the overall deployment of one's forces, has mainly been contrasted to tactics, the more immediate maneuvers in the field. Moving strategically enables Spivak to bring other figures and concepts into potential alignment with the prac-tice of the subaltern group—Marx's fetishism, Nietzsche's gene-alogy, Foucault's counter-memory, even Derrida's affirmative de-construction.

Yet the elaboration of Marxist notions of class consciousness to produce richer and more plausible accounts of subaltern conscious-ness appears constricted in Spivak's essay. One gets the sense that problems of consciousness in the "narrow" sense are never quite theoretical but are only of strategic value. As she put it in a recent interview: "[A] strategy suits a situation, a strategy is not a theory."[27] Therefore, the efforts of the subaltern historians to delineate auton-omous moments in anticolonial struggles are effectively pulled out of an extended consideration by being marked "theoretically unvia-ble," though of undoubted "political interest" (*OW*, p. 207). The point I am trying to get at is that too much is given up in such *undeconstructed* juxtapositions of "theory" and "politics," "theory" and "strategy"; we lose the full force of her suggestion that the desire to claim "a *positive* subject-position for the sub-altern might be reinscribed as a strategy of our times" (*OW*, p. 207).

The nexus of theory and politics is clearly not straightforward or simple. As Spivak herself has returned to it in painstaking and at times self-critical length in the context of the relations between feminism and deconstruction, perhaps a look at those arguments will help locate my dissatisfaction with "Deconstructing Historiog-raphy" more carefully and productively.[28]

In the course of revising her position, Spivak's major emphasis is to warn against the *conflation* of theoretical and political moves.

Thus, when Derrida makes Nietzsche's "woman" one of the names for undecidability, Spivak criticizes her earlier view that, as a feminist, she must question Derrida's politics because he is guilty of instrumentalizing the position of women for his deconstructive ends. Deconstruction, she now argues, is located in a *different register* from a feminist interrogation of patriarchy because it does *not* take a narrative form—it is not a description of the position of women in philosophy. Rather, deconstruction is about the suppression and precomprehension of difference necessary for any act, thought, or narrative, a precomprehension "which we cannot get a handle on"[29] but which deconstructive readings make manifest. "Woman" in deconstruction is strictly nominal—the term Spivak uses is *catachresis*, a metaphor without adequate referent—one way (among others) of naming the lack of a foundation for truth claims. Derrida's "woman," therefore, is not the subject of feminism as we might conceive of her in the women's movement or in feminist theory.

Spivak's corrective gesture is salutary and persuasive. But whereas she wants to prevent the reduction of deconstruction to a narrative, to warn against confusions between the dislocating maneuvers of deconstructive "theory" and feminist attacks upon "unmarked" patriarchal epistemologies or the instabilities wrought by feminist politics, my concern stems from the other direction—*after* according deconstruction its structural level of operation, don't questions of feminism, politics, and strategy return with even greater force, precisely because they are *not* equivalent to, subsumed under, or narrativized by "theory" as she understands it? If "woman" is, indeed, a catachresis, a concept-metaphor without adequate referent, and, moreover, if feminists often further conflate political and epistemological considerations, then, as feminists, we have to work in many different registers simultaneously. Our investigations, therefore, are as much conditioned by the effects of the women's movement and the work of feminist scholarship as by the realization that "woman" has also been one of the names for undecidability.

Unlike the male deconstructivist, whose efforts can remain parasitical upon a philosophical tradition inherited in a straightforward and unproblematic manner and who has been able to keep the

historical and institutional marks of his text more or less transparent, the feminist deconstructivist has a more obviously composite task to perform.[30] In other words, I do not wish to detract
from Spivak's warning that our patterns of thought are caught within
structural binds and metaphysical traps, perhaps especially so when
we are motivated by political and strategic considerations. I am only
arguing for an equal emphasis upon the ways in which our questions
move within and between levels of abstraction, forms of analysis,
and institutional constraints. The texts we read, the traditions of
theorizing (feminist, postcolonial, and so on) we harness to our
projects, the impasses we name—all have a great deal to do with
strategies, including those fashioned in the past and whose consequences we now inherit and have to contend with.

It is time to bring these reflections back to "Deconstructing
Historiography." Should we now read the "subaltern" as yet another name for the economy of undecidability, a catachresis like
"woman"? If so, then we would indeed have to distinguish between
the "subaltern" who becomes "the predicament of all thought, all
consciousness" and the subalterns of Indian history and not collapse
theory and politics, theory and strategy. As before, however, there
is every reason to work these levels and layers together, in irreducible complicity but not equivalence. At the level of "theory," we
should ask ourselves what difference is inaugurated when the em-
blem of the fundamental alienation of all consciousness is the subaltern in colonial India rather than an exemplar from the Hegelian
paradigm. What destabilization of the authority and self-contained
character of Western philosophy is wrought by going so far afield to
provide an embodiment of its universal claims?

Moving to more specific considerations that go beyond the very
privileged connotations of theory as deconstruction, we would then
need to conceive of alternate configurations of subaltern agency
rather than come to a halt with "theoretically unviable" and, one
should add, politically unsatisfactory notions of strategic essentialism. If I have understood Spivak correctly, it is in the face of
undecidables such as her notion of cognitive "success-in-failure,"
the lack of an ultimate criterion to ground our interpretations, that
further strategies must be risked and accounts rendered.

To take one example, in an essay contained in an early volume of *Subaltern Studies*, Ranajit Guha meticulously plots the failures of colonial, nationalist and even Marxist historiographers in their construction of history as the narrative of a single Subject—whether it be the Raj, the will of the state, the Indian National Congress, or class struggle.[31] A deconstructive reading would no doubt alert us to all the difficulties that attend Guha's claims regarding what he calls "the specificity of rebel consciousness."[32] At the same time, this very specificity makes subsequent analytical demands upon the reader, demands that do not end with the kind of contrast deconstructive readings often propose—the contrast between some unchanging essence and a purely differential notion of identity. For one is still prodded to *account for* those positive aspects of subalternity—religiosity, territoriality, combinations of sectarianism and militancy, contradictions of solidarity and betrayal—that historical discourses so far have naturalized, trivialized, or missed out altogether. Even the demand that "the rebel as the conscious subject of his own history" be no longer treated exclusively as a "contingent element in another history with another subject"[33] can surely be fruitfully explored by investigating the *double* sense of "subject"—being subjected to processes of domination, as in Foucauldian analyses of subjectification, as well as the excesses, resistances, and more active makings of subjectivity. That no simple lines of distinction or forms of measurement for such an ambivalent subject exist calls for both deconstructive and political interventions in the remaking of history.

Near the close of "Deconstructing Historiography," Spivak touches upon the problematic figure of woman in the work of the subaltern group. The problem, as she sees it, lies not with a lack of documentation on women's participation in the histories being reconstructed but with the historians' overall nonrecognition of the *instrumental* role women play in enabling the emergence of coherent analyses. Notions of femininity, for instance, often provide a metaphoric and discursive basis for insurgent mobilization. Or, to take another example, in order to affirm the village solidarity achieved by rebel groups in their construction of a common ancestry, what gets passed over are the women "acquired by marriage" from elsewhere, who must consequently be "drained of proper identity" (*OW*, p. 220). Focusing on the female subaltern in these ways, therefore, disrupts notions of territoriality and community that achieve their coherence at her expense.

Is this why, two years after her analysis of *Subaltern Studies*, Spivak comes to offer an interpretive essay on the gendered subaltern to this collective of historians? "A Literary Representation of the Subaltern: A Woman's Text from the Third World," along with Spivak's translation of Mahasweta Devi's story (originally written in Bengali), makes for an excellent counterpoint to the essay I have just been discussing.[34] Via a movement that is at least double-edged, a negotiation between fiction and theory is staged here, which could serve to deepen and transform some of the questions that emerged out of the transaction between theory and historiography. In order to compare the different strategies adopted and to explain how they can make the disparate structures of theory more visible, it will be necessary to provide the briefest of summaries of Mahasweta Devi's story.

"Stanadayini," meaning "Breast-Giver," tells the multilayered fable-like narrative of Jashoda, poor Brahmin wife and "professional mother" (*OW*, p. 222, in English in the original), who first prospers as the wet nurse for the innumerable children of a wealthy household, (many of whom subsequently leave to make their own way in the world), only to die unclaimed and alone of breast cancer. There is enough to invite an allegorical reading of this narrative, and not only because Jashoda is also the name of the Hindu god Krishna's foster mother. As Spivak herself succinctly encapsulates such a reading,

[l]ike the protagonist Jashoda, India is a mother-by-hire. All classes of people, the post-war rich, the ideologues, the indigenous bureaucracy, the diasporics, the people who are sworn to protect the new state, exploit and abuse her. . . . [In addition,] the ideological construct "India" is too deeply informed by the goddess-infested reverse sexism of the Hindu majority. As long as there is this hegemonic cultural self-representation of India as goddess-mother (dissimulating the possibility that this mother is also a slave), she will collapse under the burden such a self-representation permits (*OW*, p. 244).

Spivak, however, embarks upon an unexpected theoretical strategy. Instead of reading "Breast-Giver" as parable, she privileges *literality* over allegory. This means that one can raise questions around Jashoda's possible subject position as a *subaltern woman*, rather than allowing her to disappear completely as the instrument and metaphor of the nation. Already we can glimpse an initial response to the instrumental position in which "woman" was placed in many of the contributions to *Subaltern Studies*.[35]

Such a literalizing move enables a remarkable orchestration, a space into which feminist theories can travel and be interrogated by the translated narrative. One by one, dominant strains within recent Western feminism—variously (and problematically) titled as Marxist-feminist, liberal feminist, French "high" theory—take their stand and are examined for what they can offer by way of illumination.[36] At first glance it appears as though it is essentially the limitations of these theories that get emphasized as the theories are questioned by a piece of fiction. This is all the more surprising when we recall how theory traveled in the previous essay, where at one point it was so "successful" that the subaltern could become a model for the deconstructive method. If anything, one would have expected Western feminisms to have at least as much—if not more —relevance for an Indian writer's fictional woman as does the practice of deconstruction for a subaltern historiography.

A closer reading of Spivak's strategic negotiations with Western feminisms, however, would revise any initial sense of their limitation, in the sense of their simple inapplicability. I have been trying to indicate that we are in a much better position to explore the partial and composite structures of theories when their inability to travel easily is most obvious. One reason deconstruction traveled so "successfully" in the previous essay, I suggested, had to do with its philosophical level of abstraction, a level sufficiently general to make it feel unencumbered by, even indifferent to, questions of context, for instance. As against this, most feminist theories have had to be forged at different, often conflictual levels of abstraction. This has not necessarily made these theories more immediately aware of their own totalizing and homogenizing tendencies. When such an awareness has been forthcoming, moreover, it has too often taken a relativizing turn—an increasingly common practice is for dominant feminisms to be marked as "Western," "middle class," and, less commonly, "white," and then go on as before. Spivak's essay can offer something else.

A critical transaction between, for example, the work of a selection of U.S. and British Marxist-feminists, on the one hand, and Jashoda's position as a professional mother supporting a crippled husband, on the other, reveals the following: The Marxist-feminist texts are shown to circulate unevenly among different levels of abstraction and themes, such as the insertion of the labor theory of value into sexed reproduction, the specificity of the unequal exchange structuring all motherhood, and historical explanations for the transition from precapitalist into class society. In other words, the assumptions and considerations of these theories range as much from the most *abstract* formulations of value theory, some explicitly cross-*cultural* claims about mother-centered infant care, to *historical narratives* on the nature of capitalist and imperialist social formations. This simultaneous use of economic, cultural, and historical registers is what makes these theories *composite*. When brought to bear on the "cacophony" and "singularity" of Mahasweta Devi's narrative, at times these theories have to be reversed (Jashoda produces the means of subsistence while a child-bearer, rather than being dependent on her husband), at times they stall (as it becomes clear that the imperialism under consideration in a British feminist text is taken to be continuous with capitalism), and at times they reach a "strained plausibility" (in the protagonist's transition from a domestic to a "domestic" economy, from the unpaid labor expended on her own family to the sale of her labor power through surplus milk) (*OW*, pp. 247–252).

In these and her subsequent stagings of feminist theories, Spivak does not really elaborate upon her decision to foreclose on the question of the narrative's allegorical intent (which, we were given to understand, also represented the author's reading). But instead of having to choose between a Jashoda who can either stand for a subaltern woman or be the metaphorical bearer of the nation, it remains possible, in the spirit of the subaltern historians, to reinscribe the gendered subaltern *into* the making and unmaking of the nation. However pronounced the suppression of the gendered subaltern in most colonial and postcolonial histories may be, there is no reason to opt out of theorizing this particular failure. Furthermore, the special complexity of Jashoda's subject position as a subaltern, given that she is at once Brahmin in caste but a servant in class, may well be another contentious issue where dominant Western traveling theories will throw no light. We need to look elsewhere, or produce some of our own.

Perhaps because the partialities of both Marxist and liberal feminisms (*OW*, pp. 253–258) lead them to ignore crucial aspects of sexuality, Spivak also stages a section entitled "'Elite' Approaches: 'Stanadayini' in a Theory of Woman's Body." The privileged theorist she considers on questions of pleasure, or *jouissance*, turns out to be Jacques Lacan—someone who was not, though he could quite possibly have been, included among Skinner's practitioners of "grand theory." Although Spivak's choice may have been provoked by the unique position Lacan has occupied in the constellation of French feminist theory, I am more interested in seeing how a grand theory structured by psychoanalysis travels differently from those we have considered so far.

To begin with, Spivak ties together Lacan's general propositions on the status of the unconscious with the experience of an "excess" over knowledge, the excess of jouissance:

The unconscious presupposes that *in* the speaking being there is something, somewhere, which knows more than he does. . . . As against the being upheld by the philosophical tradition, that is, the being residing in thought and taken to be its correlate, I argue that we are played by *jouissance*. Thought is jouissance. . . . There is a jouissance of being.[37]

The extreme interest these considerations have engendered among feminists lies in the special position "woman" occupies in Lacan's scheme of things: "[W]hen thought thinks itself a place that cannot be known, that always escapes the proof of reproduction, it thinks according to Lacan, of the jouissance of the woman" (*OW*, p. 259). The first value in Spivak's redescriptions of Lacanian psychoanalysis for feminism lies in her ability to hold onto *both* senses of jouissance: forms of excess in *general*—the excess of being over consciousness—on the one hand, and a more *narrowly* defined orgasmic pleasure for women, on the other. Unlike Lacan, she is unwilling to privilege the former and trivialize the latter. Thus, the psychoanalytic theory that is brought to bear on the narrative "Stanadayini" already has a two-tiered *composite* structure to start off with.

At a specific level, Mahasweta Devi's text seems to emphasize either the silence of woman or the inscrutability of her sexual pleasure. Jashoda only emphasizes the priority of her husband's desire, never referring to her own. Spivak also attends to a separate "minor" incident, where the cook of the household gives in to a lustful son's attack, saying, "Yah, do what you like." When he is subsequently worried that she might "tell," her response is, "What's there to tell?" (*OW*, pp. 222, 263). Of course, we may well wonder what else the "excess," the inability to speak, is concerned with—we are surely up against questions of coercion and consent during rape that are impossible to answer, as much as we do not have a language for women's pleasure.

Where might the second sense of jouissance, the more general form of excess, be located? The narrative site Spivak recovers is not Jashoda's psychic unconscious but her body, with her cancerous breast becoming that "other" place which ultimately knows more than she does:

The speech of the Other is recorded in a cryptic sentence. It is a response to Jashoda's last "conscious" or "rational" judgment: " 'If you suckle you're a mother, all lies'. . . . *The sores on her breast kept mocking her with a hundred mouths, a hundred eyes*" (*OW*, p. 260).

During a brilliant analysis of this passage and subsequent ones, Spivak's essay subjects psychoanalysis to further transformations in its composition. In an uncharacteristic culturalist move, she claims that the Judeo-Greek underpinnings of this theory, its constitutive narratives of castration, Adam, and Oedipus, must make way for what she calls "Hindu regulative psycho-biographies." Having been "subalternized" by the master narratives of psychoanalysis, a specifically Hindu conception of "sanctioned suicide" might be recovered, she feels, and offer more productive interpretations of Jashoda's death (described in the story as the death of God) than does Lacan's heritage of Judeo-Christian monotheism (*OW*, pp. 261–262).

For the more limited purposes of my argument here, it is less necessary to evaluate the plausibility of such a theoretical turn.[38] It seems far more important to point to the incredibly heterogeneous and composite structures of traveling theory that thereby demand recognition in this essay, in some contrast to the previous one. There, deconstruction was more or less the dominant traveler into the field of historiography, supplemented no doubt by a notion of strategy, but one that remained unduly constrained by its essential-ist form.

Spivak's differing negotiations in the two essays I have read together illuminate many of the possibilities and difficulties in thinking about partial and composite traveling theories. As claimed in the beginning of this chapter, "theory" is by no means exempt from the profound effects of the West upon postcolonial subjects, even if it would clearly be a mistake to therefore club theory to-gether with what Spivak has called the "enabling violations" of colonialism. The task is to make the most of its dislocating and subversive potential for us.

Whereas in "Deconstructing Historiography" one had the dis-tinct impression that the subaltern historians were being assessed by deconstruction, the remarkable structure of the "Stanadayini" essay lies in the fictional narrative's empowerment as interrogator and disrupter of different modes of Western theory in order to make such theory interpret postcolonial contexts more fruitfully. The latter essay further demonstrates the analytical and political pro-ductivity of *discrepancies* rather than congruences between colonial or postcolonial concerns and those of the contemporary West.

Is it possible and, moreover, useful to undertake such interroga-tions within the West, in the very development of certain trends of theory, without necessarily having to seek out an "other" from elsewhere? This is what I shall be attempting in the following section on Freud and psychoanalysis.

The Contradictions of Psychoanalysis

Psychoanalysis, . . . which has travelled ev-
erywhere during the course of my long life,
has not yet found a more serviceable home
than in the city where it was born and grew.
　　　　　Sigmund Freud, *Moses and Monotheism*

Let me begin by dispelling some possible doubts. Why choose to look at Freud, who lived, worked, and wrote in the early part of this century, so much before the institutionalization of "theory" in contemporary academia? For one thing, Freud is being read today in precisely those fields centrally involved in the production of theory —literary criticism, cultural studies, film theory, feminism, some anthropology—and much more so than in his own disciplines, medicine and psychology. Though predating "theory," Freud is now intrinsic to theory. Especially since the advent of Lacan and post-structuralism, his name evokes all the authority and controversy that accrues from having become the grand theorist of sexuality.

The next question that might arise concerns my emphasis on Freud rather than Lacan. It is Lacan, after all, who has been such a key figure in the psychoanalytical wing of theory, a prominence that has transformed feminism and postcolonial analysis, among other things. My reasons are quite specific. Though it opened up the field to a whole new set of possibilities and consequences, the reconceptualization of psychoanalysis largely derived from Lacan also has resulted in a kind of amnesia regarding the extraordinary heterogeneity of Freud's writings. Contemporary rereadings of the Freudian corpus alert us to its textual and linguistic qualities, but without paying sufficient attention to what his writings are textualizations *of*. My point is that Freud's work lends itself to a particularly rich exploration of the data-ladenness of theory, more so, I would contend, than that of Lacan, which shares something of the level of abstraction characteristic of deconstruction.

Unlike the previous discussion of Spivak's negotiations, made possible by her transactions between Western and Indian theoretical contexts, this section has a much more modest aim in view. By taking a step back, so to speak, within the genealogy of theory, rather than engaging in questions of its travel elsewhere, I hope to dispel any sense of the unitary nature of psychoanalysis's beginnings, as well as to highlight some of the contradictory impulses that course through those early texts. Doubts today regarding "how labile psychoanalysis is, how far its boundaries can expand to incorporate issues of social difference into a discourse useful, if not for changing the social order, at least for theorizing this order's intervention into the production of diversely gendered subjects,"[39] are so widespread that such a retrieval from the past need not be redundant. Probing the differing units of analysis, interdisciplinary crossings, and social embeddedness of Freud's analyses will point us in a more enabling direction for flexible feminist and postcolonial appropriations than do claims such as that "Freud's resistance to a culturally inflected psychoanalysis are overt and infamous."[40]

The briefest of examinations of the resources and methods constituting the Freudian corpus is enough to undermine any conviction one may have held regarding its homogeneous structure. His better-known essays interpret transcriptions of dreams, jokes, constructions of stages of development in childhood, case histories, and excursions into the beginnings of culture and religion. What differences are introduced by such a construction of his theory? It is precisely through all these "cases" that he came to propose and revise his theories of the psyche; they have left their sedimentations on the distinctions between conscious and unconscious activity he was developing. *Jokes and Their Relation to the Unconscious*, written five years after *The Interpretation of Dreams*, is an illuminating instance of this process of differential composition.[41]

In *The Interpretation of Dreams*, Freud was at great pains to make a convincing case for the existence of the unconscious by arguing for its crucial explanatory role within the complex production of a dream. Mediating between the conscious and unconscious, the dream-work (comprising creative mechanisms of condensation and displacement, censoring considerations of representability and secondary revision) ensured, he believed, the dissimulation of wish-fulfillments that might otherwise prevent the continuation of sleep. It is these theoretical fictions that formed a resource or reservoir in his subsequent attempt to interpret the peculiar inventiveness and effectiveness of jokes. Not unlike the dream-work, the joke-work was assigned to the unconscious—that structure which one cannot know but which Freud felt compelled to supply—and similar techniques were elaborated to analyze the double meanings, caricatures, travesties, and comedy underlying forms of wit.

What stood out for me, though, was the extreme self-consciousness and care with which Freud organized his arguments. Emphasizing the necessarily partial and fragile process any inference from dreams to jokes must entail, he warned that if

from an inference of this kind, one is led, not to a familiar region, but on the contrary, to one that is alien and new to one's thought. . . . [i]t can only be regarded as 'proved' if it is reached by another path as well, and if it can be shown to be the nodal point of still other connections.[42]

To my mind, this is an excellent example of "traveling theory" within a delimited analytical space. The *analogy* between the dream-work and the joke-work is a good one precisely because its partial value is recognized: Although the structuring effects of the unconscious are carried over, as it were, from Freud's more detailed and familiar interpretations of dreams into the less well-understood mechanisms of jokes, there is no question of forgetting the differential levels of composition separating the two spheres of inquiry. For he is even more acutely aware that the contrasts between jokes and dreams are thrown into sharper relief by the very desire to compose them along similar lines:

A dream is a completely asocial mental product; it has nothing to communicate to anyone else. . . . Not only does it not set any store by intelligibility, it must actually avoid being understood, for otherwise it would be totally destroyed; it can exist only in masquerade. . . . A joke, on the other hand, is the most social of mental functions that aim at the yield of pleasure. It often calls for three persons and its completion requires the participation of someone else in the mental process it starts. . . . A dream still remains a wish; a joke is developed play (*J*, p. 238).

Thus, the advantage of reading *The Interpretation of Dreams* together with *Jokes and their Relation to the Unconscious* is the extent to which their composite layers of theorizing are rendered manifest. Given the precariousness of Freud's claims concerning the unconscious—with most of this realm forever repressed and unknown, and the rest knowable only through its effects upon conscious activity—we must hold on to the fact that Freud's theories are about different modes of access to an *interface*—between the conscious and the unconscious, between institutions and fantasies—and are not about some isolatable structure of the mind.

In the case of dreams, this interface is analyzed by positing the mechanisms of the dream-work, working backwards and forwards between the compressed, alien entity of the dream, disturbing residual thoughts from the immediate past, and much older, repressed infantile wishes. Where a conscious thought is revised for a moment by the unconscious to erupt again into perception in the condensed and indirect form so often found in jokes, it appears plausible to speak of a kind of joke-work in analogous fashion. But the very similar characteristics of economy and indirection that dreams and jokes share must, in the case of jokes, be explained within a unique social process, a complex intersubjective space requiring both objects and allies. Much of Freud's study is taken up with detailed explorations into the possible psychic/social interfaces involved in the formation as well as the reception of jokes, processes that result in the creation of social solidarity, psychic accord, and pleasure between speaker and audience, over against an "other," the joke's butt.

This is not to say that the social dimension of things is somehow absent in *The Interpretation of Dreams*; far from it. The many examples described and analyzed in that immense book are pervasively scored through by the intertwining significations of sexuality and class—the pressures of social status and professional advancement, forms of sexuality within "companionate marriage," the ambiguous situations of servants and prostitutes. However undeniably pivotal the position of sexuality is here as elsewhere, the special anxieties and intellectual aspirations of the middle class of Freud's time are not just fully evident but are on occasion explicitly discussed—the section devoted to examination dreams being a case in point.

The social spaces depicted in the joke book are more immediately part of the analysis. Moreover, they are strongly structured by unequal relations of power, especially where "hostile" jokes are concerned—those aggressive or defensive jokes that mark rebellion to authority or ridicule of the powerless, depending on where one is located in a cultural milieu that does not permit more direct forms of confrontation. We may not always fully agree with Freud in the way he works class distinctions into his analysis: in the discussion of dirty jokes, for instance, he seems to imply that because "civilisation and higher education have a large influence in the development of repression," the greater the social and educational status of men and women, the more they need "refined obscene jokes," rather than the "coarse piece[s] of smut" (*J*, p. 145) of peasants and barmaids, to undo the repudiation of sexuality.[43] More suggestive, if undeveloped, are his occasional forays into issues pertaining to ethnicity and race. Freud's own identity as a Jew appears to have determined his choice of examples from among Jewish jokes. He remarks about their "self"-directed nature, the need for Jews in Germany to counter the "brutal comic stories" (*J*, p. 157) coming their way by producing jokes that are at once self-critical and defensive, or, more accurately, that defend by criticizing a Jewish national identity on its own terms. Due perhaps to the tenacious stereotype of money, a whole group of Jewish jokes deals with the relations between poor and rich Jews, epitomized by the recurring twin characters of the beggar and the baron.[44]

It is this range of "data-ladenness" that tends to drop out of sight so often in contemporary accounts of what psychoanalysis comprises. A "minor" text like *Jokes and their Relation to the Unconscious* is rarely mentioned. Today, key passages in *The Interpretation of Dreams*, especially those concerned with the mechanisms of the dream-work, have traveled far afield, often being generalized to the point where they don't bear any of the marks of their original context. Think of how the processes of condensation and displacement have been semiotically and linguistically revised by the concepts of metaphor and metonymy, so much so that one is no longer able to distinguish between the workings of the dream apparatus and the structures of language more universally. Even as excellent a discussion as Kaja Silverman's *The Subject of Semiotics*, which goes to considerable lengths to maintain the distinctiveness of Freud's

contributions, ultimately treats the interpretation of dreams inter-
changeably with analyses of novels and films—they are exhausted
as instances exemplifying the general effects of signification.[45] As
the result, we hear too little about how Freud's evolving conceptions of the interaction of the conscious and the unconscious were
themselves structured by the "examples" he focused on rather than
determined autonomously as a general thesis.

The relation of cautious inferential tacking between contexts that
connect the study on dreams with that on jokes is one of many that
run through Freud's work. However, a countertendency is also in
evidence—some of his texts are equally marked by strategies of
containment, attempts to foreclose on the "others" he is considering, to conflate levels that must be held apart. An example of this
kind, in my estimation exemplifying theory travel that "fails" precisely because of its apparent "success," is his study *Moses and
Monotheism*, which he undertook toward the end of his career. At
this time in his life, he appears to have been preoccupied with a
particularly ambitious project: establishing a nexus between the
practice of psychoanalysis, on the one hand, and the writing of
history on an epochal or monumental scale, on the other. The
psychoanalytical "family romance," by which the son would replace
the father in a narrative of dispossession and membership, is re-
enacted in this text by Freud, the Jew, in his relation to the primal
father, Moses. The historical culmination of the psychoanalytical
institution itself also seems to be at issue here, its "non-place" in
Nazi Germany at the time of Freud's writing in 1937.

Everything in this remarkable text, composed of three essays,
revolves around Freud's heretical claim that "Moses was an Egyptian." Such a blasphemy must be defended again and again—hence
his repeated incursions into the subject via the origin myths of
national heroes, the relation of Judaism to the uniqueness of monotheism, and the nature of religious consciousness more generally.
Above all, however, Freud's efforts concentrate upon "the kernel of
historical truth" that needs to be salvaged "in the face of the in-
coherence and contradictions clustering around the heroic person
of Moses."[46]

For Freud, this quest for history is grounded in the hope for the kind of certainty that rests on evidence, one that is obtainable by the isolation and rejection of subsequent "textual distortions" from the original tradition (*MM*, p. 52). However shrouded in the distant past the figure of Moses might be, the point is to determine as unequivocally as possible that this leader and, indeed, maker of the Jews must have been an Egyptian governor who imposed a short-lived monotheistic religion (raised to universal status by the then Egyptian emperor) onto an outlying Semitic tribe. Whereas the emperor's successors were responsible for the demise of this religion within the imperial realm, the Jews themselves finally rose up against the Egyptian Moses' alien laws and killed him. At least two generations later, Freud surmises, during their return from Egypt to Palestine, the Jews were influenced by a new and very different deity, "the volcano-god Jahve," who, however, "lost his own character and became more and more like the old God of Moses" (*MM*, pp. 77–79).

Even as Freud wishes to have facts, "established historically," to support such a narrative, he also takes simultaneous recourse to "the work of hypothesis" (*MM*, p. 73). What this implies only becomes clear in the last of the three essays, where a series of sections are devoted to aspects of another narrative that Freud can lay a distinctive claim to—the psychoanalytical account of the successive stages of development that sons undergo in order to attain adulthood. Just as this developmental process involves traumatic infantile experiences, the Oedipus complex, a latency period, and a return of the repressed, so too, Freud contends, should Judaism be thought of in terms of mass psychology, as a kind of collective neurosis, with an archaic beginning, the repudiation and murder of the father Moses, and the later obsessive penetration back into conscious memory and tradition of the God Moses had imposed. Even though he acknowledges that such a "translation" is difficult to make and that the realm of mass psychology is one where he is "not at home," Freud still defends his inferences from the individual to history as "very complete, . . . approximating to identity" (*MM*, p. 90).

Let me first clarify where my difficulties with this form of theory travel do not lie. To begin with, the introduction of psychoanalysis into conventional historiography brings into view a profoundly important approach to past events. His explicit avowal of a "presentist" perspective to supplement the search for evidence, where all history—whether of a particular person or a people—is constantly in the process of being reconstructed *backwards* in light of one's present desires and problems—is a crucial corrective to his own initial thrust toward somehow recapturing the past "as it actually was." Therefore, my objections have less to do with Freud's specific rendition of the "family romance" as a possible analogy for his fractured and ambivalent relation to Judaism. Freud's perspective could, after all, be contrasted or countered by relating other conceptions of the predicament of identity with the hybrid experiences of loss and recovery undergone by the Jews in Egypt. This is what Zora Neale Hurston attempts in allegorizing the African-American experience of slavery within her text *Moses, Man of the Mountain*.[47] Again, I am tempted to suggest the perhaps far-fetched possibility that Jewish history can be rendered legible through psychoanalytical accounts of a daughter's (rather than a son's) problematic developmental history, where the "incoherences and contradictions" of femininity might offer a more multivocal view of what counts as tradition, alienation, and identity.

The real problem as I see it lies in the totalizing reach that Freud demands of the analogy he brings into play. The conflations between the individual and the collective, past and present, historical evidence and psychoanalytical fantasy, are so thorough as to close off all other modes of access or supplementary accounts. When a *single* analytical thread is made to tie up the ambivalences and contentiousness structuring the history of many centuries and peoples, with no room for a more complex weave, the partial and composite potential of psychoanalysis is suppressed. (In fact, Freud's analogy of the individual masculine psyche in this text even misses the more composite analysis of subjectivity he developed in the analysis of dreams.) It is one thing to privilege a particular narrative of identity over others, quite another to make it the structural basis for history at large. The reciprocities, but also the discrepancies, between different modes of dislocation are rendered transparent, resulting in a foreclosure on the alterity of history. Freud's search for historical underpinnings is unnecessarily thinned down and robbed of any extended understanding of how *collectivities* are produced by the analytical closure into which it is forced. Questions of national memory, the relation of orality to writing, and the very profundity Freud attaches to monotheism over against any other religious form (to name only a few issues) demand going beyond the analogy Freud supplies, not unlike the more careful transactional moves he made so much earlier in his career.[48]

This countertendency within the psychoanalytical corpus has often bequeathed us with what Rosalind Coward has described as "sterile polarizations"[49] in such intellectual fields as anthropology and feminism. Again and again, the debate regarding the viability of psychoanalytical insights in these areas has run aground by being couched in terms of an either/or choice between universalism or relativism: either we must believe that the Oedipus complex applies everywhere, or we must uphold the sealed boundaries of culturalist explanations.[50]

An acute example of the kind of impasse that has occurred within Western feminist theorizations is the exchange between Jacqueline Rose and Elizabeth Wilson.[51] Interestingly enough, their debate on the value of psychoanalysis for feminism took analytical shape around conceptions of psychoanalytical theory and its "other"— namely, social and historical theories. On the whole, this struck me as a potentially promising move, particularly when we recall Freud's own insights in the studies of dreams, jokes, and, later, Moses. For it should be obvious by now that it is hardly a matter of *opposing* a psychoanalytical perspective with, say, a social or historical one in some dualistic manner but rather of recognizing the specific contours of the psychic/social interface that are required in relation to the complex subjects that constitute our life and our projects. Neither side of such an interface takes the place of the other—there can be no question, therefore, of rendering one or the other, such as the psychic and the historical, effectively *superfluous*. Where such dualisms or conflations exist, they need to be set aside. Jacqueline Rose herself has pointed to a number of examples: sociological views of the mere internalization of gender identity lose sight of the crucial mechanisms of the unconscious; an emphasis on the "in-between" status of fantasy does not (yet) "show us the fully social import of the concept of the unconscious."[52] How fantasies are fully at work within social and historical institutions—the family, schools, the law—is what needs to be demonstrated.

What makes the debate between Rose and Wilson even more worthy of attention are the lessons to be learned from the pervasively different ways psychoanalysis is perceived and evaluated by them as *feminists*. Thus, for Wilson, psychoanalytical contributions to the construction of gender identity are closed, deterministic, and only serve to emphasize the inescapability of phallic power for women. Only in the strictly social and historical realm, therefore, can feminists hope for signs of an alternate identity: "Yet it is possible to imagine that personal identity could be, in a society in which male power did not dominate, organized around some other principle. There could be an adult sexual identity constructed around a different symbolic differentiator."[53] For Rose, by contrast, what lies at the heart of psychoanalysis is not the inexorable working of human psychic development but almost the reverse: the "recognition that there is a resistance to identity at the very heart of psychic life."[54] If anything, it is when so-called psychoanalytical accounts of gender acquisition become sociological and forget the recalcitrance and complexity of the unconscious that they tend toward the kind of fixity, universality, and inescapability that Wilson is protesting against. Indeed, Freud's importance in the history of psychoanalysis lay precisely in showing that the hysteric was not an isolated example of degeneracy, the unfortunate product of early industrialization and the rise of a new class, but rather revealed identificatory mechanisms of the unconscious that we, too, partake of.

It is at this point, however, that instead of picking up momentum and clearing new ground, the debate falls apart. By claiming that attempts to draw in sociological and historical considerations rest on an unreflective empiricism, with which neither psychoanalysis nor feminism can have much in common, Rose effectively banishes them from the fray. Because Wilson considers material and social conditions to be the only factors allowing a properly feminist imagination full rein, she cannot see what psychoanalysis might offer her.

Because neither Rose nor Wilson seems prepared to accept the partiality of their claims and allow for the fact that, as feminists, our questions, desires, and, therefore, our analytical strategies are posed at different levels, the conversation halts just when it should have begun. What should have been at stake is the recognition of the mutual implication of different levels of analysis, even within the *same* culture and for the most well-known subjects of feminism, white middle class women.

And yet, beginning with Juliet Mitchell's classic exposition from 1974, *Psychoanalysis and Feminism*, right up to ongoing efforts intent on reworking the relationship embodied in Mitchell's title, feminists have been equally concerned with finding ways to "move beyond" "stagnant issues in feminist, psychoanalytical thinking."[55] Mitchell's conclusion to a book that effectively introduced psychoanalysis to many feminists both in Britain and elsewhere is filled with the desire to ask the right kinds of questions—as much of the production of an oppressive system of sexual difference as of psychoanalytically informed methods to explain it. Rather than engage in a search for the origin of it all, she says, psychoanalysis points out how we need to begin with where we are *now*—that is to say, with a realization that the past structures the present in manifold ways. Indeed, she believes that Freud's strength and weakness lay in the very "presentism" I alluded to earlier, which is less concerned with writing a social history of the past than in mythologizing the past for his time and concerns.[56] She therefore goes along with him some of the way: "[I]nfantile phantasy, 'primitive' tribal rites, 'invented' historical accounts, psychoanalytical reconstructions, are all the same thing—each an explanation of the other at a different level."[57]

As a feminist, however, Mitchell also finds it necessary to step outside Freud's self-referential texts and try to locate psychoanalysis's emergence at a historical moment in the West when the structuring effects of kinship relations were giving way to the complex stratifications of classes in capitalist society. Her suggestion—and I think it is a brilliant one—is that "it is against the background of the *remoteness* of the kinship system that the ideology of the biological family comes into its own."[58] In other words, and following from this, only when the so-called exchange of women between families can no longer be so simply assured must the heterosexual monogamous family unit be culturally produced and legitimated. Just how this unit is reproduced through the constitution of subjects and objects of desire within it has been psychoanalysis's central concern. Here, then, would be a way to read and recompose Freud's persistent concern with infantile sexuality, masculinity, and, especially, femininity. Wilson is simply mistaken in imputing a one-dimensional deterministic view to Freud in these matters—the uncertainties, risks, contradictions, and incompleteness of his successive incursions enabled an extended deconstructive reading of his analyses of women, such as that in Luce Irigaray's *Speculum of the Other Woman*.[59] Moreover, his narrative of femininity, of how women who start out as "little men" are finally made to occupy the normal heterosexual place in the cultural order, is severely truncated. Freud's attempt to account for her "sex change"—namely, the shift in desire from a daughter's primary love, the mother, to the father—turns out to be so protracted and diffuse that we hear next to nothing about the *subsequent* substitution that would have to occur from the father to some other male figure to assure her successful entry into adult society. Attempting to explore such questions requires less a rejection of psychoanalysis than the production of more composite interpretations—at once psychoanalytical, feminist, and social—of the forces at work in the reproduction of identities, a psychoanalysis supplemented as much by Foucauldian genealogies of sex as with more specific investigations into "the invention of heterosexuality."[60]

Another example of such a tacking between levels of analysis would be Mary Poovey's study of the uneven development of gender in mid-Victorian England.[61] Reading both literary and historical documents of that period, she especially concentrates her attention upon the growing rise of single women in middle class society and the sense of potential threat they posed to the changing social order of the time. Here psychoanalysis enables her, for instance, to analyze the position of the governess in *Jane Eyre*, a figure who is deeply ambivalent about her social, financial, and affective dependencies. It is in the dreams of the protagonist and the composition of the novel itself that Poovey reconstructs moments of hysteria neither the author nor her characters consciously acknowledge.[62]

When the subjects of feminism come from "elsewhere," our questions and efforts will be redoubled, because we can expect more discrepancies than congruences between theories such as psychoanalysis, on the one hand, and colonial and postcolonial women, on the other. But we are not well served here by misleading notions of *cultural diversity*. One reason the relative/universal opposition in anthropology and cultural studies seems to be particularly badly posed is because it hinges on an image of "cultures that live unsullied by the intertextuality of their historical locations," as Homi Bhabha has so nicely put it.[63] A better response to being the hybrid subjects of a relation of cultural difference is to enunciate the partial and composite value of dominant Western theories without losing sight of the "subalternizations"—not to speak of "sanctioned ignorances"—that have maintained the authority of the West.

In the foregoing pages I have been trying to develop some considerations around the manifold structures and deployments of "theory." The extremely uneven and fragmentary nature of my remarks may be an indication of how much further we need to go. My goal has not been to "trash" some theories and applaud others. Instead, I have sought to call for a closer examination of the theories we depend on and of how they structure the institutional nexus of power/knowledge within which we work.

In a number of departments and disciplines, "theory" appears to occupy a place that until recently was the prerogative of philosophy. Perhaps because the tradition of Western philosophy has been constituted along such well-worn lines of succession, opposition, and inheritance, it offers a clear self-conception of its boundaries and levels of abstraction for those who wish to work within and against its norms. The force field of theory has benefited considerably from this philosophical tradition. It has inherited a penchant for metatheory especially evident in the growing vigilance toward the *foundational*, rhetorical, and linguistic structures governing a given argument or text.

But it is equally true that the kinds of theory I have been considering—such as deconstruction and psychoanalysis—are not what a significant number of departments—take sociology, anthropology, or history—mean by the term. They have their own traditions and criteria of what counts as theory, with methodological imperatives unique to those disciplines, and the degree to which they have felt compelled to attend to what "we" mean by it has been fitful. Moreover, the travel into what this chapter has been identifying as "theory" has been lopsided—whereas the search for metaphysical presuppositions and rhetorical strategies has occupied a dominant position, poststructuralist theory has engaged considerably less with the elements of sociohistorical analysis.

All these considerations take on a special significance for those of us whose projects are tied up with subjects until recently hidden from history and analytical inquiry. Because they have never been "sovereign," the subjects of colonialism, race, class, gender, and sexuality are still coming into language at different, intermediate levels of analysis. Not surprisingly, the greatest amount of work on these themes has taken place outside the realm of philosophical investigation, sometimes prior to the constitution of "theory." The sense I have is that the field of theory has yet to come to grips with this situation; to rewrite our projects in theory's terms is not an adequate response. My suggestion in this chapter has been to partialize our theories, and watch for their levels of composition, as a way forward.

Though my own directions of inquiry emerge from a desire to see Western theories travel better so as to illuminate the conditions of subjects for whom they were not made, this recognition of the mutual implication of different levels of analysis is equally urgent for Western subjects. This was why I chose to exemplify the more or less partial and composite theories of Spivak, as well as examples from Freud and feminist psychoanalysis. Given the range of questions and possibilities of "travel" Juliet Mitchell manifested in her earlier work, it is surprising to find her subsequently less interested in pursuing such lines of inquiry. In the course of an interview in 1988, she talked of the lag between "inner" and "outer" realities, "the problem . . . that a sociology cannot be made to match the very different structures of the unconscious,"[64] as a reason to avoid such

conjunctions, whereas I have been trying to argue that psychoanalysis itself is constituted by these very discrepancies and in-
congruities. More to the point, these interfaces need to be investigated further as contradictions that are productive for feminist
work. But perhaps Mitchell is changing directions yet again, this
time in favor of a less confined psychoanalytic feminism. She now
appears concerned with a recovery of the socialist dimensions of her
early book *Psychoanalysis and Feminism* that readers completely
missed.[65] To take another example, in his detailed analyses of
Thatcherism in Britain, Stuart Hall is forced to question "the trans-
historical speculative generalities of Lacanianism," where "the formation of subjectivities . . . is accomplished in the same series of
resolutions." As he puts it, " . . . there is all the difference in the
world between the capacity to use Language *as such* and the appropriation and imaginary identity between particular *languages* and
their specific ideological and discursive universes."[66]

Both of the epigraphs to this essay have pointed to the source of
our difficulties and the possibility of moving beyond it. Whereas
Tey Diana Rebolledo incisively demands that we demystify the
power of "theory" and learn instead to internalize and reconstitute
theories in light of our themes and problems, de Certeau has called
for an interdisciplinary crystallization of new subjects and methods.
Paradoxically enough, it is by paying more rather than less attention
to the divisions and hierarchies presently conditioning our projects
that partial and composite theories can aim toward the possibility of
a transdisciplinary, perhaps even decolonized horizon.

Chapter Three

Women, Patriarchy, Sex, Gender

U.S. Feminist Theory in Historical Perspective

The more a thing is torn
the more places it can connect.
Meredith Stricker, *Island*

I find I am constantly being encouraged to pluck out
some one aspect of myself and present this as a meaningful whole, eclipsing or denying other parts of self. But
this is a destructive and fragmenting way to live. My
fullest concentration of energy is available to me only
when I integrate all the parts of who I am.
Audre Lorde, *Sister Outsider*

In the course of the previous chapter's discussion on the status of
theory, feminist theory as such was unevenly and sometimes only
marginally at issue. In this chapter I will attempt to rectify that imbalance by examining more closely how some of the arguments
made so far can be extended and revised in the light of recent developments within feminist scholarship. Once again, my thoughts and
questions have been overwhelmingly framed by the real, if provisional, effects of years of (dis)location in the United States. Not
unlike "theory," or even academic work in general, research by or
about women also comes in disproportionate quantities from this
particular sector of the globe—so much so that the equally significant work by feminists living elsewhere must contend with the
effects of Western dominance in such a field as well.

As I tried to indicate in chapter one, just what arrives in other
places is itself a product of the relations of power and marginality

that structure the circulation of knowledges *within* nations such as the United States. As recently as 1991, feminist critics of literature in India had to confine their awareness of a book on black women writers to a footnote. Even here, the book had by no means come independently, if belatedly, through the circuits of international distribution networks; rather, it was brought to these theorists' notice by their U.S. publisher.[1] I do not think the situation has decisively changed in the intervening years.

There is every reason, therefore, to open up certain aspects of U.S. feminist theory—to review some of its claims, debates, and concerns with an eye to providing a potentially richer and, perhaps, more critical sense of the U.S. field. If it was not entirely misleading to refer to an entity called "theory" in the last chapter, how do matters stand among feminists in the U.S. academy? Ever since the latter part of the eighties, and increasingly since the onset of the nineties, mention of the trends, changes, and impasses in the last two decades of U.S. and European feminist theoretical work are being heard. Feminist research has been emerging within almost any discipline one might name—if mainly in the social sciences and the humanities—and with little danger of being segregated inside Women's Studies programs; it is a vast and heterogeneous field that would take many books to adequately explore. One entry point could be to attend to the modes of classification available, the ways in which feminists have been identifying themselves, their work and one another. Thinking along these lines, I discovered the following: National identifications within the United States don't seem to count for much; distinctions according to traditional political positions, such as Marxist or socialist, liberal or radical feminist orientations, are still in use, though much less so than before; questions of race and ethnicity have been insistently foregrounded by women of color; and lesbian feminism is becoming more visible all the time. The most prevalent style of self-identification, however, is by disciplinary affiliation—feminists in the academy are historians, literary and film critics, sociologists and political theorists, anthropologists and psychologists, philosophers (occasionally) and scientists (rarely).

These somewhat pat observations, however, provide little inkling of the uneasy but profound effects such differing and evolving identifications have been producing, especially for feminist subjects who cannot be contained within any one of these descriptions neatly, whose very subjectivities are conditioned, promoted, or denied by the mutual effects of and power relations between such strands of identity and difference. For there are other ways to try to allude to that fleeting space called the historical present. The nineties in the U.S. have become a time scored through by expectation and disillusionment, as "we" are increasingly conscious of the divisions within and between us and of the possibilities and limits of their articulation through the traditions and terms of feminist theorizing hitherto valorized. There appear to be no readily available frameworks in order to articulate and respond to difference and conflict. In the context of a discussion of the uneven reception of *This Bridge Called My Back* within Anglo-American feminist scholarship, Norma Alarcón interprets the theme poem of that volume, Donna Kate Ruchin's "The Bridge Poem," as the eloquent expression of a predicament that is not the author's alone:

In my view, the speaker's refusal to play "bridge" [the dream of helping the people who surround her to reach an interconnectedness that would change society], as an enablement to others as well as to the self, is the acceptance of defeat at the hands of political groups whose self-definition follows the view of self as unitary, capable of being defined by a single "theme." The speaker's perception that the self is "multiple," and its reduction harmful, gives emphasis to the relationality between one's selves and those of others as an ongoing process of struggle, effort and tension.[2]

The twin epigraphs to this chapter also express something of that "struggle, effort and tension" around the fragments and connections, the levels and institutions of difference constitutive of contemporary U.S. feminism.

In the present chapter, I shall attempt a very limited assessment of how these experiences are being played out theoretically—that is to say, what importance has been assigned to the reinvention of the *concepts* structuring feminism itself. A great deal of intellectual hope has been lodged in the potential meanings and articulations of feminist categories of analysis. I by no means want to diminish that

hope. But in order to confront, let alone move beyond, the reproduction of unitary rather than multiple feminist subjects, feminist
theorizing must *historicize* itself. Building on scattered remarks
from chapter one, together with my claims in favor of partial and
composite theories initiated in chapter two, I am therefore arguing
here that feminism needs a more explicitly fostered exchange between feminist categories and a sense of historicity.

But first, what have been the presumptions, questions, and arguments about the nature and scope of the concepts of feminist theory? A number of terms might come to mind—Woman and women,
sex and sexual difference, femininity and patriarchy. In the last so
many years especially, one concept in particular has been gaining
immense ground. Theorists from many disciplines, feminists anx-
ious to overcome earlier hurdles and impasses, are speaking the
language of *gender*.

The Explosion of Gender
as a Category of Analysis

The clearest indication of the pervasiveness of gender in contemporary feminist work—and, one should add, in research more generally—is the degree to which its meaning tends to be *presumed*
rather than questioned for its conceptual role. At the same time,
though, articles and books have been getting published that make
gender itself the subject of analysis, thus attempting the difficult
task of placing the very terms of one's method at the center of
analytical attention.

Looking up the etymological genealogy of the word "gender" in
the context of contributing this keyword to a German Marxist dictionary, historian of science Donna Haraway starts her entry as
follows:

The root of the English, French, and Spanish words is the Latin verb
generare, to beget, and the Latin stem *gener-*, race or kind. . . . The
substantives "Geschlecht," "gender," "genre," and "genero" refer to the
notion of sort, kind and class. . . . The modern English and German words,
"gender" and "Geschlecht," adhere closely to concepts of sex, sexuality,
sexual difference, generation, engendering, and so on, while the French

and Spanish seem not to carry those meanings readily. Words close to "gender" are implicated in concepts of kinship, race, biological taxonomy, language, and nationality.[3]

Indeed, as she goes on to sum up, "'gender' is at the heart of constructions and classifications of systems of difference."[4] Conclusions of a similar nature have been echoed in other studies as well. Joan Wallach Scott, a historian, the literary theorist Elaine Showalter, and the film critic and semiotician Teresa de Lauretis all have pointed to the classificatory connotations emanating from the notion of gender—grammatically and morphologically, with de Lauretis adding a cautionary note about the differing proximities of grammar and sex in a number of European languages.[5] And the French philosopher Derrida, commenting on Martin Heidegger's near silence on these matters, distinguishes between "the Geschlecht" and "Geschlecht," where Geschlecht can connote "sex, race, family, generation, lineage, species, genre/genus."[6]

Gender is not only richly intertwined with other meanings when investigated along etymological and linguistic lines. In the context of exploring "the science question in feminism," Sandra Harding, among others, has emphasized the symbolic meanings associated with gender—meanings that she feels undergird more specific conceptions of gender identity and gender relations. Gender symbolism, as she calls it, is analytically so crucial because

gender difference is the most ancient, most universal, and most powerful origin of many morally valued conceptualizations of everything else in the world around us. . . . As far back in history as we can see, we have organized our social and natural worlds in terms of gender meanings within which historically specific racial, class, and cultural institutions and meanings have been constructed. Once we begin to theorize gender—to define gender as an analytical category within which humans think about and organize their social activity rather than as a natural consequence of sex difference, or even merely as a social variable assigned to individual people in different ways from culture to culture—we can begin to appreciate the extent to which gender meanings have suffused our belief systems [and] institutions.[7]

I will be examining the effects of Harding's comments in greater detail in the next section. At this point I am only interested in underlining how she, too, places an immense amount of analytical weight on gender, a term, moreover, that is rather new. For, as Haraway discovered, gender exploded into common usage only after the seventies. She was able to monitor the "explosion" by verifying the phenomenal rise in keyword entries under gender during the last twenty years of social science academic research in the United States. Using sociological and psychological abstracts as her case studies, she found that the number of entries in sociological work increased from none at all between 1966 and 1970 to 724 between 1981 and 1985. The figure for the same periods in psychology jumped from 50 to 1326.[8]

Coinciding as it does with the emergence of feminism as a social movement, there can be no denying the political reasons behind the pervasiveness of a term that we can now practically take for granted but that was effectively unknown a generation ago. But to my mind, the most interesting aspect of gender use has yet to be touched upon. Feminists of various persuasions and with remarkably diverse disciplinary backgrounds are debating "the rise of gender" (to use Showalter's expression) not so much against an earlier, prefeminist era but *within* feminist theory itself. Positioning themselves inside the complex field of feminism in terms of their intellectual and political frames of reference, some of these theorists are attending to or privileging the category of gender over against other concepts that have also been part of a vocabulary for the study of women.

Let me start by looking at some of the ways an emphasis upon *women* has become problematized in light of a gendered perspective. In her extensive study of the relationship between feminism and anthropology, published in 1988, Henrietta L. Moore first points to the uniqueness of the discipline of anthropology. It may well be the only discipline where women have *not* been traditionally ignored. The problem facing a new generation of researchers who entered the discipline in the early seventies expressly as feminists therefore had more to do with how women were represented in the older ethnographic accounts. The new "anthropology of women," as it came to be called (and anthologized in such well-known collections as *Women, Culture and Society* and *Toward an Anthropology of Women*),[9] was consequently less caught up with correcting for a lack of empirical data than with interrogating interpretive presuppositions that left women present but "muted." But —and this is the important moment in Moore's reconstruction of feminist anthropology's history—it was not until the "anthropology of women" was able to make room for gender that its feminist potential could be more fully realized:

> Feminist anthropology is more than the study of women. It is the study of gender, of the interrelations between women and men, and the role of gender in structuring human societies, their histories, ideologies, economic systems and political systems. Gender can no more be marginalized in the study of human societies than the concept of "human action" or the concept of "society." It would not be possible to pursue any sort of social science without a concept of gender.[10]

The problems inherent in an emphasis on women had to do with its exclusionary and marginalizing effects within the discipline, foreclosing on a potential critique of the theories and methods structuring anthropology *as a whole*. Not unlike the claims made by Sandra Harding earlier on, the promise of gender for feminist theory when undertaken from an anthropological perspective should lead to a fundamental reconceptualization of the terrain of feminist research, such that one could now expect feminist anthropology to move beyond kinship, labor, and the household (chapters three and four of Moore's study) into, for example, questions of women and the state (chapter five).

Speaking of and about women also runs the danger of presuming a set of common meanings and connections when such meanings are precisely what need to be explored. The danger grows when women become the subject of analysis in a universalizing way. Feminist anthropology, however, has been more conscious than many about such issues, drawing as it does from a discipline whose very conception of itself has come to rest on the truths of cultural difference. At least around questions of culture, then, women have not been taken as a category that goes unquestioned.[11]

But this cannot be said for other traditions and disciplines. Speaking from the intersections between feminism, poststructuralism, and semiotics in 1987, de Lauretis has put forward her reasons for developing a new theory specifically concerned with gender. In feminist work from the sixties and seventies that she draws from, *sexual difference* circulated as the key term of intervention central to questions of subjectivity and representation, especially as it was foregrounded in film theory and literary criticism. It is this very notion (as well as others de Lauretis considers derivative, such as women's culture, mothering, feminine writing, and femininity), once so enabling, that has now, she feels, turned into a limitation for feminism. For, in the first instance, sexual difference constrains feminism "within the conceptual frame of a universal sex opposition, . . . which makes it very difficult, if not impossible, to articulate the differences of women from Woman, that is to say, the differences among women or, perhaps more exactly, the differences *within women*."[12] Following from this, the earlier privileging of sexual difference cuts off alternative routes for the conceptualization of newly emergent feminist subjectivities, especially since the eighties, "subject[s] constituted in gender, to be sure, though not by sexual difference alone, but rather across languages and cultural representations; subject[s] en-gendered in the experiencing of race and class, as well as sexual, relations; subject[s], therefore, not unified but rather multiple, and not so much divided as contradicted."[13] Toward such an end, she proposes a conception of the "technology of gender" by critically rewriting Michel Foucault's analyses of the "technology of sex." Foucault's incursions into the history of Western sexuality—the technologies of sex at work in discourses, institutions, and practices, and especially through processes of subjectification—can, she argues, be fruitfully revised from a contemporary feminist perspective, where sex and gender are no longer coterminous. Introducing gender into his analytical apparatus would therefore not only call for a questioning of his biases—the degree to which his considerations were structured within an unmarked masculine frame—but, more important, bring into play a theoretical construct at once more ambivalent and more open to reevaluations of feminist analyses in the face of other women's understandings of their social and sexual condition.

We thus have at least two theorists who have staked their claims on gender by turning a critical eye backwards to an earlier, more restrictive, more homogenizing period in feminist intellectual history. If, for Moore, the limitation for a newly emergent feminist anthropology lies in its initial privilege on "women," it is the universalizations and blind spots contained in an unmodified use of sexual difference among poststructuralist feminists that de Lauretis finds most wanting.

Judith Butler is another figure on the contemporary map who has questioned previous feminist paradigms. Her criticisms, often overlapping with those we have heard already, can perhaps be distinguished by their more insistently philosophical focus on the foundations of feminist politics. Not only has feminism required a subject upon which to ground itself *before* being able to initiate its interests and goals, she argues, but this subject has further been a universal one. If such an assumption once rested on a presumedly universal conception of *patriarchy*, taken to be oppressive of all women, that particular notion no longer enjoys much credibility, according to Butler. However, other terms, such as women and sex, have been considerably harder to displace—as much in their ontological function as in their ethnocentrism.

Butler is insistent in her demand that feminists in general do without such foundational categories—for rather than being the conditions of possibility for our politics, at this point they may actually be in danger of threatening it. As she puts it,

[o]ntology is not a foundation, but a normative injunction that operates insidiously by installing itself into political discourse as its necessary ground. . . . The internal paradox of this foundationalism is that it presumes, fixes and constrains the very "subjects" that it hopes to represent and liberate.[14]

Rather, then, than looking for *grounds* in our theories and vocabularies, it behooves us to find ways of creating what Butler calls *gender trouble*, ways of disrupting the connections that bind sex, gender, and desire into a natural and universal order. Neither a noun nor a set of free-floating attributes, gender is produced through convergences among culturally and historically specific sets of relations. Where Gayle Rubin outlined her pathbreaking analysis of "the sex-gender system" in 1975, the mechanisms by which biological sex was transformed cross-culturally into social gender,[15] and Catherine MacKinnon in 1981 resolutely retained the language of sex and sexuality,[16] Butler turns the argument around: by making "sex" the *effect* of gender, a legitimation subsequently imposed in order to fix the socially contingent through recourse to an unquestioned biology, "the distinction between sex and gender turns out to be no distinction at all."[17]

There are a number of other considerations around gender that could be touched upon.[18] But for my purposes, I would first like to pull back at this point and find a way to take stock of some of these claims, coming from such different angles as they clearly do. One pair of statements seems to be echoing in many places. First, unlike Woman or women, relations of gender are to be found everywhere (it is not possible to study anything without the concept of gender, as Showalter puts it). Second, and again in some contrast to earlier feminist concepts, gender is not universalizing and homogenizing in its presumptions and purview—indeed, the theorists we heard were particularly self-conscious about wanting gender to highlight the differences among and within women. (To refer to Showalter once more, "talking about gender is a constant reminder of other categories of difference, such as race and class, that structure our lives and texts.")[19] The crucial issue from my vantage point is, how have these combined claims been recognized and subsequently worked through? I cannot emphasize this question enough, because how well gender "travels" depends entirely on how self-reflexive one is in following up on such methodological insights.

The first consideration underlines the mistake of equating gender with women. Instead, it indicates a more general *relation*, one that structures institutions, symbols, and practices that on the face of things may have nothing to say about women. For example, Joan Scott unravels E. P. Thompson's *The Making of the English Working Class* to show how his definition of class was crucially constructed in gendered terms, relying on representations of masculinity to convey its meanings.[20] It is not women alone who have hitherto been naturalized and thus rendered invisible—rather, the successful working of ideology must ensure that we do not see gender relations *as a whole*. With the wisdom of hindsight one can now detect the flaw in such a pathbreaking analysis as Simone de

Beauvoir's, which—having so brilliantly demonstrated the effects of equating "woman" with "the sex," "the other," the one confined to immanence—barely interrogated the first sex, its masculinity draped in Sartrean transcendence or a Marxist humanism.[21]

The second consideration, however, appears to be incompatible with the previous one, or at least to pull us in a different direction. It reiterates the *specificity* of gender, the realization that conceptions of gender alone cannot accomplish all the work. Moreover, these very conceptions are transformed by one's cultural and historical contexts of investigation. Can, then, the twin pulls of gender—namely, of wanting to extend feminist analyses into hitherto unexplored spheres of inquiry and of recognizing that feminists are only concentrating on part of the story—be explicitly worked through? I would like to think so, though the implications for the status of gender as a category of analysis might well appear paradoxical. For the consequences, as I see it, lead to an effective *demoting* of gender as a central and foundational category. If I might carry over some of the considerations from the previous chapter, this concept, too, needs to be examined for its own partial and composite meanings. This means *both* holding onto the partiality of gender for feminists and going *outside* this notion to explore the histories, symbolisms, and political stakes of other terms in their irreducible relation to feminism. Only then can a more genuinely nonhomogenizing and nonuniversalizing—that is to say, composite—analysis be achieved.

Indeed, it is already necessary to go beyond the concept of gender at precisely those intractable sites where it seems most central, stable, and foundational to the rest of culture—in the engendering of subjects within modern Western households, in the family. As Butler persuasively argues in *Gender Trouble*, the reproduction of gendered dispositions within the family cannot be rendered intelligible without *additional* concepts—namely, those of heterosexuality and homosexuality. For a consideration of gender relations alone cannot achieve the necessary denaturalization of heterosexuality and a concomitant questioning of the social and psychical taboos on homosexuality. Why, she asks, have we so often presumed that there are only two genders?

But if the potential of gender thus indispensably depends upon its articulation with other categories, a better sense of the relationships between gender and other terms of analysis is clearly called for. Now it may well be that a sense of fatigue is evident in the oft-repeated demand to integrate gender with "class, race, ethnicity and sexuality." Such fatigue, I suggest, is premature. Iris Berger has made the point quite forcefully: " . . . in the absence of analytical clarity, the litany of 'race, class and gender' threatens at times to become a formulaic reiteration of belief rather than a source of innovative or systematic insights."[22]

Feminist theorists who wish creatively to address a broader audience than has been possible so far not only must cease to impose an agenda based on the primacy of gender but also must begin to look into the often *divergent* forms and historical constraints accruing to such categories.

In order to provide an indication of the kind of problematic I have in mind, a brief examination of another major category of analysis may help. Writing at this particular historical juncture, no one can avoid confronting the glaring retreat of class from the political and intellectual agendas of the day. Probably the strongest indication of such a state of affairs is to be found in the embattled status of Marxism and socialism as viable and credible frameworks of political struggle and historical change—certainly in the nations of the West and increasingly elsewhere as well. One specific field where this situation has produced quite evident effects would be contemporary U.S. feminism.

I have already mentioned how a number of theorists found that the new analyses of gender enabled, or at least coincided with, the emergence of more heterogeneous feminisms than had been possible before. However, the history of Marxist or socialist feminism in the West may not fit this narrative so easily, or at least not in a simple way. Among the best-known texts to have foregrounded the relationship between feminism and Marxism is surely the collection of essays edited by Lydia Sargant in 1981, *Women and Revolution, A Discussion of the Unhappy Marriage of Marxism and Feminism.*[23] What the text taken as a whole enacts is a debate over the levels of generality and specificity that need to be characteristic of feminism, though *without* benefit of either the developed analyses around gender that have subsequently come to be so much a part of feminist discourse since the eighties or the poststructuralist and philosophical critiques of foundationalism and essentialism more common today.

If only because the overall framework of their discussion hinges on the perceived *dominance* of Marxism, leading to variously conceptualized demands for *more* feminist space, it is hard to believe how so much could change in barely a decade. At least one major participant in those discussions, writing less than ten years later, has come to feel that the term "socialist" no longer actively names U.S. feminism for the nineties.[24] Occasionally speaking the language of gender but more commonly relying on the conception of patriarchy, these contributors around 1980 differed over how best to strengthen feminism's as-yet fragile political and theoretical status within the "larger" struggle against capital. How autonomous is capitalism from patriarchy—should one speak of two systems, closely but not necessarily intertwined, or one? Whether or not capitalism is gender-blind, wouldn't one still need to go beyond the framework of Marxism to account for the origins and persistence of patriarchy? Or is feminism dependent on using and transforming key Marxist concepts, such as class, the division of labor, and the question of history, to get feminist analysis off the ground? And what of the issues of racism and gay and lesbian liberation—how did the debate remain so narrowly defined as to bypass sexuality and the distinct dynamics of black feminist analyses, for instance? These are some of the themes circulating within the book.[25] Even though only preliminary in scope and too often bogged down by the need to assert that a given category or institution be recognized as more basic than the rest, their questions struck me as quite compatible with contemporary desires to see feminism both broaden and enrich its terrain. The major and obvious difference is that whereas the earlier socialist feminists felt themselves up against a monolithically and narrowly defined system called capitalism, today's theorists are voicing similar doubts about the legacy of feminist analyses!

This brief glimpse into a textual moment in the history of U.S. Marxist-feminism should therefore make us pause before too quickly ascribing a one-dimensional past to feminism in favor of a more multivalent and contradictory present. It is not irrelevant that just when we are being reminded of the manifold connotations and symbolic mobilities of gender and are hearing constant allusions to the differences of race, class, and sexuality, class analysis is actually in a state of decline, despite its roots in such an extensive tradition of Marxist exegesis and scholarship.

My purpose in specifying the retreat of class from contemporary feminist concerns is to make us more historically aware of the changing grounds of feminist theory, where certain legacies live on while others are effectively written out of collective memory. Both because it is so crucial at the present time to take questions of difference seriously and because the need for such analyses has never been more strongly felt, I am attempting in this chapter to examine in some detail how feminist theories claiming to be all about heterogeneity are actually constructed. If questions in the last chapter circled more generally around the levels of abstraction and disciplinary affiliations characteristic of theories such as deconstruction and psychoanalysis, it is the irreducibly partial and composite potential of gender—that is to say, its double inheritance of what de Lauretis has called "the essential difference"[26] of feminism *together with* the active integration of differences among and within women —that occupies us here. For I can think of no set of issues with better prospects of traveling into and engaging with the complex field of feminism in India.

But in order for such a potentially productive encounter to take place, we need something other than Judith Butler's passing comment in *Gender Trouble*, where she says:

The theories of feminist identity that elaborate predicates of color, sexuality, ethnicity, class, and able-bodiedness invariably close with an embarrassed "etc." at the end of the list. . . . What political impetus is to be derived from the exasperated "etc." that so often occurs at the end of such lines? This is a sign of exhaustion as well as of the illimitable process of signification itself. It is the *supplement*, the excess that necessarily accompanies any effort to posit identity once and for all.[27]

At one level, I cannot agree with her more, especially in light of her excellent critiques of misleading binarisms that conceptualize identity as either completely determined or arbitrarily chosen. And, of course, any desire to provide a picture "once and for all" is, and should be, doomed to failure. But the call for more many-layered and contradictory feminist work has developed at least in part in light of Norma Alarcón's allusion to the difficulties and disillusionments that have accompanied the "ongoing process of struggle, effort and tension" for multiple subjectivities within ideological and academic worlds more given to prioritizing (if not monological) strategies than to demonstrations of excess. Precisely because Audre Lorde's demand for the integration of all her fragmented identities in the epigraph is an impossible one, it becomes all the more necessary to guard against images of excess and supplementarity that seem to speak of identity in terms of a surfeit, a play of too many options that only run out from exhaustion. After Butler has shown at considerable length that there aren't and shouldn't be necessary guarantees in the making of subjectivities, that "we" are the effects of contingent practices, what historical spaces and times are available for more "excessive" constructions and destabilizations, for whom, and with what consequences?

In other words, the task of a theoretical exploration into the significations of difference and power is made infinitely more complicated when references to heterogeneity may still be covering up homogenizing moves. It is obviously no longer the case that questions of multiplicity are simply invisible or suppressed. In the rest of this chapter I develop my overall argument about the analytical and historical constraints inhibiting the articulation of difference. The following section attempts to understand what can get passed over in the very claim to have successfully broached the integration of gender with other categories. On that basis, a more forceful elaboration of the intertwining themes of history and the unequal trajectories of feminism's concepts of analysis can be staged.

"Curious Coincidences" or Analogical Detours?

Sandra Harding, whose work has already been referred to, is one of the theorists to have examined the complex configurations of gender in its relations to other structures of inequality. The quotation from her important study *The Science Question in Feminism,* where she contrasts the pervasiveness of gender symbolism with the historicity of other forms of difference, already hints at such concerns: "As far back in history as we can see, we have organized our social and natural worlds in terms of gender meanings, within which historically specific racial, class and cultural institutions and meanings have been constructed" (*SF*, p. 17). In order to see how this assertion is subsequently followed through, I would like to move into one of the later chapters of her book, entitled *Other "Others" and Fractured Identities: Issues for Epistemologists.*

In that chapter she lays out in some detail what initially struck her as "eerie" and finally sounded "suspicious:" the "curious coincidence," as she called it, between the worldviews and forms of identity variously ascribed to African, Native American, and Chinese peoples, on the one hand, and to women, on the other. Whereas a number of feminists, many of whom were influenced by psychoanalytical object relations theory, have been redeeming a sense of femininity that is relational, subjective, and in deep connection with the social and natural world, completely independent anthropological and third-world texts have highlighted just these sorts of characteristics for *their* subjects. To take but one example from the literature she looked at, here is her summary of the black economist Vernon Dixon's delineation of a specifically African worldview:

The individual gets his sense of self and can determine what it is only through his relationships within the community. Because the self is continuous with nature, rather than set over against it, the need to dominate nature as an impersonal object is replaced by the need to cooperate in nature's own projects. Coming to know is a process involving concrete interactions that acknowledge the role of the emotions and values in gaining knowledge (*SF*, p. 170).[28]

One of the feminist theories Harding compares these considerations to is Nancy Hartsock's proposal of a uniquely "feminist standpoint" arising out of women's special material activity as contributors to subsistence, with motherhood playing a definitive role:

Motherhood in the large sense, i.e., motherhood as an institution rather than experience, including pregnancy and the preparation for motherhood almost all females receive as socialization, results in the construction of female existence as centered within a complex relational nexus. . . . [G]eneralizing the activity of women to the social system as a whole would raise, for the *first* time in human history, the possibility of a fully human community, a community structured by connection rather than by separation and opposition.[29]

But haven't Africans, according to Dixon, already epitomized just such "a fully human community"?

The most interesting moments emerge in the course of Harding's methods for dealing with this "curious coincidence." Ascending to a metadiscursive level of abstraction—not unlike the philosophical level often characteristic of "theory" outlined in the last chapter—she is able to pinpoint the kinds of conceptual schemes at work in each case, though they are not always explicitly acknowledged. Where the African literature is structured around the binary opposition "European/American/Western" versus "African/non-Western" (distinctions between male and female remaining unmarked terms), the feminist texts move between "masculine" and "feminine" poles (and with few further qualifications). Furthermore, it is the forms of subjectivity of the "masculine" and of the "Westerner" in each of the literatures—autonomous, individualistic, self-interested, and fundamentally isolated from other people and from nature—that turn out to be most identical. Her explanations for this and the consequences she draws are swift and clear: both women and Africans have, perhaps unwittingly, fallen into an insidious trap. Rather than having discovered an identity they can legitimately call their very own, they have been defined and subjectified as the conceptual "other" in opposition to the imperializing Western male, through a process of negation.

As partial analyses go, this level of explanation has definite strengths. It prevents anyone from ever forgetting the structuring effects of the *relations* of domination—whether these be the relations to the West wrought by colonialism or the relations of gender produced within patriarchy—for the development of any identity. There is surely no direct route outside these hierarchically organized binary oppositions bequeathed upon the world at least since the so-called Enlightenment. Moreover, because these conceptual schemes emanate from the same central nexus of discourses, small wonder that they sound so surprisingly alike.

But Harding cannot stay satisfied with this kind of explanation, nor should she. Instead, she continues her train of thought by introducing a series of considerations at various levels of analysis. Her questions and doubts range from noticing the way such contrast schemas work by overemphasizing certain differences at the expense of others, asking just *who* the subjects in each of these literatures might be, to wondering further what kind of emancipatory potential such worldviews actually contain. She also does not neglect to mention that the very success of an explanation for these (or any other) parallels between Western/third-world and masculine/feminine distinctions is predicated upon rendering invisible those subjects who straddle *both* dichotomies—namely, women within third-world countries. Should African and Native American women, for instance, think of themselves as doubly in connection with their social and natural worlds?

Having raised issues such as these, one would expect Harding to move more self-consciously between levels of analysis in order both to position herself more directly and to follow up on some of the questions she has foregrounded so well. What seems necessary at this stage would be a more multilayered and composite situating of the literatures she is comparing from her vantage point as a Western feminist concerned with the pervasiveness of gender in its relation to questions of race, class, and culture.

But the effective connections she ultimately sanctions take her down a rather well-worn road. A major emphasis in the text, one that takes up a significant portion of the chapter, is that Western feminists would do well to pay good attention to the history of Africa, in particular to its experience of colonization and cultural imperialism, because it has been so exemplary in the "othering" process. The very notion of "Africa," after all, only came into existence when it was forced into modern world history as a continent to be governed and exploited. In other words, the history of its name has been the history of its being so named by the West.

So far, so good. However, though there are moments when she

acknowledges that "we are assigned to different subjugations by our single set of rulers" (*SF*, p. 176), what finally gains the upper hand in the analysis is her desire to use the experience of Africa in order to clarify the relations of gender more directly. For Africa's colonization is so plain to see: "The original social process of creating the genders is lost to our view in the distant mists of human history, but the original creation of the races is entirely visible in relatively recent history" (*SF*, p. 175).

Therefore, it does indeed become possible for Harding to provide a coherent explanation for the "curious coincidence," and I shall quote from it at some length:

With the coming of imperialism to Africa, decisions about what labor Africans would perform and who could benefit from it were wrested from Africans and transferred to Europeans and Americans. Henceforth, Africans would work to benefit Euro-American societies, whether as diamond miners, as domestic servants, as the most menial of industrial wage laborers, or as wage or slave labor on plantations in Africa or America . . .

Similarly, the emergence of masculine domination among our distant ancestors can be understood as the transfer of the conceptualization and control of women's sexuality, reproduction and production labor to men— a process intensified and systematized in new ways during the last three centuries in the West (*SF*, pp. 187–188).

In other words, Harding effectively shifts her analysis from the status of a coincidence to that of an *analogy*. By taking a detour, as it were, through the history of colonialism, the narrative of African peoples' subjectification can be made to stand in for and speak to Harding's subjects of feminism.

Because I introduced questions of analogy in the discussion on Freud in the last chapter, it would be worth linking up Harding's moves here with the examples I already touched upon. To recall briefly, I presented an analogy as a theoretical move from more familiar to relatively unknown terrain in order to understand how a set of relations evident in one sphere might illuminate the other. The cases that came up for examination were the differences between Freud's analyses of the dream-work and joke-work, on the one hand, and his attempt to view religion, especially Judaism, as a mode of collective neurosis, on the other. My reasons for preferring

Freud's analogies between the structuring role of the unconscious in dreams and jokes to his more reductive reading of *Moses and Monotheism* centered around the greater open-endedness of the former: he never lost sight of the partial meaningfulness of such "travel" nor of the subsequent ways in which the differences between jokes and dreams at other analytical levels were brought more sharply into focus. It was precisely when he seemed to have forgotten this in later life, such that the obsessions and compulsions of individual neurosis could be rendered equivalent to the Jews' commemoration of their Mosaic "father," that my difficulties began.

How do those concerns bear up in this context? It seems to me, for a number of reasons I will try to elaborate on, that Harding's moves veer more closely toward a reductive identification of colonial and gender relations, leading to the effective flattening of a series of questions that might have otherwise led her analysis into new directions. As it stands, her call for a "unified field theory" capable of bringing the "laws of tendency of racism" together with the "laws of tendency of patriarchy" (*SF*, p. 186) reads like a tag. Rather than to have such overambitious and, indeed, questionable aims (what could it mean to wish for a unified field theory "quite as impressive as that of Newton's mechanics"?) (Ibid.), everyone would be far better served if Harding would be more accountable to the analytical connections she does valorize and the consequences that follow from them.

To begin with, discovering analogies between race and gender is nothing new. Nancy Stepan has made a preliminary but telling investigation into the powerful structuring role such analogies have played in the history of Western science from the eighteenth century into the present one. Perhaps because scientists first singled out "race" as their subject of analysis, after which their attention turned increasingly to sex and gender as well, the direction of comparison appears more often to have been from the former to the latter. As Stepan puts it: "So fundamental was the analogy between race and gender that the major modes of explanation of racial traits were used to explain sexual traits."[30] Stepan cautions anyone from wishing to simply step outside the analogical and metaphorical structures of those arguments, however debased and strained they may sound, in favor of some immediate access to the subjects themselves, and a great deal of poststructuralist theory would support her here. I, too, would hesitate before making demands for a purely literal-minded reading of things, though there are times when such readings can be undertaken with illuminating effect.[31] But my point is a slightly different one. I don't think our options are restricted to the wholesale acceptance or rejection of analogies, with nothing further to say. As Hayden White has made abundantly clear, analogies, like other rhetorical devices, are tropical rather than logical instruments, which means that, depending upon their contexts and effective histories, they work *strategically*. The tropical element

is the process by which all discourse *constitutes* the objects which it pretends only to describe realistically and to describe objectively. . . . [T]roping is both a movement *from* one notion of the way things are related to another notion, and a connection between things so that they can be expressed in a language that takes account of the possibility of their being expressed otherwise.[32]

Precisely because the "swerve" of a particular trope is not governed by logical consistency—indeed, according to White, even the logical syllogism in its move from major to minor premise is not—there is a moment where "nothing but the *decision* to move"[33] is at issue.

Aida Hurtado, among others, has pointed out how parallels and comparisons drawn between white women and black men by early feminist suffragists in this country actually "pitted white women against Black men in a competition for privileges that erased Black women altogether."[34] Because analogizing moves between race and gender have such a long if problematic history, one might be led to the conclusion that discourses around the construction of racial and colonial subjects enjoy at least the same hearing in the West as do those on the histories of sexuality and gender. And, in fact, because an analogy travels by carrying over an analysis or set of relations from *more* to *less* well-known terrain, one could even expect a certain eminence, if anything, to "the laws of tendency of racism," as Harding put it. However, today this is by no means the case. Within the United States, at least one major contributor to the contemporary understanding of this country's "racial formation" has found many reasons to speak of "a pervasive crisis of race,"[35] born in some measure by the wholesale *denial* and recoding of structures of racism and injustice in the political climate of the seventies and eighties. In spite of the insistence of women of color and their recognition that "something about the subject makes it hard to name,"[36] questions of race remain troubling, if not intractable, with far too little serious engagement and analysis from white feminists. Is this because, as law professor Patricia Williams so acutely put it, race has become a "phantom word"?[37] It is within this context, therefore, that one would need to assess Harding's strategy of foregrounding the violent naming of Africa in order that contemporary white feminists question the alleged discovery of femininity for themselves.

Having been instructed by the "coincidences" between race and gender relations at a more general level of abstraction, a more far-reaching strategy could then be to examine how these relations intersect or, better still, *articulate*[38] with one another at other levels of analysis, thus coming a step closer to producing a more composite sense of the histories of different women. The need for such composite articulations may seem more urgent and obvious to me as a postcolonial feminist, for whom the transformative relations of both colonialism and patriarchy need to be rendered legible, rather than being erased by superimposition. U.S. women of color may well feel even more written out of Harding's tropical moves, not only since she does not seem to be directly addressing them but also because her treatment of "Africa" bears too little relation to the history of U.S. race formations. But there is more. Harding's analogy actively prevents Western white women, her main audience, from coming to terms with *their* imbrication within racism and colonialism—there is simply no room within the analysis we have heard for such women to question their own "unmarked" identities. For the most part, the promise Harding began with—namely, of bringing the pervasiveness of gender into relation with other forms of difference—never really materializes.

Harding's subsequent book, *Whose Science? Whose Knowledge? Thinking from Women's Lives*, is somewhat differently structured and deals more intensively with questions of science. Race is now

unambiguously perceived as a fundamental category structuring
social life and marking everybody in the first and third worlds,
especially so-called colorless "women and men of European descent."[39] Most promising of all, conceptualizations must, she argues, emerge from different and contradictory social locations. At
the same time, however, her thought continues to be driven toward
a common destiny for everyone and a single theory to undergird it:
"If feminists wish to integrate race, class and gender issues, they
must transform our largely separate theories about the origins and
natures of gender, race and class hierarchy into a single theory."[40]

One cannot dispute the necessity of finding links in the conditions governing our discrepant lives, such as the connections between the overdevelopment of the West and the de-development of
the Third World, as she puts it. But her urge to rush ahead, think
comprehensively for the entire globe, and recruit everyone to feminism and other countercultural politics also makes for a certain
carelessness. One hears next to nothing about the conditions under
which such a theory might be conceivable, nor of the very different
implications it would have for different peoples.

The Science Question in Feminism, Harding's earlier book, is in
many ways more interesting because of its more loosely stitched and
open-ended qualities. If I seem to have been dwelling on her use of
analogies unduly, it is because Harding's work brings out the consequences in an exemplary way. I by no means want to give the
impression that she is alone in having foreclosed on potentially
more fulfilling and multiple analyses.[41] In fact, feminists with almost
diametrically opposed conceptions of the (dis)locations of women
make remarkably similar analogous moves, with concomitant conflating effects. Think, for instance, of the use of the privileged figure
of "exile" among some Western feminists as a way of describing
women's extreme marginalization from the social and sexual order
of things. Luce Irigaray (who also draws from the Freudian psychoanalytical corpus, but with profoundly different implications than
the object-relations theorists whom Harding cites), distinguishes
between (heterosexual) men and women in terms of the condition of
exile that is specifically only true for women. For it is only women
who are exiled from their first love objects, their mothers, a condi-

tion for which they can never compensate in subsequent relations with men. Addressing a man in the course of an interview, she says, "You are not in exile: you remain in continuous relation with your first object, with your first love, with your first attachments. If you displace them, it would be according to your laws: the language, the culture you have made."[42] So, too, in a recent collection of essays entitled *Womens' Writing in Exile*, Jane Marcus has this to say:

Feminism is a natural medium and method for the examination of exile, for, in its explicit position of otherness, it places the critic in the position of exile, aware of her own estrangement from the center of the discipline, awkwardly measuring just how much marginalization she is willing to bear.[43]

Marcus does, however, worry a bit that the privileging of exiles could in turn expel those who stay at home; she also wonders whether "exile" applies more to some than to others. But her question ("Is the political refugee from Siberia more of an exile than a lesbian poet in Iowa or a woman of color in a white culture? Can the loss of language be compared to the loss of nation?")[44] is posed rather archly, if not in an objectifying form, and quickly dissolved. Here, again, my point is not simply to call a halt to such metaphorical moves (as if that were even possible) but rather to see what gets valorized and what suppressed in the process. For the figure of exile as it is used here works by relating the more literal image and knowledge of exiles who have had to leave the second and third worlds and are now in the West, on the one hand, with the relations of otherness that a first-world woman—usually white—experiences from her home, language and sexuality, on the other. The very different and discrepant dislocations in each case are once again papered over, as are possible ways of articulating the kinds of ex*patria*tion at work for women "at home" outside the West. Precisely because Irigaray's repeated analyses of a woman's outsider status do ring true (the overwhelming absence of figurations and images by which she might represent herself, such that she seems condemned to borrowing signifiers without the ability to leave her own mark on them),[45] I would expect her to be especially sensitive about the metaphors to which she does then lay a claim.[46]

In many ways, questions from the previous chapter on the structures of theories—their composition within intellectual fields scored through by relations of power, disciplinary hierarchies, and unequally privileged levels of abstraction—returns even more sharply in this context. But whereas the problems we encountered earlier centered more closely on the kind of authority "theory" has been institutionally granted as the successor of philosophy, our difficulties here are of a slightly different order. As I have already mentioned, Western feminism, especially at this historical juncture, is directly caught up within a double tension. The first concerns the ongoing desire, both politically and conceptually, to enable the emergence of new subjects—the subjects of feminism— through the disruption and destabilization of an antifeminist system. Many concepts have been proposed to highlight this process, the most recent one focusing on the mobilizations of gender. But because the creation of new concepts is dependent upon borrowing from and rewriting preexisting ones, theorists have sought "to give a direction"[47] to their analyses through the use of parallels, analogies, and so on. That women have undergone a kind of colonization and suffer a kind of exile have been two examples.

At the same time, however—and this is the second aspect of the double tension—the future of feminism, more than ever before, hinges upon the ability to actively integrate questions of difference and specificity, again both politically and conceptually, into its structures. It was because the use of analogies and metaphors to strengthen feminism in the first case ran *counter* to the second desire to make more room for differential and multiple subjectivities—whether of white women, women of color, or women from colonized nations—that Harding's promising conception of "fractured identities" in the *Science Question in Feminism* remained largely unsubstantiated.

As I understand it, the imperative most deeply fueling the search for powerful images in feminism is the desire to pull women out of the invisible and the inert—that is to say, out of nature and the naturalizable—into *history*. Thus, Harding may well be effectively saying that women's subjugation is as historical as the events of racism and colonialism; Irigaray's caution in the passage we heard concerns the fundamental social, symbolic, and sexual reordering that would be required to bring women into history when they have so systemically been assured a position outside it. But hasn't the promise of gender—especially over against other concepts such as woman, sex, and patriarchy—also had centrally to do with its historicizing potential? Moreover, when we pause to think about it, aren't conceptions of difference and heterogeneity best captured by the realization that what distinguishes us most from one another are our differing historicities? How, then, do theoretical maneuvers and categories of analysis resonate with and alert us to questions of history?

Taking Historicity Seriously

Unfortunately, the contemporary institution of "theory" has not always been an enabling one in developing the imbrication of feminism with problems of history. In an important exchange of views with Linda Gordon, for instance, Joan Scott has made a powerful case for the liberating effect of poststructuralism—especially Derridean deconstruction—in rewriting the historical record from a gendered perspective. Gordon, by contrast, has been less enamored of what appears to her as an unnecessary inflation of such "theory," even when it is made to bring the category of gender more fully into view:

It is arguable that because of the primacy of gender in human acculturation, any study attentive to language will notice how gender becomes a trope for all differentiation, alienation, individuation. However, feminist scholarship about gender additionally requires a critical stance, a standpoint that questions the inevitability or desirability of particular gender meanings. I would wager that the impetus toward such a critique comes, not from a particular analytical method, but from the political impulse of the scholar.[48]

Elsewhere, Gordon has claimed that what might distinguish the field of women's history has less to do with method—whether it follow poststructuralism or the more well-established parameters of political and social history—than with the subject matter of feminism, the complex distinction and relation between being female and being feminist.[49]

I expected to learn something about the specific status of *history* from this exchange, about how theories and methods, whatever they may be, are brought into a reciprocal relationship with our sense of ourselves as historical beings. Perhaps because they were both historians, however, this was one area that was not in itself part of the debate—it was, so to speak, already *assumed.*[50] Furthermore, the kinds of theories, such as deconstruction, that were most discussed have very little, if anything, to say about history.

Gerda Lerner, another influential feminist historian, has in fact pointed out how impoverished the interplay between feminism, theory, and history has been:

Most of the theoretical work of modern feminism, beginning with Simone de Beauvoir and continuing into the present, has been ahistorical and negligent of historical scholarship. This was understandable in the early days of the new wave of feminism, when scholarship on the past of women was scant, but in the 1980s, the distance between historical scholarship and feminist criticism in other fields continues.[51]

If this is the case, then perhaps a prior question is needed: what *conceptions* of history were either being assumed (by practicing historians) or left unexplored beyond rather loose uses of the term (by feminists elsewhere) such that questions of history have not been more strongly foregrounded?

We obviously need a more active sense of history that does not rest exclusively on the past, in and for itself, but that negotiates between the past and the *present*. The past *claims* us, and we are accountable to that claim—otherwise why engage in the rewriting of history in the first place? According to Juliet Mitchell, one of the most valuable lessons of psychoanalysis for her is the multilevel effort at reconstruction necessary at certain moments in a patient's life, the recollection of personal history based on fragments of memory, where time past and time present are one.[52]

From my perspective as a feminist concerned with the possibilities and limits of theories and concepts, their partial and uneven, if composite, qualities, conceptualizing history opens out that spaciotemporal field of signification where our theories and questions can have their fullest play. For one thing, theories tend to be structured around a *single* pair of binary oppositions—male/female, whiteness/color, colonizer/colonized, home/exile, straight/gay, and so on. One of the "models" for bringing them together has been to allude to the intersecting *axes* of race, class, gender, and sexuality. For me this conjures up the image of a multidimensional geometrical field constituted with "race," "class," "gender," and "sexuality" as a starting list of coordinates. Barbara Johnson has, on occasion, diagrammed a two-dimensional space structured by race and gender,[53] and Harding herself spoke of a unified field theory. Such a framework can have its attractions, although it already runs into problems of depiction when the "axes" become too numerous. But I have a more fundamental distrust of the imagery of axes. To begin with, speaking this way gives one an entirely misleading sense of their parity and mutual symmetry with one another. As I shall continue to demonstrate, this is by no means the case. Furthermore, and because it is so difficult to imagine what such a multiaxial model would look like, the chances grow that it will effectively collapse through the search (and discovery) of parallels, analogies, and metaphors between them.

Given such difficulties of responsibly mapping identities, one response has been to turn away from theory altogether. I would like to make a plea for something different. Because categories of analysis themselves are loaded with their effective histories, part of the historicizing task must be to realize that notions of race, class, gender, and so on are not reducible concepts. For example, "gender" today does not, say, simply refer to some putative, isolatable relation between men and women but is caught up within, has taken into itself, and is therefore data-laden by a network of connotations, histories, and political positions. In fact, the discussion so far—the transformation of earlier feminist concepts such as those of sex, patriarchy, femininity, and so forth by gender, feminism's relation and debt to Marxism,[54] and the development of gender through analogies like those of colonization and exile—only scratches the surface.

Witness the degree to which the hold of "nature" on feminist theory and politics has been loosened: the radical efforts of feminists in science have made us less allergic to biology by demonstrating its constructedness as "a social discourse open to intervention";[55] other deconstructive efforts reveal the naturalizing function of sex in its apparent contrast to gender. Gender today is deeply inscribed by a political and intellectual history that includes a wide range of uto-pias and positive affirmations of difference (regardless of whether one would subscribe to Elaine Showalter's stage-like approach of the "feminine," the "feminist," and the "female"). Thus, this con-cept has been released into new possibilities, especially through the proliferation of gender analyses in the U.S. academy, together with the emergence of the "identity politics" of the eighties and nineties.

When one reflects over the comparative composition of "class" in the West, a rather different configuration becomes visible. I have already remarked on the sense of decline—some would even say collapse—of Marxism in the contemporary world. Few seem pre-pared to echo Sartre's claim that Marxism is "the one philosophy of our time which we cannot go beyond."[56] Marxism appears, quite simply, to have lost much of its authority. This is not to deny that significant studies concerned with feminist analyses of class haven't been written in recent years. Notice, though, that the ones more commonly referred to are by and for women of color in the United States or the Third World.[57] Once dominant debates on the rela-tions of feminism and patriarchy to political economy, the division of labor, and questions of ideology are now on the sidelines; the kind of studies on comparative worth that Heidi Hartmann, among others, is presently engaged in appear to have become cocooned within a professionalized subfield, with few connections to broader feminist orientations. Why have analyses of class become the prerogative of feminists in the social sciences, especially economics and sociology? There are surely no "natural" restrictions to its significance in other fields.

But perhaps U.S. feminism is also producing and witnessing a shift in the frameworks underpinning class analysis, from a central concern with the structuring effects of capitalism and the possibili-ties of socialism to the beginnings of a certain identity politics with distinctive contours of its own. One place where such a shift appears to have already been accomplished—but without being reflected upon—is in the anthology *Conflicts in Feminism*. (The editors of

this book are otherwise acutely self-conscious of their new temporal
location in the United States at the onset of the nineties, within
an increasingly hostile larger climate, and in a feminist milieu of
"intense mutual criticism and internal divisiveness.")[58] That class
should be paired with race in both of the essays in the volume
dealing with the subject[59] may be of some interest in itself; more
decisively new, however, is the *form* in which it makes an appearance. Questions pertaining to class are overwhelmingly ap-
proached through such modes as autobiography, personal history,
and narratives of childhood—that is to say, through the experiences
and subject formation of feminists from poor, working class backgrounds, who are now acknowledging their distance and proximity
to middle class norms. It is by virtue of the presence of such
feminists in the academy that class is an issue, rather than through
political perspectives held earlier by unmarked (middle class?) feminists from the Left. Indeed, what have feminists made so far of our
most easily used, yet least analyzed, marker of social location,
cultural hegemony, and economic anxiety—the middle class? According to Barbara Ehrenreich, "there is even a problem of what to
call this class."[60]

Picking up from the few remarks already made regarding the
place of race in the Western intellectual field, contemporary references to "race, class, and gender" barely allow one to suspect that
the nineties are inheriting the failure of theories about race, especially their failure to capture its crucial role after the struggle for
civil rights in the United States. There has quite simply been "an
inability to grasp the uniqueness of race, its historical flexibility and
immediacy in everyday experience and social conflict."[61]

Just consider the practice of placing "race" in quotation marks,
when neither gender nor class calls for such circumscription. The
very concept itself seems to suffer from a profound confusion, so
much so that many attempts at clarification fall prey to its contradictions:

Race has become a trope of ultimate, irreducible difference between
cultures, linguistic groups, or adherents of specific belief systems which—
more often than not—also have fundamentally opposed economic interests. Race is the ultimate trope of difference because it is so very arbitrary

in its application. The biological criteria used to determine "difference" in sex simply do not hold when applied to "race." Yet we carelessly use language in such a way as to *will* this sense of *natural* difference into our formulations. To do so is to engage in a pernicious act of language, one which exacerbates the complex problem of cultural or ethnic difference, rather than to assuage or redress it.[62]

In this passage from the editorial introduction to the well-known special issue *"Race," Writing, and Difference*, Henry Louis Gates, Jr., is propelled not just to pry race apart from other, presumably more meaningful categories of difference—those of culture, language, ethnicity, economic status—but to turn it inside out, as it were, to expel it from its place within the natural order of things. "Race" must be shown up in all its arbitrariness. It is as though the enormous burden of the racial discourses and practices of domination of the nineteenth century, especially the legitimizing role of the sciences, can only be countered by doing away with the reality of the concept altogether. In a similar vein, Anthony Appiah is entirely engrossed in his determination to find a "true criterion" for racial identity by rejecting such logically inadequate "sociohistorical" elements as descent, slavery, memory, and discrimination in W.E.B. Du Bois's writings. "Race" is repeatedly reduced to the "grosser" features of biology—the differentiations of "color, hair, and bone" —which, by the contemporary standards of science, are without genetic basis and, more important, bear no social consequences.[63]

To my mind, these attempts at overkill end up marginalizing, if not missing, the very spaces within which race must primarily be addressed and overcome—the spaces and politics of everyday life where identities, and the histories that subtend them, are reproduced. Contextless logical argument or proofs of arbitrariness are not the best responses to the questionable ways in which race was provided with a "substance."[64] Instead of striving to reduce race to an empty or illusory notion, perhaps one must take on its irreducible imbrication with other concepts, not excluding such "unviable" markers as skin color. As Patricia Williams has it,

I wish to recognize that terms like "black" and "white" do not begin to capture the rich ethnic and political diversity of my subject. But I do believe that the simple matter of the color of one's skin so profoundly affects the way one is treated, so radically shapes what one is allowed to think and feel . . . , that the decision to generalize from such a division is valid. Furthermore, it is hard to describe succinctly the racial perspective and history that is my concern. . . . I don't like the word "minority" (although I use it) because it implies a certain delegitimacy in a majoritarian system; and if one adds up all the shades of yellow, red, and brown swept over by the term, we are in fact not. I prefer "African-American" in my own conversational usage because it effectively evokes the specific cultural dimensions of my identity, but . . . I use most frequently the word "black" in order to accentuate the unshaded monolithism of color itself as a social force.[65]

Such preliminary explorations into the intersecting and contradictory careers of some of the key concepts upon which U.S. feminism depends should make the need for a greater historical sensibility urgent. It is our histories—populated by those subjects and institutions that have constituted as much as altered them—that most powerfully enable one to interrogate concepts and theories for their partialities and levels of abstraction. And, in a reciprocal manner, theories are fully meaningful when they in turn engender partial and composite histories. Depending on how our identities are constituted by "unmarked" privileges and the marks of otherness, depending on which subjects have played more central and marginal roles—depending, that is, on where we are *located* in the active process of uncovering sanctioned ignorances—the process of reconstruction can become almost unrecognizably different. If a historian like Joan Scott can *presume* a history that culminates in her present, Hortense Spillers must not only strive somehow to make her history visible but also do so against the grain of dominant connotations of gender and by taking on board the incoherences and illegibilities of race.

As might be recalled from chapter one, Spillers is motivated by the unabated naming, even today, of the black woman as the cause of the plight of the black family. It is this situation in the present that forces her to undertake a commemorative rereading of African American historical texts and to reinscribe the category of gender by making it signify upon captive bodies. Because gender meanings— whatever their more widespread classificatory connotations—still veer toward what Spillers calls "sex-role assignation, or the clear differentiation of sexual stuff,"[66] fundamental revisions are necessary if the history of African American women is to gain any real intelligibility.

This does not mean, however, that gender ceases to have any meanings at all in this context. On the contrary, it points to the need for new theorizations and historizations forged through the intricate relations of power between many subjects in their ideological locations—not just among African American men, women, daughters, and sons but through complex forms of domination by white men and white women as well. At times, Spillers presses "theory" into service: in order to play a meaningful role, Lacanian psychoanalysis, for instance, must be transformed—some would say deformed—to produce the lineaments of the law of the white father. How, therefore, can one even begin to disentangle race and gender in their intrinsic co-implication for any analysis of the legacy of slavery? As Patricia Williams insists,

[a]lthough the "bad black mother" is even today a stereotypical way of describing what ails the black race, the historical reality is that of careless white fatherhood. Blacks are thus, in full culturally imagistic terms, not merely unmothered but badly fathered, abused and disowned by whites. Certainly the companion myths to this woeful epic are to be found in brutalized archetypes of black males (so indiscriminately generative as to require repression by castration) and of white females (so discriminately virginal as to wither in idealized sexuality).[67]

From Spillers's perspective, the task becomes one of "actually *claiming* the monstrosity of the female with the potential to 'name,' "[68] claiming the task to radically rewrite a history of dispossession.

As so many black feminists have had to repeat over and over again, it is not that the category of "woman" is so steeped in universalism that white feminists commit an imperializing act by using the term without further qualification. The titles of at least two books have taken up Sojourner Truth's call "Ain't/Ar'n't I a Woman?" to show how "woman" was actively constructed as an ideological and material representation through an active process of exclusion. Qualifying for womanhood turns out to have carried quite specifiable, if unmarked, racial and class connotations in the history of the

United States.[69] Indeed, according to Hazel Carby, "woman" was a figure of such power that a major narrative device in the literature of black women intellectuals following emancipation from slavery centered around the possibilities and limits of "passing." Therefore, she says, "we need more feminist work that interrogates ideologies for their racial specificity and acknowledges *whiteness*, not just blackness, as a racial categorization."[70] Or, if I may put it this way, merely in order to do justice to a term like "woman" from a *feminist* perspective, it is necessary to undertake further analyses that would render its historical embeddedness within racial and class ideologies explicit. Such a step is all the more imperative today, when questions of class, race, and whiteness lead such a subterranean, if turbulent, existence.

Aida Hurtado has extended these issues for women of color as a whole, demonstrating how constructions of womanhood that are at least "dual" continue to be developed simultaneously. Where white women, as a group, are subordinated to white men through *seduction*, women of color, unable to fulfill white men's need for racially pure offspring, are socially and sexually constituted in relations of *rejection*. "Class position, of course, affects the probability of the awards of seduction or the sanctions of rejection."[71] Almost as though she were in conversation with Sandra Harding, Hurtado contrasts the relatively greater access to privileges for white women under such conditions (not the least of which is a substantial tradition of feminist theory and scholarship in the academy) to the one area where she feels white women are at a disadvantage. This would be the process of "reclaiming—or perhaps it is more accurate to say, in inventing their identity" in relation to history. Women of color, whether through the events of conquest and genocide, slavery or exclusion, have recourse to collective memories of "a past, a tradition, and sometimes a religion or culture."[72]

Perhaps Hurtado's foregoing remarks do discern important reasons that "history" has preoccupied some more than others. But I would hesitate in thus reducing the meaning of history to the plotting of the "before" and "after" of an event or origin, especially for feminists. Questions surrounding the "origins" of patriarchy are no doubt crucial ones, but in order to be fully historical they must be framed more explicitly within the context of the person asking them, as what is being contributed to is an effective "history of the present," a tracing of the impress of history in the present. Much the same could be said, too, of the methodological implications of what Joan Kelly identified as "the basic concerns of historical thought: 1) periodization, 2) the categories of social analysis, and 3) theories of social change" in the restoration of women to history and history to women.[73]

Someone might well intervene and ask at this point whether all this emphasis on our divergent historicities, the demand to examine the specific trajectories of categories of analysis—indeed, the overall drift of my reservations against conflations and analogies—is not in danger of lapsing into essentialism. But then, shouldn't the very deployment of notions of difference and history (rather than identity and nature) be sufficient guarantees of one's antiessentialist credentials? Queries such as these make it amply clear that there is nothing self-evident or transparent in the invocation of history as such. At the same time, taking historicity more seriously than U.S. feminism has done so far could potentially advance, if not transform, the debate around essentialism and antiessentialism that has been miring feminist theory and politics within a "dangerously sedimented opposition,"[74] as Diana Fuss has called it. Let me therefore conclude this discussion on history's place by tacking it onto the issue of essentialism.

Even though the idea of the "essence" of a thing is about as philosophical an issue as one could come across and the naming of "essentialism" and "antiessentialism" developed from poststructuralist theory's deconstructive undoing of the essences of this metaphysical tradition, today these terms circulate far more outside the discipline of philosophy than within it. It is among feminists, gays and lesbians, Marxists, and theorists of race, ethnicity, and colonialism that these positions have been taken up, attacked, and defended. Although still overwhelmingly tilted in favor of antiessentialism, the proportion of those who have also been calling for a revision of this trend is growing.

There have been many reasons to believe that essentialism is a problem to be overcome. It is often used, for instance, to signal the place where something can be taken as "given," whether because of perceptions of what is natural and therefore unchangeable or due to presumptions of what is simply beyond question. According to Arthur Brittan and Mary Maynard, "'essentialism' makes the task of explanation very easy indeed."[75] Or rather, it marks the vanishing point of an explanation in the face of what is either wittingly or unwittingly taken for granted. A commitment against such essentialism, therefore, is a decision that further accounts are required—for if matters aren't *essentially* so, then the antiessentialist must come up with reasons why they aren't otherwise.

This attitude has been an extremely productive one, politically and intellectually. At the same time, however, the accusation of "essentialism" has been going out to rather opposite effect, as a sanction of dismissal shored up by the conviction of one's own theoretical superiority. In the first extensive study of this issue, Diana Fuss has managed to disentangle a number of interconnected but distinct questions that were beginning to get obscured. She begins by noticing how deeply co-implicated conceptions of essentialism and antiessentialism are so that "the logic of essentialism can be shown to be irreducible even in those discourses most explicitly concerned with repudiating it" (*ES*, p. 2). Attempts among social constructionists, for instance, to deessentialize the sphere of the natural by bringing it into history may only be *displacing* "the encounter with essence" onto sociality rather than actually dissolving it. Second, and this is equally overlooked, the problems of essentialism and universalism are often run together, so that moves toward more concrete and heterogeneous subjects of analysis are taken automatically to imply an antiessential attitude. But, as Fuss points out, "hasty attempts to pluralize do not operate as sufficient defenses and safeguards against essentialism."[76] Thus, the language of historicity, or the reference to multiple subjectivities, do not in themselves necessarily imply an antiessentialist position. In the course of successive chapters on Derrida and Lacan, Luce Irigaray and Monique Wittig, African American literary theory, and gay and lesbian politics, Fuss, therefore, looks for the modes of deployment of essentialism and antiessentialism in their permutations and combinations, especially keen to demonstrate how essentialist arguments or assumptions structure the most avowedly antiessentialist texts.

Nonetheless, the strength of her arguments also reveals the limitations of her level of theorizing, coming from a purely deconstructive position as it does. The tendency to view her task in terms of the need to raise "the discussion to a more sophisticated level," which means "taking the analysis *up* to another *higher* register" (*ES*, pp. 20–21, emphases added), prevents her from sufficiently taking into account the levels at which her "case studies" operate.[77] In spite of an explicitly announced desire to show how "the radicality or conservatism of essentialism depends, to a significant degree, on *who* is utilizing it, *how* it is deployed, and *where* its effects are concentrated" (*ES*, p. 20; emphasis original), she ends up, more often than not in an *a priori* mode, "redress[ing] the critical imbalance between essentialism and constructionism, while [her] own position balances precariously between the two" (*ES*, p. 40).

Though I agree completely that the issues Fuss investigates do not (and, I would add, should not) go away when we move from more abstract to more specific and multiple levels of analysis, I do believe they are transformed thereby. Because subjects have discrepant histories and political stakes, shifts toward discernibly "essential" formulations versus moves in opposition to them become key issues of contention that can no longer be exclusively governed by generalized deconstructive maneuvers. It is as historical subjects rather than as philosophical ones that our politics take shape, our differences matter, and the fluidity or fixity of our identities begin to count. Our accounts and accountabilities to one another become significant and productive alignments or fundamental disagreements emerge because the history we live is finite. Whatever one's position within relations of domination or one's dependence on theories and concepts forged elsewhere, a sense of historicity at work in the present should make it impossible to conceptualize "our" histories as nothing but the failed versions of the History of those in command.[78] Of course, it remains absolutely crucial to submit one's conception of history to scrutiny—to see whether one is subscribing to more "essential" ideas of continuity or "antiessential" notions of destabilization and change—and, further, to consider how each of these orientations can turn out to be less impermeable than one might have thought. To appreciate just how divergent conceptions of history can be, I might juxtapose Carl Degler with Michel Foucault:

Only in history can a cause, or an issue, or a social group gain an identity, a sense of who or what it is.[79]

The purpose of history, guided by genealogy, is not to discover the roots of our identity, but to commit itself to its dissipation.[80]

But if, as Foucault continues, the point is "to make visible all of those discontinuities that cross us," "creat[ing] danger in every area,"[81] there must be a prior commitment to the subjectivities, if not the identities, of those for and with whom we undertake such genealogies, without which the very purpose he speaks of becomes unintelligible.

A reader of Fuss's book gets very little sense of her stakes, of what it means to read as a feminist, discuss the unequal positions of gays and lesbians in the construction of homosexuality, or witness the frayed connections between African American literary scholarship and the black community—"the dilemma of the black intellectual," as Cornel West has so succinctly enunciated it.[82] Perhaps this is because she is ultimately concerned with preserving the antiessentialist imperative of never coming to rest, always looking out for binary oppositions to destabilize, never pausing to reflect on her own position and location, her historical embeddedness, one that is never alluded to, let alone deconstructed.

Because Fuss refers to philosophers such as Aristotle, Locke, and Heidegger when defining questions of essence, it is worth remembering that there is all the difference in the world between Locke's discussion of the essences of gold and triangles, on the one hand, and the kinds of subjects Fuss focuses on. I doubt whether we have essences in the more or less straightforward fashion that chemical substances or geometrical figures do. Less doubtful, if hard to pin down, are the histories preceding us. They remain, for lack of a better term, essential, especially as we spend our entire efforts working against their effects in order to break with the injustices of the past. Toward this end, we also inherit unequal political and intellectual traditions that we are actively engaged in recomposing and rewriting. As Patricia Hill Collins has excellently expressed her conception of what is needed from the historical perspective of black feminism,

developing adequate definitions of Black feminist thought involves facing th[e] complex nexus of relationships among biological classification, the social construction of race and gender as categories of analysis, the material conditions accompanying these changing social constructions, and Black women's consciousness about these themes.[83]

In the course of this chapter, I have been concentrating—too cursorily, no doubt—on some of the general aspects of U.S. feminist theory. My particular concern has been to plumb the potential of the category of gender, in its double tension with the effective history of feminism and with contemporary desires for a more analytically rich and politically accountable feminist space. It has been my contention that it is necessary to produce articulations both with other terms of analysis and with an active sense of history for such a promise to be fulfilled. My own examples have been less than adequate, and this surely reflects my own ignorance of the field. If I have remarked upon the declining significance of class and the uneven place of race, I have said nothing about sexuality. The revolutionary naming of sexuality as a primary locus of women's oppression is a legacy of an earlier, more strongly represented radical feminist writing; today, issues about sexuality have largely developed into an internal debate within the lesbian community. At neither stage have I come across sustained responses from heterosexual feminists among either white women or women of color. As a heterosexual feminist who owes her understanding of "compulsory heterosexuality" to this radical lesbian tradition, I wonder about the nature of this silence. In the naming of identity, "heterosexual" may well be the most unmarked category of all.

Perhaps, then, my considerations are indicative of the challenges ahead. Because I strongly believe that questions of identity and difference in feminist theory are not the special prerogative of some women more than others, the overall discussion so far has been of a more general nature. But because each of us must work through the intrications of feminism, theory, and history from our particular vantage points, it is now time to turn back to my situation and project, the subject of the next chapter.

Chapter Four

Closer to Home

Feminism, Postcolonial Locations, and the Politics of Representation

> But while it is true that history only answers the ques-
> tions which are put to it, it by no means follows that we
> get the answers we expect.
>
> Stree Shakti Sanghatana,
> *"We were making history . . ."*

In the construction and development of the last two chapters, I have
sometimes occupied the position of a potential "immigrant" in the
United States, including myself in debates whose relevance for a
different setting was not always uppermost in my mind, debates to
which I had had limited or no access before. At other moments, the
subject position structuring the text has been more discernibly
that of an "anthropologist in reverse," a participant-observer in
the worlds of U.S. feminism and theory, so to speak, whose interest went beyond considerations of basic translatability to thoughts
about better and worse forms of travel.

The subject positions framing this book, however, are multiple
and include the questions and self-questionings of a "native informant." It is the predicaments and peculiarities embodied in this
position—not just in the naming of our relation to the West but in
the search for a *response* to that relation—that I shall be focusing on
more closely here. Whereas the previous chapters were formulated
and even considerably revised within the United States, the following lines bear the stamp of return, having been produced within,
and consequently also *by*, the context of contemporary India. It will
therefore be possible to begin a demonstration of my overall claims

about the inescapability of questions of location for postcolonial feminist theorizing and politics.

Locations play a *constitutive* role in structuring the frames of reference within which we develop our projects, a role that deserves to be more fully analyzed. This includes our institutional and disciplinary affiliations, the milieu of intellectual debate, the "background practices"[1] and grain of everyday life, not all of which can be rendered explicit. Indeed, the very nature of ongoing intellectual production could be described as an interplay between what becomes a problem for thought and what is allowed to go without saying. Such an interplay takes its cues from one's location (or so I would like to contend), the site of one's questions and interventions, the place of accountability.

I must confess to a sense of urgency in counterbalancing my own—and postmodern—privilegings of conditions of dislocation— being rootless and mobile, no longer in connection, away from home—with the issue of location. This has to do with the profoundly unequal ways in which some places are valorized over others, often without further comment, and all the more so where the work of scholarship is involved. Thus, when Edward Said discusses the "overlapping territories" produced by colonialism in his most recent writing and points out the "discrepant experiences" that thereby ensue in the postcolonial world, his humanistic affirmation of both East and West as mutually interdependent realities serves, perhaps unwittingly, to dilute the nature of the problem.[2] It therefore bears repeating that the West represents the kind of placeless place able to extend its frontiers well beyond the particular geographic region called the West and in so doing to disable the development of non-Western spaces as viable alternate locations for postcolonial political and intellectual engagement.

In the opening chapter, the "native informant," or rather "the impossible mix of anthropologist and native informant," came to stand for a subject position interpellated by precisely this uneven relation between spaces. "Anthropologist" and "native informant" serve to mark the degree to which the uncovering of sanctioned ignorances by postcolonials, even Said's elaboration of the need "to think through and interpret together experiences that are discrepant, each with its particular agenda and pace of development, its own internal formations, its internal coherence and system of external relationships, all of them coexisting and interacting with others,"[3] can still be governed by the West and its demands.

Stressing the forces that prod even a resisting postcolonial feminist along Western routes for the mapping of "Eastern" places is one reason to take recourse to the terms of anthropology. At that level, the "native informant" has stood for a subject position of refusal, a refusal to reduce the space of home to a place one visits, mines for its resources, and then leaves in order to complete the process of feminist production elsewhere. However, a more positive set of reasons also motivates the following intervention within the specific discipline of anthropology as a way to restate and provisionally conclude my arguments. For the career of feminist anthropology in the West, as well as its significantly different status in India—when reconsidered from within the Indian context—has enabled me to make a fresh exploration of the necessity of a locational intellectual politics in our frenetically globalizing world.

Can There Be a Postcolonial Feminist Ethnography?

Anthropology is one discipline in the West today that can be called an afflicted field—critiques from the perspectives of colonialism, poststructuralism, and certainly feminism have affected the self-conception of ethnographic practice like no other field. The question "can there be a feminist ethnography?"[4]—among a host of other formulations indicative of the prevalent sense of disquietude—has emerged from this critical confluence in a way that has not been witnessed elsewhere in the academy. (Even when parallel doubts are raised in other fields, such as in feminist history, feminist philosophy, and so on, they carry neither the same sense of burden nor the promise of something radically new.)

The following contribution to the debate between feminism and ethnography is provisional and tentative. It is unlike Lila Abu-Lughod's discussion about the possibility of a feminist ethnography, which begins with the remark that this is one of those rare occasions when her arguments will have to stick without "stories from the field." For her readers are left in no doubt that those stories already exist—indeed, we are already given glimpses of the book-in-the-making that constitutes the "practice" of the "theory" she is about to offer.[5] I can provide no such alibis; what follows does not have the benefit of prior fieldwork as the discipline defines it. However, I do not think this omission represents a limitation for the arguments I am about to make. It certainly has not prevented me from critically reflecting on ethnographic practice, nor even from hypothesizing about the alternative forms a postcolonial feminist ethnography might take.

If Western ethnography—whether feminist or otherwise—has been standing under a cloud for some time now, at once fearing and planning for its future, I would like to hazard some guesses as to why this might be so. To begin with, while many problematic aspects of the anthropological discipline and its relation to feminism are being productively examined, the issue of location I have just been emphasizing is receiving scant attention. On the face of it, this is quite surprising. In considerable contrast to other disciplines, after all, anthropology obtains its distinctive identity through the institutional and conceptual movement between places, the writing of cultural difference, whereby an elsewhere "there" can be evoked "here." As far back as the sixties, moreover, commentators had begun to remark upon the kind of systematic asymmetry within which the discipline came to be conceptualized, shaped, and sustained. If anything exposed anthropological practice, it was, as Talal Asad reminds us, an acknowledgement of its rootedness "in an unequal power encounter between the West and the Third World which goes back to the emergence of bourgeois Europe, an encounter in which colonialism is merely one historical moment."[6] Along with Mina Davis Caulfield, it is not my intention to equate the complex (colonial) process whereby "members of the Western European and American educated elite" could study "natives . . . made safe for ethnography"[7] with anthropology itself. Rather, I have been asking myself why an awareness of the imbricated relationship between anthropology and power has not really been named as a relation of asymmetry between locations, quite apart from what the consequences of such a naming might be.

Addressing the issue of location, it seems to me, would require coming to terms with the *nation* and *nationalism*, which have been dormant—or negatively construed—subjects in the Western intellectual field.[8] Interestingly enough, though, it was precisely nationalist movements in the third world and the creation of independent nation-states out of erstwhile colonies that transformed the colonial world into the postcolonial one, thus fundamentally altering the geopolitical configuration within which a discipline such as anthropology had its beginnings. The combined effect of such global historical sea changes—coupled with a certain theoretical and political inattentiveness to, if not avoidance of, the nation—has, I think, contributed to the distinctive turbulence characteristic of contemporary ethnography, especially feminist ethnography.

Let me elaborate this claim by looking at some of the directions the debate among feminist ethnographers has been taking. Though epistemological issues about the universality of gender oppression or the applicability of Western binaries such as the public/private and nature/culture oppositions are of longer standing, I am specifically interested in the recent spate of self-reflexive and critical discussions around the scope of ethnographic practice for feminists. Dating from the late eighties, these essays are structured by the influences Western feminism, poststructuralist theory, and critiques of colonialism have exerted on the discipline of anthropology and by the controversies that ensued.

An early intervention is Marilyn Strathern's much discussed "An Awkward Relationship: The Case of Feminism and Anthropology." The extreme value of her essay lies in the shift she achieves from narrowly theoretical considerations to questions concerning "the nature of investigators' *relationship to* their subject matter"—that is to say, "the social constitution of both feminist and ethnographic practice."[9] What comes to view is the unexamined background of a community of practitioners with mutually dependent positions in the intellectual field, even though they also hold conflictive social interests. In spite of the many points of convergence between feminists and anthropologists, Strathern's central argument is that the basic position of a feminist anthropologist is an "awkward" one, as she must draw upon conceptual frameworks that "mock" one another's presuppositions.

This is so because the respective "others" for feminism and anthropology occupy very different places within their communities. If feminism's "other" comprises the institutions of patriarchy and male domination, it is distant other cultures that the ethnographer seeks to represent. Thus, from a feminist perspective that emphasizes the need to expose, if not undo, relations of oppression, the idea of a collaborative relationship between anthropologist and informant, and especially the ideal of multiple authorship inspired by the inroads of poststructuralist theory into the discipline, is a delusion:

> There can be no parity between the authorship of the anthropologist and the informant: the dialogue must always be asymmetrical. Whether the prime factors are the colonial relations between societies from which both anthropologists and informants come or the use to which the text will be put, the social worlds of the anthropologist and the informant are different.[10]

Moreover, anthropology can mock the feminist impulse to create one's self in opposition to or separation from patriarchal structures. An externally achieved anthropological perspective would show how deeply feminists remain bound up within the values and presuppositions of their own culture. Strathern, however, is not interested in resolving such challenges; she believes they arise from worldviews incommensurable with one another. Hence her special use of the notion of *mockery* to evoke the lack of meaningfulness of each set of questions outside their own domain; the feminist anthropologist she has in mind would, presumably, just have to live with this irreconcilable tension.

It is uncommon to find someone so prepared to refuse any easy methods for the resolution of conflict. Strathern is surely right in making the strongest possible case for the difference in the traditions that feminism and anthropology represent. In their reading of the essay, Frances E. Mascia-Lees, Patricia Sharpe, and Colleen Cohen consider her parallel designation of men (in feminism) and non-Western peoples (in anthropology) as "the other" a potential source of obfuscation about the nature of the difference: one might be led to forget that these "others" occupy *opposite* positions of power in their respective institutional contexts.[11]

My questions to Strathern come from a somewhat different direction. Having thus delineated the professional and political space of the feminist ethnographer as beset by opposing interests, is it enough to stop with the skewed parallel between anthropologist and native informant, feminism and patriarchy? Isn't it far more problematic that in this set of paired oppositions the native informant is the only element unambiguously hailing from the non-Western world, whereas the other three seem rooted in the West? In another essay, Strathern mentions in passing how "certain apparent dichotomies between writer, audience and subject have folded in on themselves"—Melanesia today is at once peopled by informants and by readers.[12] Mascia-Lees, Sharpe, and Cohen characterize the new native informant of postmodernity as someone who "may well have heard of Jacques Derrida and have a copy of the latest Banana Republic catalog."[13]

Somehow, the turmoil affecting the anthropological discipline has thrown up distant others from non-Western places in the form of consumers of first-world products, including texts about themselves. But why has the field focused on no third-world citizens who are also *producers*, members of a community of scholars, with interests and conflicts of their own?

Such a figure never appears on the horizon because the West has remained the unspoken or, at least, underanalyzed location of the self-questioning of the discipline, of the relations between subject and other, in a way directly affecting feminist critiques. It is not as though the history of colonialism has been suppressed. On the contrary, Strathern invokes "the colonial relation between societies" in the quotation above, and Mascia-Lees, Sharpe, and Cohen claim a "sympathetic identification" with non-Western peoples based on their (feminist) "history and understanding of being appropriated and literally spoken for by the dominant."[14] Yet these analogies do not allow for the possibility that there might also be some rough equivalent to the (Western) feminist movement and its institutionalizations, with third-world peoples in the late twentieth century inheriting decades of anticolonial struggle and nation building. But beyond the naming of colonialism as the context that so decisively marked and marred ethnographic practice, third-world nations remain opaque, without political and intellectual histories or the kind of institutional structures Western scholars take for granted.

If one is not attentive, further elisions and slippages can occur. In her commentary on James Clifford's introduction to *Writing Culture: The Poetics and Politics of Ethnography*, the book that has come to play such a pivotal role in the defining of the new poststructuralist ethnography, Lila Abu-Lughod points out how the experimentation with representation tended to gloss over the fundamental source of political crisis in the discipline—the division between self and other, Western knowers and non-Western knowns. As she goes on to claim, "[e]ven when anthropology is in crisis, as many would argue it is today, and even when the focus of that crisis is precisely the self/other problem, as it is in reflexive anthropology and the new ethnography, the divide tends to remain unquestioned."[15]

The history of feminism, in sharp contrast, has repeatedly recognized the non-innocence of the self/other distinction—from Simone de Beauvoir to the contemporary conflicts around race and sexuality in the United States. An acknowledgement of the fragmented and multiple identifications of the erstwhile Western subject, no less than the realization that the other is also a self, would, she contends, address the source of the problem and disrupt boundaries far more effectively than the new ethnography. Moreover, as a "halfie," someone with prior mixed relations to the West and to her place of fieldwork, one's sense of partiality and implication across cultures can only be heightened. Despite such redoubled efforts in defense of the interconnectedness of the contemporary world and feminism's privileged place within it, here is how she concludes:

Feminist ethnographies, ethnographies that try to bring to life what it means to be a woman in other places and under different conditions, ethnographies that explore what work, marriage, motherhood, sexuality, education, poetry, television, poverty, or illness mean to other women, can offer feminists a way of replacing their presumptions of *a* female experience with a grounded sense of our commonalities and differences.[16]

Suddenly a new divide opens out—between "feminists" and "other women"—where the assumption seems to be that feminists inhabit

one world—the Western one—whereas other women live elsewhere and are *not* feminist. Why not an ethnography about being a
feminist in other places? What about ethnographies from other
places?

In the essays I have looked at so far—undergirding the irony of
Strathern, the negativity of Mascia-Lees, Sharpe, and Cohen, and
the optimism of Abu-Lughod—the sense of crisis and the unique
position of the feminist ethnographer are obvious. My own commentary has been less concerned with arbitrating between their
formulations than with driving home the consequences of the fact
that, for all their aliveness to cultural difference, they are feminists
inhabiting Western locations, the citizen-subjects of Western nations.

The experiences and displacements of fieldwork sharpen but do
not fundamentally unsettle their partiality to and familiarity with
the institutions and debates of "home." Feminist ethnographers
have not spoken in the same manner for locations elsewhere, notwithstanding the weight of "ethnographic authority"[17] legitimizing
the claim of knowing other cultures. However, and this is the more
important point I am trying to make, we need to probe the lack of
discussion around such issues of representation when differences
among women, the crisis of anthropology, and the need for a globally more responsive feminist practice characterize the present
moment. The extreme difficulty, I believe, of acknowledging a
"politics of location" that arises from national affiliation, particularly
for feminists in the West (barring important exceptions such as
Adrienne Rich), might constitute a partial answer.

Indeed, matters become even more interesting when one pauses
to reflect on a growing trend among U.S. feminist ethnographers
over the last few years: aspects of U.S. culture have become the
subject of study, their nation is the site of fieldwork. For instance, in
Uncertain Terms: Negotiating Gender in American Culture, the
editors Faye Ginsburg and Anna Lowenhaupt Tsing innocuously
mention (without further comment) that "the contributors are
American anthropologists and feminist scholars who have turned
their ethnographic gaze homeward to everyday life in their own
society."[18] Why the almost surreptitious nature of the turn toward

home? On the one hand, there may be the sensibility that it is no longer quite so okay to study non-Western cultures; on the other, a more positive tug seems to pull them toward the unfamiliar within their own everyday vicinities. In either case, the making and unmaking of nations, national boundaries, and commitments is taking place, a process U.S. feminists seem to have so much trouble contending with. U.S. feminist ethnographers who are now studying their own society appear to be particularly motivated by a sense of *accountability* (perhaps because their subjects are also citizens, members of the same "imagined community"?)[19] and evince an urgency toward confronting cultural processes affecting the most disenfranchised among them.

To take an example, I would like to argue that Judith Stacey's treatment of the question "Can there be a feminist ethnography?" with her attitude of modesty, wariness, and partial hopefulness cannot really be separated from the source of her theorizing: the choice of studying family and gender in California. As she points out, Strathern's discussion (to which I alluded earlier) tends to miss its mark, because the most common scenario in feminist ethnography is one where women set out to study other women in an ideally egalitarian mode. However, Stacey has become much more cautious about feminists' general eagerness to reduce the distance and alter relations of power between the researcher and the researched. For feminist goals of "authenticity, reciprocity, and intersubjectivity"[20] might be even more dangerous than the masculinist, objectifying methods they criticize, precisely because professed beliefs of mutual respect are apt to hide relations of authority, exploitation, and manipulation unavoidable in fieldwork. There is simply no getting away from the institutional and disciplinary power any ethnographer wields in converting fieldwork experiences into "data," nor from the fact that the product will ultimately be in her control. Unlike Strathern, however, Stacey does believe that a better dialogue between feminist ideals and postmodern ethnographic methodologies, especially those emphasizing the *partialness* of the capacity to represent self and other, are well worth the risk, if only to make feminists more self-conscious about their dilemmas and modest about their achievements.

Now it is true that there is absolutely nothing in the overall thrust of Stacey's reflections that links them explicitly with the site of her fieldwork. Nevertheless, I would contend, it is the spaces of "home" (rather than a place one occasionally visits) that sharpen problems, make insufficiencies pressing and ethicopolitical quandaries inescapable. No doubt, as Stacey observes, "fieldwork represents an intrusion into a system of relationships, a system of relationships that the researcher is far freer than the researched to leave."[21]

But her examples illustrate something else as well—the ongoing nature of many of her interactions, their open-endedness, and, most emphatically, the need for accountability in relations of inequality. There is less room for the overly neat mockery Strathern advocates or the fulsome energy of Abu-Lughod. I am trying to suggest that such measured ambivalence is more easily realizable when one is a Western ethnographer working with members of one's own national community.

Let me approach the issue of first-world ethnography with an entirely different case. Angie Chabram, a Chicana literary theorist, has explored the usefulness of poststructuralist anthropology for the unique project of creating the field of Chicano/a Studies. It is the "selves" and "others," the subjects and objects of the "oppositional ethnographies" she envisages, that make her venture so radical: Chicana and Chicano intellectuals in the U.S. academy who will study themselves.

Even the idea of such revised oppositional ethnographies (authored by national minorities from working-class backgrounds mainly) taking place within national university settings immediately suggests a break with the traditional ethnographic situation . . .

Traditionally, people of color are the objects of mainstream ethnographies written usually by male Anglo-Saxon and European anthropologists. Traditionally, mainstream ethnographies enact a radical separation between the world of scholarship—the academy—done prior to and upon return from ethnographic fieldwork, and the site of ethnographic research: the *world*. Usually the *Third World*.[22]

How is it, Chabram asks, that minority communities in the United States are so rarely perceived as having any direct connections with institutions of higher education, with Chicano intellectuals them-

selves forgetting the experiences, practices, and prehistories ("in
the fields, the border, the family, the oral tradition, factories, public
institutions, and research designs"[23]) that bind them to the larger
social and political formation and to one another?

In Chabram's essay, anthropological "theory" is pulled away from
its textual and formal strategies in order to attend to the underside
of academic activity, to the institutional, material, and cultural
constraints that make such activity conceivable in the first place.
The decisive change of terrain we are witnessing here lies in the
appearance of a new ethnographic subject—a scholar of color—who
produces a new field of inquiry—scholars of color in the U.S.
academy—thus destabilizing the self/other dyad at one of its primary sites, the U.S. nation (not the world or the third world).[24]

So, then, to reiterate my earlier question once again, if a national
focus by feminist ethnographers can have certain enabling functions, such as we have just seen, why the silence around matters
relating to the nation?[25]

The beginning of a partial answer was brought home to me while
I read Laura E. Donaldson's discussion of nationalism in *Decolonizing Feminisms: Race, Gender and Empire-building*. In just a few
pages, she is able to jump from an acknowledgment of how nationalism "historically functioned as one of the most powerful weapons for
resisting colonialism and for establishing the space of a postcolonial
identity" to an examination of nationalism's uneasy relation with
feminism to, finally, a proclamation of a deep connection between
"sexism, racism and nationalism" based on the case of Hitler's
Germany. Nationalism is thus summarily dismissed as a possible
"postcolonial feminist strategy."[26]

Even granting that there is something quite bizarre about Donaldson's equivalence between Nazism and third-world national
movements, I consider this sort of position as a symptomatic response to the conservatism that appears to have such a strong hold
over nationalism in the West: there seems to be no space here for
oppositional intellectuals and feminists to come to terms with this
aspect of their identity. The U.S. editors of a book dealing explicitly
with nationalisms and sexualities across the globe are not so much
negative as curiously undecided in their perspective on national-

ism. They do not seem to know what to do either with the power of nationalist discourse or with the differences in the relationship between nationalism and feminism at particular historical moments in the first and third worlds.[27]

U.S. nationalism is clearly something of a dilemma for U.S. feminists. The obvious problem with ceding the field to those in dominance is to run the grave risk of appearing complicitous with their formulations. There is in any case an urgent need to examine why the presence of dissident women and feminists *within* the borders of the United States—women of color, lesbians, immigrants, and so on, who now have a place in the U.S. feminist community—is forcing an accountability and handling of issues (however uneven or unsatisfactory) that has not so far been reproduced globally, across nations, and not by those perhaps most equipped to do so—namely, feminist ethnographers.

The above reflections were initiated while I was still a graduate student in the United States but needed my return to India to take fuller shape. If anyone should suppose that working and writing in contemporary India would insulate one from the contradictions, power imbalances, and ambiguities the preceding debates have been expressing, nothing could be further from the truth. Postcolonial places are rarely well defined by being called *local*, as though their boundaries were somehow simpler than the vastness of the West and its influence. But one thing is certain. The analytical, historical, and political labors necessary here, the levels of unlearning one may have to undergo, will be skewed by the partialities and possibilities such a location brings into play.

Western feminists looking in a third-world nation like India for the kind of debate we have just been following—its setting provided by uncertainties and experiments within the discipline of anthropology—might come away empty-handed. To my knowledge, the question "Can there be a feminist ethnography?" has also not been raised. This doesn't diminish my insistence that U.S. feminist ethnographers should be both more aware of their own locational bias and go on to consider the possibility of relevant institutional and political crises in other places. For the very career and legacy of anthropology, when situated within the broader making of the social sciences in colonial and independent India, would yield some rather telling results. More to the point, as soon as we think of the central problem structuring practically all the essays above—namely, the unequal production of "selves" and "others"—an immense, and immensely complicated, field opens up in the Indian feminist context. Tied up directly with this, the question now playing in U.S. feminist circles—the position of feminism across differences among women—takes on a distinctive critical and historical cast here. I can only try to hint at some of the issues involved. The rest of this chapter is little more than a sketch for a much larger project around the Indian women's movement and the emergence of feminist scholarship within and beyond the academy. Clearly, the possible avenues for a historicization of the present are multiple. Responding through the lens available to a "native informant," I sought in the previous section to interrogate repressed elements within the questions raised by Western feminist ethnographers critical of their discipline. What follows is another kind of interrogation. My point is emphatically not to provide Western readers with stories from the field in the manner of most ethnographies; to do so would quite defeat my present purpose.

Instead, in the spirit of the kinds of arguments I have been making throughout this book, it is a concern with theoretical and institutional fields—in this case, the historical field of feminism in India—that calls for representation. The reading I am about to offer of the trajectory of feminist writing in India uses the debates within ethnography as an entry point and is therefore clearly a partial perspective. Taken in counterpoint to chapter one, composed in another country and a different time, it is also an attempt to recover the contemporary history of Indian feminist politics I was earlier able to disavow.

Women, Feminists, and the Nation in India

Practically all feminist research in India that grew in tandem with the present phase of the women's movement was initially shaped by

the social sciences, where the field of economics still reigns su-
preme, followed by history, with sociology lagging considerably
behind. Whatever their status under the colonial regime, anthropology departments as such became marginalized; even major universities today may not necessarily possess one. Careful genealogical analysis is required to plot the takeover of the systematic process
of othering undertaken by colonial anthropology—through such
modes as the tabulation of kinship, the compilation of Hindu "manners and customs," the categorization of "tribes," and, above all, the
fascination with caste[28]—into postindependent India after 1947,
with its constitutional proclamation of a secular, socialist, and democratic state. If anthropology departments were made to house the
study of our tribal peoples, the *Adivasis*, or original inhabitants so
shamelessly pushed to the fringes of mainstream society, sociology
came to inherit British social anthropology and that unique "gate-
keeper" of Indian society, "homo hierarchicus."[29]

One sign of the shift in power/knowledge wrought by independence is that the census report, an anthropologically informed official document of exemplary importance if ever there was one,
stopped classifying the population according to caste. This doesn't
imply that native anthropologists and sociologists ceased to be
trained in the imperial mold: they often continued to cultivate an
attitude of distance to their own society, indeed, imaging it as
other.[30] But they did so without the kind of authority wielded by
their British predecessors; those most influential in directing government policy for the new state were the economists and planners.

At any rate, the effect in those areas touched by anthropology is
almost the flip side of the ferment in the Western discipline: they
have become largely conservative, their subject matter social rather
than political, at times ambivalent, more often inert. If history's
tasks continue to be obvious and open to renegotiation, focusing on
modern India and nationalism, extending back to earlier periods
and laterally to deal with regional specificities, much of the energy
and hope for the future was invested in economics, especially development economics. As Satish Deshpande has recently argued,
the Indian nation's most vital figuration has been that of an "imagined economy,"[31] an imaginary stretching from state-controlled
Nehruvian socialism to the horizons of the communist Left.

Though this requires the kind of detailed investigation I cannot provide here, it is unclear whether the presence of women in anthropological studies about India, or even of women anthropologists themselves, played a formative role in the emergence of feminist scholarship. Writing about the crucial function of indigenous anthropologists in the context of commemorating an international symposium on women in anthropology that took place in India in 1978, Leela Dube comments on the greater accessibility and familiarity such researchers would have to their data, leading to potentially more authentic and subtle analyses. Important as these observations are, they remain curiously contextless—one would hardly guess that they were produced here, and at a time when feminism was gaining considerable ground. [32]

However, when a context is required, an anthropologically imbued perspective appears to direct women scholars toward focusing exclusively on the difference of being an "other culture" and doing so in a manner that exhausts itself in accounts that are frozen in time and locked into local particularity. To take another example: it is not accidental, I think, that when Veena Das, a sociologist with anthropological training, offers an analysis of the work, power, and status of Indian women, she shies away from what she calls "modernization." She comes to the further conclusion that Indian women, however unequally positioned, have, in fact, access to certain forms of cultural power, such as those associated with female sexuality in Hindu thought. It is no surprise to her that feminism emerged in the West, where women had become so sexualized and segregated in the home as to give rise to a political movement to combat women's condition. Das's barely veiled implication seems to be that feminism, therefore, still belongs only there. [33]

How different, though, are even those anthropological essays that are structured not so much by manifestations of cultural otherness as by issues of development and change, where the economy plays a central role. The beginnings of feminist research in the seventies can be understood better, I am therefore trying to suggest, against the background of the dominance of the postindependence institutions and narratives around the economy, with their aims of growth, redistributive justice, and the eradication of poverty and the unique, if controversial, combination of private and public enterprise. Although it was vigorously debated, the concept of the mixed economy, with state-led planning mapping the way, constituted a veritable universe of discourse.[34] In spite of, and in part because of, the significant achievements of the first three plans, the unresolved contradictions inherent in the paradoxical mix of a state-run heavy industrial sector and unregulated consumer goods industries brought the economy into severe crisis by the late sixties. In both urban and rural areas, among youth as much as the cadres of leftist parties, forms of popular protest and struggle were launched against the state and its institutions, including the available forms of parliamentary politics. At the cost of compressing an extremely dense historical conjuncture, let me just emphasize that the contemporary phase of the women's movement, like many of the other radical movements of the seventies, owed its inception to the failure of the Nehruvian model and above all to the realization that only a tiny upper and middle class crust was reaping its benefits.

According to Neera Desai, where an earlier, preindependence generation of politically active middle class women had placed their hope on the claims of an egalitarian free India and the creation of a welfare state—to the extent that an independent women's movement was felt by many to be no longer necessary—the seventies saw the emergence of something quite new.[35] A subsequent generation of feminists were shaken by the absence of a women's perspective in the overall development process and by the indifference of planners and policymakers. That women were occasionally present in research work prior to the seventies, especially in anthropological "descriptions of [the] position of elite women in family, marriage and kinship networks,"[36] depictions of puberty rites, and so on, they dismissed. (The role conflict of the middle class working woman was a typical Ph.D. topic in sociology in the fifties and sixties, we are told.) If the initial postindependence years were a time of "complacency and acquiescence among women,"[37] reproduced in some measure in the kinds of studies that were undertaken, this was shattered in 1974 by the revelations of the report *Towards Equality*[38] produced by the Committee on the Status of Women in India:

Three decades after Independence, and after three decades of planned development, the picture of women's position that emerged was startling in its grimness . . .

Women's position was worsening in practically every sphere, with the exception of some gains in education and employment for middle-class women. Women were found in the least paid jobs, working long hours, and bearing full responsibility for the home by fetching fuel and water; by doing work in family production units, without being paid for the labour; by bringing up children and caring [for] the sick and the aged. There was growing violence against women—rape, wife battering, family violence, dowry deaths and prostitution. This was the stark reality for millions of women.[39]

There could be no stronger contrast *and* connection between "the stark reality for millions of women" and the world of the writers of the above lines. For the most part, therefore, contemporary feminism in India began its career as a particular kind of *split* subject composed of the investigating subject and the subject of inquiry, at once populated by "selves" and "others." What I am trying to get at with this potentially misleading formulation (misleading because the use of the distinction between "selves" and "others" is open to the kind of reified interpretation that would not capture the complexity of the Indian situation) is that Indian feminism was formed through an active process of representation, with the need to speak on behalf of the vast majority of the nation's women. In the face of the reneged promises of independent India, it was not possible for a tiny group of feminist intellectuals and activists to refer to the experiences and predicaments of their worlds alone. (Against this, one might recall a text central to the onset of the U.S. women's movement, such as Betty Friedan's *The Feminine Mystique*,[40] whose subjects were overwhelmingly untouched by internal disparities: "selves" were naming, analyzing, and politicizing selves. Not so with us.)[41]

An objection could well be raised here. For it is quite common to find an Indian feminist text that opens in critical appraisal, just as its Western counterpart has also come to do. "A very large part of the thinking, writing and efforts to change the conditions of life of Indian women is confined to a narrow stratum of urban, educated middle-class women,"[42] says Madhu Kishwar in her introduction to a collection of articles from *Manushi*, India's major journal about women. From a very different angle, Ilina Sen has also referred to the prominence of urban and middle class women's groups and the issues they raised, including the rise of Women's Studies in the university and of feminist scholarship more generally.[43] Now, there is little doubt that an Indian feminism was predominantly formed out of the experiences and conflicts of those middle class women who were most active in its ranks, through the contradictions of family and personal relations, of work and public spaces—in other words, within a context constituted by the institutions and knowledge structures governing their everyday lives. Moreover, many of the campaigns women's groups took up in the seventies and eighties were urban-based. One of the first major issues that gained attention was the giving and taking of dowry and the terrible atrocities perpetrated in its name—the so-called dowry deaths. In the southern Indian city of Hyderabad, the Progressive Organisation of Women launched a popular offensive against the sexual harassment of women students on roads and buses. Rural women's movements, such women's participation in other struggles and daily strategies for survival, did not, no doubt, receive the same kind of national coverage. However, the middle class backgrounds of most feminists has also, I think, been the source of some confusion.

For what I am trying to suggest is that although most feminist researchers have, indeed, been formed by their urban locations and professional identities and, further, "have often remained circumstantially quite distant from the actual lives of poor women,"[44] this did not substantially come in the way of the overall slant of their scholarship. It was unthinkable, for instance, that "Women's Studies" should be conceived of more or less autobiographically—the canvas of the nation and its "imagined community" did not allow for such a mode of approach. Even as the language of a certain kind of liberal feminism appears to have been the one theoretically available—the language of rights and of equality—it was the aspirations of socialist feminism, if anything, that occupied a privileged position. In a typical Women's Studies text, for example, the chapter on the economy is dominated by information related to women in agriculture as well as in industry, with the dilemmas of the middle class woman in employment only occupying a few pages.[45] In fact, some of the most important work by researchers has been in such key areas as rural women and the feminization of poverty.[46] Much the same can be said about studies on health, where basic nutritional needs, primary health care, and hazardous family planning techniques have been the main pressure points. Significantly enough, there have even been those who felt that a sense of priority was required: to the question, "Who are the nation's women?" the response was—India's women reside in the villages. The everyday lives of rural women occupy not just a privileged part but the entire space of Madhu Kishwar's introduction. "I have to get away from the towns to get at the heart of things,"[47] writes Gail Omvedt, and she isn't only echoing a narrowly Western sentiment. On the contrary, paying attention to the lives of women who were less privileged was often precisely the way in which a middle class movement could proclaim its *Indianness*.

The attempt to reach out to and speak for those women whom history and the nation were in danger of throwing aside has often demanded something akin to an ethnography on the part of feminist activists and researchers. This would be one way of exploring the notion of the split subject of Indian feminism that I am trying to argue for, as it is ethnographic encounters that manage to produce —and co-implicate—"selves" and "others" so uniquely. Such encounters may thus clarify the sense in which these distinctions are being used. Not many generalizations are possible, so I will briefly cite two vastly different examples—K. Saradamoni's *Changing Land Relations and Women: A Case Study of Palghat District, Kerala*, and "*We were making history . . . :*" *Life stories of women in the Telangana People's Struggle*, as told to members from the women's collective Stree Shakti Sanghatana.[48]

Saradamoni's study was a response to the report *Towards Equality* (brought out by the Government of India's Department of Social Welfare), which exerted pressure in the hope that women's integration into development would become a matter of government policy. Begun in 1977 and located in the author's home state, it combines historical investigation, surveys, and participant observation to trace the unique—and to most, peculiar—history of women in Kerala. Although this is fundamentally a conventional text governed by the constraints of "objective" social science, the nature of its subject matter presses it in another direction as well, one far less common in this genre of research: Saradamoni is also writing her own history. In a sense, two stories are going on simultaneously. The first maps different women within Kerala's agricultural economy—this is the narrative of "land, women and women,"[49] as Saradamoni expresses it at one stage, in order to emphasize the nonunitary nature of women's situations. The second narrative speaks of "land and woman"[50] and can perhaps also be called a story of the "self."

Notwithstanding Saradamoni's introduction to the broader socioeconomic order that effectively hierarchizes women along class and caste lines, it is perhaps inevitable that "land and woman" soon sets the tone, for Kerala's "woman" is overdetermined: no discussion of women in Kerala takes place without reference to the system of matriliny that characterized significant sections of society, especially among the Nayar castes. As Saradamoni observes, it would be hard to find any account of Kerala that does not deal with it—in shock, confusion, occasionally in wonder. Over centuries of exorbitant writing, I should add, matriliny in Kerala has been molded into an anthropological object of a density and magnitude that in all probability lies unsurpassed, at least in India. Thus, when one considers the kind of othering matriliny has been subjected to, realizes the absence of a feminist perspective on the issue, and takes into account Saradamoni's personal connection to her investigation as a Nayar (even though this is never explicitly articulated), it might seem almost imperative to concentrate on reclaiming its legacy for feminism and for herself.

To begin with, this is exactly what she sets out to do. Matriliny holds the narrative together—her "peep into history" and the chapter on inheritance laws are, if anything, dominated by it. Here ostensibly was a system where women and men were fully maintained by and traced descent from their mother's side, and where women did not depend on husbands but could enter into and terminate *sambandham* (relationships) with men of their caste and castes above theirs. If deviance from the conventions of patriliny was what attracted most observers, Saradamoni wants to understand how these women allowed it to change. For change it did, as the result of the new system of land ownership imposed during British rule.

A detailed discussion of this process is not possible here and may not be necessary for my more limited purposes. To sum things up all too cursorily, a lack of "alertness" on the part of matrilineal women, Saradamoni feels, must have been responsible for the way reform movements came in the wake of agrarian unrest, giving rise to new laws investing men with private property rights, normalizing the nuclear family, and setting in motion an ideology of conjugal love. The coming to power of a democratically elected Communist government in postindependence Kerala in 1956 and the land reforms it implemented in order to confiscate and redistribute land holdings above a certain size "failed to see woman and her special problems. The protected and secondary role to which she was being relegated since British rule and the ideology that accompanied [it] were cemented and given legal sanction."[51]

Having thus set the historical stage, Saradamoni proceeds to the main focus of her study, which is an analysis of the contemporary situation of women in Palghat, one of Kerala's more backward northern districts. It is now, in the mix of ethnographic observation and survey work, in the construction of the present rather than the past, that the story line splits, as it simultaneously speaks of "woman" as well as "women and women."

Differences between women in Kerala's rural economy are clear and receive corroboration at various points. Regardless of land reforms, old inequalities between erstwhile landlords, tenants, and landless laborers persist. References are made to women's responses to questionnaires, and the text is replete with tables and charts indicating patterns of land ownership, participation in agricultural activity, levels of education, employment, income, and so on.

There is no question that those who were often virtual slaves during precolonial and colonial times, the "untouchables" who owned nothing, have seen only marginal changes with the introduction of wage legislation and fixed hours of work—these landless women now depend entirely on the vagaries of the agricultural season and are forced at times to work for less than the minimum wage. Disparities between men and women appear least fixed here; surprisingly enough, among all those whom Saradamoni interviewed, these women feel most strongly the need for economic independence from their men. Small tenants are among those who gained most from land reforms, though it is somewhat puzzling that Saradamoni does not have much to say about women from such groups. A sizable percentage of women from Brahmin and Nayar landowning families may not even play a supervisory role in cultivation but are confined to household activities, almost like their urban counterparts. It is also they who are the most educated, though this has yet to translate into middle class membership. When asked about ways of lightening the burden of household work, responses ranged from modern gadgets and the need for creches to the employment of servants. None of them, Saradamoni notes with obvious disappointment, mention the possibility that husbands might do their share. Thus, all these women had and continue to have very different struggles to cope with. Perhaps most important of all, "they hardly knew each other."[52]

But, as I said, this is not the only story being told. Interrupting the discussion at many moments, a particular figure keeps arresting the author's attention and is described in the most poignant terms: the destitute upper-caste woman, often a widow. With all the land gone because of reforms and most of the men and the younger generation working independently elsewhere, her life is at the mercy of whatever comes her way. Often hailing from a poorer Nayar household and sometimes from an erstwhile Brahmin landlord's family, she symbolizes and sums up the loss of matriliny for Kerala. Indeed, it is she who signals the basic failure of a century of progress. To put it differently, this figure of abandonment and loss becomes the vehicle by which Saradamoni can identify with the past they both share; hence my designation of this aspect of the text as a kind of history of the "self."

As the narrative draws to a close, all the women Saradamoni has been evoking in such different ways stand poised before an uncertain future. What will be the effects on their lives of the ongoing breakdown of a self-sustaining rural economy and the rise of a new middle class culture? When will they find the answers themselves and find each other?

Before discussing further aspects of Saradamoni's study, let me move on to the other example I mentioned—*"We were making history . . . ": Life Stories of women in the Telangana People's Struggle.* Unlike Saradamoni, the women's collective Stree Shakti Sanghatana had no difficulty in explicitly proclaiming:

When we first chose to do this study, one of our aims was to recover our own history (we saw the women in the Telangana Struggle as founders of a history of women's action in Andhra, indeed in India itself.) . . .

Constantly with us was the feeling that this was all out of our own lives—that we had been there before ourselves.[53]

(Saradamoni's special investment in recovering a past for herself, by contrast, had to function more in the form of a subtext.)

As the result of the kind of relation that developed between the members of this urban-based group and the overwhelmingly rural women they interviewed, what might earlier have remained "data" for an analysis of women's participation in the Telangana peasant uprising from 1946 to 1951 turned into "life stories" that called out to be presented as such. The book thus consists of a selection of some sixteen interviews out of the seventy that were collected over four years; it was first published in 1986 in Telugu, the language of the state of Andhra, where they live, before an English edition was brought out in 1989. Transcribed, edited, and translated, lightly framed by background essays that both contextualize and discuss some of the problems that arise in writing about women in a political movement such as this one, these women's "voices had to be heard."[54]

Not only does the Telangana Struggle span one of the most complex periods of Andhra's history, but the women's accounts themselves, in all their evocativeness and diversity, defy summary. At considerable cost, though hopefully not entirely damaging the basic picture I am trying to convey, I shall only touch upon one thread running through all their stories—the catalyzing role of the

Communist Party of Andhra, which, however, turned from being the basic source of support for the struggle to calling for its withdrawal in 1951. Pivotal to most of the women's memories, the party is also a major focus of the authors' reflections.

The stories tell of the terrors unleashed on villages that harbored known sympathizers. Vajramma in the village of Akkirajupalli recalls, "We never slept in the same place twice . . . Each ran for her life. Was there such a thing as mother and child?" S. Sugunamma, from a bonded laborer's family, says of her first contact with the party, "I was just nine . . . when they [the party] started some classes in self-defence . . . Being a girl I felt neglected in my family and longed to get away." She goes on to emphasize just how much it came to mean to many like her—"The Party was like a large common family. We dreamt that the Communist Government would come—and all families would be communes like this." Or, as Dayani Priyamvada expressed it, "in one way, if we had no connection with the party we would have been ordinary women who knew nothing. Because of our working in the party and reading the literature, we were able to understand the problems of society, the oppression in society, the situation of women and men; we were able to understand all this."[55]

By far the most difficult sections of the women's stories center around the contradictions the narrators experienced as women, which at times seemed to go without saying, at times was painfully suffered, at others identified with sharpness and anger. Though they profess equality between men and women, it was the women in the squads who did the cooking. Single women found themselves cornered into marriage to secure protection from the advances of other men. One woman had to give away her six-month-old baby, never to see him again, because he would have been a liability to their underground forest existence, and another speaks of the "rubbish domestic life"[56] she had to endure when her first child was born. A somewhat different example focuses on the performance of a political play called *The Step Forward*. Even though prevalent norms of respectability excluded them from going on stage, the women were sure that "a step forward" could only be taken if they did not leave the female roles to men. Yet these women found themselves unable to act their parts; it "required" the refusal to eat on the part of a party leader to force them to do so.

In their commentary on problems such as these, the authors do two things. On the one hand, they take issue with the party to show the kind of double standards that operated, especially underscoring the devastating betrayal these women underwent when the movement was called off. Considering what a "magic time"[57] those years became and how often it was male comrades who opened up new horizons of possibility for women, being told to go back to their old lives was crushing. However, the authors also feel forced to confront the ideological constraints structuring women's own sense of their worth in the very attempt to name areas of experience hitherto left unsaid and still largely unsayable. The example of Acchamamba, who may well have been one of the world's first "barefoot doctors," disturbs them in particular. Acchamamba's story focuses far more acutely on the daily harassment involved in sharing out food fairly and on the occasions when she had to defend herself against painful and unjust accusations of having affairs. One hears next to nothing about her skill and fame, the knowledges and practices that constituted her medical expertise: "This is a problem we have to face. How do we evaluate women's work when not just the official records but the women themselves, continually make distinctions that devalue and marginalise their importance?"[58]

The very emphasis the authors place on their task as listeners rather than analyzers allows for many levels of identification—here is a women's organization living in the same area whose members have also been uniquely formed by an ongoing tradition of leftist politics. In more ways than one, therefore, they share a common language. And yet, however much they may try to play down their evaluative role, the difference that the women's movement has made in their lives is equally inescapable. Unlike the women struggling at the turn of independence, the members from Stree Shakti Sanghatana also have another language—that of contemporary feminism: they can, therefore, name the relations of power between men and women and point to sexuality and reproduction as one of patriarchy's most intractable sites, in a way those women could not.

This difference, even distance, between the women being interviewed and those doing the interviews does not, however, imply a lack of rapport or sense of community. The same could be said for Saradamoni. However much feminism may be weighted on one side and so produce its own version of "selves" and "others," this is simultaneously undone by viewing feminism as the tie that binds. When will they find it? asks Saradamoni. "We were tracing a lineage,"[59] say the members of Stree Shakti Sanghatana. The point is to make the state and the Left more accountable toward the processes that have "cemented," as Saradamoni phrased it, these women's disablement; it is also to retrieve, through the act of retelling, their rightful place in history and the making of the nation. Everything else recedes.

Feminism and the New Middle Class

Having tried to argue that the subject of feminism in India was never single or unitary, I may now be somewhat clearer in explaining how feminist research, through its priorities of representation, contributed toward the shaping of this split subject. When it came to writing about India's economy and society, urban middle class feminists have been insistently foregrounding women from rural, poor, and backward areas in the midst of the struggles of women from their own class. To recall what I said earlier, this privileging of non-middle class and non-urban women needed to be understood against the background of the Nehruvian model of socialism, or, to be more accurate, the failure of its imagined economy.

At least since the mid-eighties, but more completely with the onset of the nineties, however, the social imaginary hitherto sustaining the nation—for its apologists as much as its radicals—has begun to give way. One palpable sign of this fundamental change is that some feminists have been shifting their analytical attention from the flawed policies of development and the repressive measures of the state to a realm much closer to home, perhaps too close for comfort: the sphere of the middle class as part of an ideologically dominant order. It is not that feminists had no initial place in their scholarship for women like themselves. Middle class women's problems found expression in a number of areas, ranging from the law and family violence to the inflationary rise in consumer prices. The shift has to do with the self-reflexive manner in which the middle class woman is being thematized for the first time. Even more interesting is the fact that, when first self-consciously articulated, she has come to us from the past—to be more specific, from colonial India in the nineteenth century.

By far the most well-known book to have brought her to our attention is the anthology *Recasting Women: Essays in Colonial History*, edited by Kumkum Sangari and Sudesh Vaid. Writing as the eighties were about to draw to a close, Sangari and Vaid speak of "the obtuseness of the present."[60] Alongside the more "invisible" (but, I would add, by now also more familiar) economic processes that have marginalized most women, "visible" developments— growing communal conflict, the politicization of religion, the re-emergence of a "traditional" practice such as widow immolation in the heart of modern India—appear to have propelled feminists into a new field of inquiry, that of cultural history. According to the editors, this has occurred because history enables the kind of integrated approach to "questions about the inter-relation of patriarchal practices with political economy, religion, law and culture"[61] that eludes contemporary analysis.

In their remarkable introduction, Sangari and Vaid display a compelling desire to provide the fullest possible picture and represent women across different classes and communities. It is a serious limitation to them, therefore, that the essays in the collection focus mainly on the middle class and always on the Hindu community. As they rightly insist, "it is not possible to understand a dominant class or religious community without locating its relationship to other strata or religious groups."[62] However true these observations might be, in terms of the perspective I am trying to make room for they are also misleading. To begin with, only six of the ten essays are biased in favor of the middle class, and just three carry out their analysis without active reference to women from other groups. But more to the point, might not the *explicit* emphasis on middle class women, the direct focus placed on the "self," be what is most innovative about these historical essays?

Let me even suggest that part of the "obtuseness" of the present relates to the extreme difficulty of examining one's own class in sufficient detail when that class has, until very recently, been surreptitiously functioning as the norm. Within the Nehruvian imaginary, the middle class marked itself as modern, privileged, and elite. So also feminists eager to represent India's women—in the villages, at the wrong end of development, suffering the injustices of the state or the limitations of leftist politics and so on—have been doing so while rendering their own identities within the dominant culture largely *transparent.* In the two examples we looked at, both the members of Stree Shakti Sanghatana and Saradamoni locate themselves in their respective texts through processes of identification with women from rural backgrounds whose class positions were often at variance with their own.

Now, in contrast, the past framing the Sangari-Vaid essays provides the context for a discussion of the "new woman" who emerged at the interface of colonial subjection and an incipient nationalism and who, ironically enough, may not always be feminists' preferred choice in constructing a lineage. We are told about the shaping of a newly reinvented Hindu-Aryan identity, a modern Indian spirituality and quest for tradition, middle class respectability, and the cultivation of a tasteful ethnicity over against lower class depravity, all of which were critically predicated upon "our" female ancestors.

If these genealogical excavations undertaken in the eighties have disturbed feminists in the way that all "histories of the present" are bound to do, developments in the nineties are disorienting us even further. Just how deep the unexamined claims of a modern secular democracy could go has been brought home in no uncertain terms by a series of "events" whose violence none were prepared for—riots, even self-immolations, by elite students protesting against reservation quotas (affirmative action) in government jobs for backward castes; the demolition of a mosque at the "birthplace" of the mythological Hindu god Ram, followed by some of the worst communal pogroms against Muslims the nation has witnessed; and a "revolution from above" that is sweeping away an "outmoded" socialist state to usher India into the new global order of liberalization. Whatever the irreducibility of these processes—and they are as much irreducible as fundamentally co-implicated with one another—the middle class is crucially negotiating and shaping them in each case. This class, moreover, *is* the nation now (and not just its representative), out to save it from "casteist" policies favoring those marked backward, countering the "appeasement" of its Muslim and minority populations, and bringing true sovereignty via the mechanisms of the capitalist market rather than through "inefficient" planning and a "welfarist" state.

As a result, the language of politics, of justice denied, has been redeployed to sanction the right to dominance, openly and unabashedly claiming the space of the postcolonial nation as middle class, upper-caste, Hindu, and less obviously male, yet still speaking in terms of secularism and democracy. Part of the disorientation for feminists, therefore, has surfaced in their being forced to interrogate their own identities, affiliations, and practices, those aspects of the "self" that could remain transparent and go unmarked. At the end of their extensive study of the Indian women's movement—the first of its kind—Nandita Gandhi and Nandita Shah flounder in their discussion of religion and communalism. Is religion not an oppressive patriarchal force, something to be blanked out of one's mind? they ask. "But there is no way we can escape it in everyday politics, electoral wrangling and indeed in the lives of women."[63] Even greater uncertainty has been produced by the realization that the very forces of communalism, caste oppression, and the new economic order not only boast of visibly assertive women in their ranks but speak the language of feminism itself. How does one respond, ask Susie Tharu and Tejaswini Niranjana, when allegations of sexual harassment are used to justify attacks on Dalits by upper caste men? Or when population planners invoke women's empowerment in their campaigns to introduce highly risky injectable female contraceptives and hormonal implants into India?[64] As a consequence of these and similar developments, the boundaries marking feminism and feminist community, "selves" and "others," even politics itself, are all in the process of being redrawn.

It is too soon to expect anything like an extensive treatment of these issues. Let me cite one example that once again bears some of the qualities of an ethnography and that enacts the dilemmas being named here. In response to the contemporary communal tide, Tanika Sarkar, a feminist historian, set out in 1991 to interview members of the Rashtrasevika Samiti in New Delhi, the less well-known women's wing of the Rashtriya Swayamsevak Sangh, or RSS, a seasoned cadre-based organization of the Hindu Right. According to her, extremely recent developments among these women are bringing about something unprecedented: the older, more familiar symbol of inspiring motherhood is ceding ground to a new figure of vibrant militancy with "a trained, hardened, invincible female body," a mind of her own, and a sense of exhilarating possibility. Even the larger context of communalism has seen women on the center stage of riot scenes, as dynamic leaders in their own right, or courting arrest by the thousands in the cause of liberating Ram's birthplace at Ayodhya.[65] Haunting Sarkar's entire discussion is a single question: Could it be that this new communal phase is more enabling than the leftist women's movement?

Listening to the women from the Samiti talk about how their organization's greatest value lies in the exposure it has brought to a world beyond the home, witnessing the strong sense of solidarity and supportiveness among members, Sarkar feels forced to examine just what sort of feminism is involved here, if feminism it is. She weaves back and forth between her own position as a feminist on the Left and the complex forms of self-empowerment these women are enacting. Radical women's organizations are "vertical" in structure, she tells us, "reaching out to less privileged sisters as soon as they form themselves,"[66] especially in rural and laboring areas, in contrast to the "horizontal" modes of mobilization of women into the Rashtrasevika Samiti. Thus, the breadth of the older "split subject" is held up against this new class subject, whose actual membership is relatively very small, even if they have the advantage of strong cohesion within a homogeneous social milieu.

Most explicit within the Samiti is the theme of becoming empowered and militant in order to fight the enemy—Muslim lust. Sarkar, however, also discovers something less open to view—self-protection from the enemy within, from a potentially hostile *Hindu* environment. One version of the origin of the organization—not the official one, of course—has it that its founder witnessed a young girl being raped by (Hindu) hoodlums in the presence of her helpless husband.

Moreover, Sarkar realizes that these women come mainly from

upwardly mobile trading and service sectors of the middle class, precisely the ones with which feminist organizations in the seventies and eighties have had prior experience around family violence, divorce suits, and dowry deaths. In employment these women are bound to encounter further harassment and discrimination. Vociferously against a "traditional" practice such as sati, they even evaluate the women's movement in positive terms in spite of "official" denunciations of its corrupting western influence.

Doesn't all this, then, clearly add up to a feminist consciousness? No doubt, says Sarkar, but of a "bourgeois" kind: "The new Hindu woman is . . . a person with professional and economic opportunities, secure property ownership, legal rights to ensure them and some amount of political power to enforce these rights."[67] More critical now, Sarkar shows how these new citizens in fact blunt the edge of feminism by adopting a "neutral" position on issues: home life is to be preserved and not broken; intercaste and intercommunity marriages are permitted, but only if the family agrees. Caste is denounced by the dropping of last names and promotion of community dining but never discussed. Class is an area of silence.

According to Tharu and Niranjana, it is this "neutrality effect"[68] that feeds into and in turn is upheld by the nationalism of the Hindu Right, a nationalism indeed less fundamentalist than bourgeois. They emphasize just how hegemonic the new Hindu woman may become, rapidly entering a new middle class "common sense." If Sarkar loses her sense of disturbance and by the end of the essay has placed all confidence on "the more aware and sensitive forms of Left democratic and feminist movements"[69] to counter communal hatred and genuinely address caste, class, and gender oppressions, Tharu and Niranjana insist on the prior need to excavate the alliance between the new Right and the subject of liberal humanism. For the question is whether "our" claims to secularism and democracy have not also been undergirded by this very subject.

If we just step back for a moment and contrast the sense of feminist community that emerges here with the kind of examples I took up earlier, the difference is overwhelming. The fact that both the self and the other, the knower and the known, are feminist has become a source of disturbance and distanciation, if not disidentification. Under the previous dominance of the imagined economy, when the socialist claims of the Indian nation were being actively interrogated, "privileged" feminists were reaching out to and identifying with their more distant sisters in the name of social, economic, and gender justice for "all" women. Today, as a reconfigured hegemonic culture occupies center stage, with feminism having become a part of this culture, feminists are forced to scrutinize their immediate worlds in a new way. It has become painfully clear to some, at least, that the assumption of a secular India was just that, an assumption.

Thus, when Lila Abu-Lughod writes about how notions of the "self" and the "other" are far more complex than much of anthropology, including experimental anthropology, would allow, she is absolutely right. Just consider the way in which the dominant subject in India was formed under the aegis of colonialism and with the coming of national independence:

The shaping of the normative human-Indian subject involved, on the one hand, a dialectical relationship of inequality and opposition with the classical subject of western liberalism, and, on the other hand, its coding as upper-caste, middle class, Hindu and male. The coding was effected by processes of othering/differentiation such as, for example, the definition of upper-caste/class female respectability in counterpoint to lower-caste licentiousness, or Hindu tolerance to Muslim fanaticism and by a gradual and sustained transformation of the institutions that govern everyday life. Elaborated and consolidated through a series of conflicts, this coding became invisible as this citizen-self was redesignated as modern, secular and democratic.[70]

At the same time, let us not forget the incredibly disabling and immobilizing forms of othering that continue to be produced in the late twentieth century, when even third world nations like India are busy celebrating the possibilities of the agentive "new woman." Within the ambit of the hegemonic constructions of Hindu nationalism I have just been discussing, there is no room, for instance, for the Muslim woman. Indeed, as Tharu and Niranjana point out, "[t]he Muslim woman is caught in a terrible zero-zero game. She cannot really be woman any more than she can be Indian. As woman and as Indian, she cannot really be Muslim."[71]

The fact that right-wing women publicly proclaim Muslim men to be the main enemy can produce the worst of antagonisms between Hindu and Muslim women. Newly reconstituted contradictions and patterns of exclusion along class and caste lines are also actively setting upper caste and middle class women against those who are lower caste and poor. What unites the often very different forms of othering at work here—and, most important, what makes them unprecedented in postindependence India—is that these processes are openly legitimized by the newly articulate middle class and, indeed, may not even appear as problems at all.

How might feminists on the Left, more accustomed to political initiatives and forms of scholarship that leave essential aspects of their own identities out of the frame, situate themselves today? Angie Chabram's project around a proposed "oppositional ethnography" by Chicana/os in the U.S. academy comes to mind here. What would such a project look like in the Indian feminist context? Chabram focuses on the invisibility of marginalized people of color, but a different kind of invisibility is at issue among feminist activists and academics in India—the extent of "our" Hindu, middle class, and upper caste presence. Beyond just "naming" that which could hitherto pass unmarked in the feminist community, such an ethnography might be able to elaborate the *contemporary* meanings and practices that are attached to these markers. Under the sign of a specifically Indian modernity, in which vicinities and spaces of our everyday lives have they been suppressed? Where have they lived on? And what of feminists whose identities diverge from this norm?

The contemporary feminist field is far more complex than these loosely formulated questions would suggest. Conflicting forces, whose charge and direction are as yet poorly understood, are bringing new constellations of the West, of gender and the nation, into view. The present has not grown any less obtuse, and the Indian women's movement itself is entering its most challenging phase yet. These preliminary explorations have nonetheless made it possible to put forward two related arguments that I believe to be relevant not only for the United States but also for India: first, locations fundamentally structure our work and our politics in ways that tend to remain obscured; second, it is the failure to theorize the nation that has contributed most to the poor appreciation of our locational partialities.

One way of plotting the difference in the intellectual fields of the two nation-spaces—the way chosen in this chapter—is to see how ethnography plays in each context. To repeat a point made earlier, no ferment motivates the discipline of anthropology (or, for that matter, sociology) in India, at least not yet. The "ethnographies" I foregrounded by way of illustration were produced by feminists from economics, history, and English literature departments or by feminists located outside the academy. This certainly doesn't prevent aspects of Western debates from being relevant here, whether they are specifically attached to feminist ethnography or arise out of the broader tensions and conflicts characteristic of U.S. theory and feminism discussed in chapters two and three. It is vital, though, to appreciate just why.

The potential relevance of such debates has much more to do with the palpable and disruptive political developments overtaking Indian feminist praxis than with a desire to go "experimental" or be up on "theory." Indian feminists committed to egalitarian principles in the face of an ethos ready to condone inequalities are being forced into greater self-reflexivity about their aims, their methods of critique, and their alliance politics. We are now in the process of articulating a new—less transparent and more modest—politics of representation in our claims to speak from the perspective of India's "other" women.

More composite forms of theorizing the Indian feminist context demand an examination of our extraordinarily disparate conceptual apparatus and the divergent careers of gender, sexuality,[72] class, caste, community, and region. We are only beginning to sense the chasm that separates our relative facility with respect to some of these terms over against the repression, opacity, and sanctioned ignorance governing others. Can the insights of "theory" and the debates of Western feminism be useful in this process? No question.[73] At the very least, the unequal positions of the concepts structuring U.S. feminist theory can alert us to some of the difficulties involved. On a more positive note, I would like to think that some of the impasses and conflicts, especially around the question of race and the demands of U.S. women of color, could be illuminating analogies that would travel well, if handled with care, into our contemporary situation.

I am unable to say more (yet) in this regard. In a paradoxical sense, for Western debates to travel better into third-world spaces, the axis of the West—its position as obvious and ultimate source of reference—would first have to be displaced or, at any rate, redirected. This book—not excluding the present chapter—has been too deeply formed in the Western light, or under its shadow, to be able to initiate the next steps.

It is time to conceive of travel differently—between third-world nations, for instance, or between third-world spaces in the West. Unlike Mascia-Lees, Sharpe, and Cohen, who only seem to view travel negatively, I would, therefore, like to suggest that we conceive of it afresh—in both the third world and in the first.[74] Precisely when the hegemony of the United States over the rest of the globe appears more "natural" than ever, it could be important for U.S. feminists to travel in search of perspectives that might otherwise elude them as citizens of the world's only superpower. More to the point, Western feminists need to reconsider what they are out to learn from the distant places they visit. Instead of developing ever more theoretically sophisticated twists on the cross-cultural construction of gender,[75] why not attend also to *feminist* voices from elsewhere? How are women's issues situated? Who represents them? What institutions advance their cause? What impasses beset them?

Questions such as these might point to a more viable—and accountable—international feminism than claims either to our universal oppression or to its obverse, our global sisterhood, have hitherto allowed.

Notes

Chapter One: Postcolonial Feminists
in the Western Intellectual Field

1. Foucault, "The Political Function of Intellectuals," trans. Colin Gordon, *Radical Philosophy* 17 (1977): 12.

2. Foucault, "Politics and Ethics: An Interview," trans. Catherine Porter, in *The Foucault Reader*, ed. Paul Rabinow (New York: Pantheon Books, 1984), p. 374, emphasis added.

3. Lâm, "Feeling Foreign in Feminism," *Signs* 19, 4 (1994): 890–891.

4. For other discussions about the position, location, and history of feminist scholars of third-world origin in the first world, see Chandra Talpade Mohanty, "Feminist Encounters: Locating the Politics of Experience," *Copyright* 1 (Fall 1987): 33–44; Lata Mani, "Multiple Mediations: Feminist Scholarship in the Age of Multinational Reception," *Inscriptions, Traveling Theories, Traveling Theorists* 5 (1989): 1–23; Ruth Behar, "The Biography in the Shadow," *Translated Woman: Crossing the Border with Esperanza's Story* (Boston: Beacon Press, 1993), pp. 320–342; Kamala Visweswaran, *Fictions of Feminist Ethnography* (Minneapolis: University of Minnesota Press, 1994).

5. B. B. Misra, *The Indian Middle Classes: Their Growth in Modern Times* (London, New York, Bombay: Oxford University Press, 1961), pp. 10–11.

6. "Discussing Modernity, 'Third World,' and *The Man Who Envied Women*," with Laleen Jayamanne, Geeta Kapur, and Yvonne Rainer, *Art and Text* 23/24 (1987): 44.

7. Macaulay, "Indian Education" (Minute of the 2nd of February 1935), in *Prose and Poetry*, ed. G. M. Young, (Cambridge, Mass.: Harvard Uni-

versity Press, 1967), pp. 719–730. In Macaulay's formulation, this class was defined by its *differential* status: "a class of interpreters *between* us and the millions whom we govern—a class of persons Indian in blood and colour, but English in tastes, in morals and in intellect" (p. 729, emphasis added). It would be worth investigating how this differential identity has changed.

8. See Gauri Viswanathan's study, *Masks of Conquest: Literary Study and British Rule in India* (New York: Columbia University Press, 1989), p. 3: "The history of education in British India shows that certain humanistic functions traditionally associated with literature—for example, the shaping of character or the development of the aesthetic sense or the disciplines of ethical thinking—were considered essential to the processes of sociopolitical control by the guardians of the same tradition."

9. Nandy, *The Intimate Enemy: Loss and Recovery of Self under Colonialism* (New Delhi: Oxford University Press, 1983), p. xii.

10. For some varying assessments of this process based on different historical periods and levels of analysis see Lata Mani, "The Construction of Women as Tradition in Nineteenth Century Bengal," in *Cultural Critique* 2, 7 (Special Issue: "The Nature and Context of Minority Discourse") (Fall 1987): 119–156; Veena Mazumdar "The Social Reform Movement in India from Ranade to Nehru," in *Indian Women from Purdah to Modernity*, ed. B. R. Nanda (New Delhi: Radiant Publishers, 1976); Meredith Borthwick, *The Changing Role of Women in Bengal 1849–1905* (Princeton, N.J.: Princeton University Press, 1984); Partha Chatterjee, "The Nationalist Resolution of the Women's Question," in *Recasting Women: Essays in Colonial History*, eds. Kumkum Sangari and Sudesh Vaid (New Delhi: Kali for Women Press, 1989), pp. 231–253; and Radha Kumar, *A History of Doing: An Illustrative Account of Movements for Women's Rights and Feminism in India, 1800–1990* (New Delhi: Kali for Women Press, 1993).

11. Chatterjee, "Colonialism, Nationalism and Colonised Women—the Contest in India," mimeo, p. 16. For a slightly altered version, see Chatterjee, "The Nationalist Resolution of the Women's Question," p. 246.

12. Jayawardena, *Feminism and Nationalism in the Third World* (London: Zed Books; and New Delhi: Kali Press for Women, 1986), pp. 107–108.

Susie Tharu has this to say about prominent women during the nationalist struggle:

Individual women, especially those who came from families that had risen economically and socially during the colonial regime, were able to develop, move close to and sometimes even achieve leadership and power (often held tenaciously), for a very old and deeply rooted ideological sanction had been obtained for the growth. However, the women who emerged from this phase, often were . . . vociferous about the traditional role of women. . . . These women rarely admit the real oppression of women in our society, for they believe the way out of it is open to any who has the strength and talent to try, and of course the virtue to succeed.

See "Tracing Savitri's Pedigree: Victorian Racism and the Image of Women in Indo-Anglian Literature," in *Recasting Women: Essays in Colonial History*, eds. Kumkum Sangari and Sudesh Vaid (New Delhi: Kali for Women, 1989), pp. 263–264. See also Radha Kumar's account of the Indian women's movement. According to her, at least by the 1930s, national leaders such as Sarojini Naidu and Begum Shah Nawaz were taking exception to the "Westernized Indian woman" because of her misplaced feminism (Kumar, *A History of Doing*, p. 88). Such an equation of feminism in India with the West, by the way, is one that repeatedly goes out as an accusation and continues to haunt the Indian women's movement right up to the present.

13. See Joanna Liddle and Rama Joshi, *Daughters of Independence: Gender, Caste and Class in India* (London and New Delhi: Zed Press, 1986), especially chapter 17, "Education: The Path to Emancipation?" for first person accounts by Indian women with professional occupations.

14. An excellent example of such a view of an Indian woman's subjectivity is Rama Mehta's *The Western Educated Hindu Woman* (New York: Asia Publishing House, 1970).

15. The term "sanctioned ignorance" comes from Gayatri Chakravorty Spivak's powerful critique of Michel Foucault's position as a self-contained Western intellectual. She focuses on his "blind spot" concerning the techniques for the appropriation of space that ravaged the colonies during precisely the same historical period that held his attention, but for other matters. His excavations remained with the new inventions of power-in-spacing in the European theater alone—in prisons, asylums, and hospitals—through Jeremy Bentham's panopticon. See her essay "Can the Subaltern Speak?" in *Marxism and the Interpretation of Culture*, eds. Cary Nelson and Lawrence Grossberg (Urbana and Chicago: University of Illinois Press, 1988), pp. 271–313. Her point is well taken. A major purpose of this study, however, is not to stop with the production of sanctioned ignorances amongst Western intellectuals but to examine our own as well.

16. Rich, "Notes toward a Politics of Location," in *Blood, Bread and Poetry: Selected Prose, 1979–1985* (New York and London: W. W. Norton and Company, 1986), p. 211.

17. Maxine Schwartz Seller, ed., *Immigrant Women* (Philadelphia: Temple University Press, 1981), p. 5.

18. Ibid.

19. Cherríe Moraga and Gloria Anzaldúa, eds., *This Bridge Called My Back: Writings by Radical Women of Color* (New York: Kitchen Table, Women of Color Press, 1983).

20. "It can be difficult to be generous to earlier selves, and keeping faith with the continuity of our journeys is especially hard in the United States, where identities and loyalties have been shed and replaced without a tremor, all in the name of becoming American"—Rich, "Notes toward a Politics of Location," p. 223.

21. Quintanales, "I Paid Very Hard for My Immigrant Ignorance," in *This Bridge Called My Back*, p. 151; emphasis added.

22. This phrase is the title of Moraga's foreword to the second edition of *This Bridge Called My Back*.

23. The relatively insignificant numbers of these immigrants, overwhelmingly Sikh (but called "Hindus" or "ragheads") was due to systematic racial discrimination by the U.S. government and the Immigration and Naturalization Service (INS). This was backed by a strong, predominantly working class movement for "Asiatic exclusion" that was securely in place by the time of their arrival on the Canadian and U.S. West Coast. The first immigrants were men, with women only joining in considerable numbers after 1946. There is now a growing body of literature on their history in this country—see for example Joan M. Jensen, *Passage from India: Asian Indian Immigrants in North America* (New Haven and London: Yale University Press, 1988); *South Asians in North America: An Annotated and Selected Bibliography*, ed. Jane Singh, Occasional Paper No. 14, (Berkeley: University of California Press, 1988); Sucheta Mazumdar, "Punjabi Agricultural Workers in California, 1905–1945," in *Labor Immigration under Capitalism*, eds. Edna Bonacich and Lucie Cheng (Berkeley: University of California Press, 1984), pp. 549–578. At a total of around 1,500 prior to World War II, the Indian-American community has shot up from 10,000 in 1965 to close to a million in the intervening years.

24. According to newspaper reports at the time, a group calling itself the "dot-busters" (the "dot" referring to the practice among Indian women to wear a red spot, or *bindi*, on their foreheads) claimed responsibility for a series of assaults on businesses and individuals from the Indian community in Jersey City beginning in October 1987. In some reports, the assailants were identified as belonging to Jersey City's other minority communities. Their demand was that "Indians get out of town."

25. Takaki, *Strangers from a Different Shore: A History of Asian Americans* (Boston: Little, Brown and Company, 1989), p. 476. For an excellent study of the place of Asian-Americans in contemporary U.S. education, see Dana Y. Takagi, *The Retreat from Race: Asian-American Admissions and Racial Politics* (New Brunswick, N.J.: Rutgers University Press, 1992).

26. I borrow this phrase from Teresa de Lauretis's book *Technologies of Gender: Essays on Theory, Film, and Fiction* (Bloomington, Ind.: Indiana University Press, 1987).

27. Rich, "Disloyal to Civilisation: Feminism, Racism, Gynephobia," in *On Lies, Secrets, and Silence: Selected Prose 1966–1978* (New York and London: W. W. Norton and Co., 1979), p. 290.

28. Here is an interesting aside concerning the differential working out of the power webs between the sciences and technology, on the one hand, and the social sciences and humanities, on the other, in terms of the relative proportions of Indian women students in these disciplines: while the number of such women in India (as in the United States) decreases sharply from the humanities to the "hard" sciences, the select group making its way to the United States is stratified in the opposite direction— most of my female peers graduate with degrees in engineering, medicine, the sciences, and economics.

29. Foucault, "Intellectuals and Power," in *Language, Counter-Memory, Practice: Selected Essays and Interviews*, ed. Donald F. Bouchard (Ithaca: Cornell University Press, 1977), pp. 205–217.

30. Spivak, "Can the Subaltern Speak?" p. 273.

31. Scott, "Locating the Anthropological Subject: Postcolonial Anthropologists in Other Places," in *Inscriptions, Traveling Theories, Traveling Theorists* 5 (1989): 75–85.

32. Michele le Deuff, "Women and Philosophy," in *Radical Philosophy* 17 (1977), cited in Meaghan Morris, "A-mazing Grace: Notes on Mary Daly's Poetics," in *The Pirate's Fiancee: Feminism, Reading, Post-modernism* (London and New York: Verso, 1988), p. 43.

33. Haraway, "Situated Knowledges: The Science Question in Feminism as a Site of Discourse on the Privilege of Partial Perspective," *Feminist Studies*, 14, 3 (1988): 584.

34. Ibid., p. 583.

35. Stephen Heath, "Male Feminism," in *Dalhousie Review* 64, 2 (1986): 270. A little further on he briefly engages with the possibility that men take up their very masculinity in response to feminism's challenge ("Pornography is the theory and rape the practice"). But he subsequently shies away, and the essay becomes increasingly noisy. It is as though the shift from "universal" to "masculine," though easy to name, is still being resisted.

36. For a range of early examples that are framed precisely by the relations between and conceptions of different groups of women within the United States, see Mary Daly, *Gyn/Ecology, The Metaethics of Radical Feminism* (Boston: Beacon Press, 1978); B. Ruby Rich, "Feminism and Sexuality in the 1980s," Review Essay, *Feminist Studies*, 12, 3 (Fall 1986): 525–561; *This Bridge Called My Back*; Elly Bulkin, Minnie Bruce Pratt, and Barbara Smith eds., *Yours in Struggle: Three Feminist Perspectives on Anti-Semitism and Racism* (New York: Long Haul Press, 1984). This kind of

cross-questioning has been taking place elsewhere as well: the Nigerian critic Chikwenye Okonjo Ogumyemi addresses in turn Buchi Emecheta in London, white feminists, and, more interestingly, Alice Walker in her essay "Womanism: The dynamics of the contemporary Black female novel in English," *Signs* 11 (Autumn 1985): 63–80. Gayatri Spivak, the diasporic woman abroad, is questioned by university women in India in an interview that was reprinted as "The Postcolonial Critic" in Sarah Harasym, ed., *The Postcolonial Critic*, pp. 67–74. In the 1990s, the modes of address and forms of interrogation between feminists have become even more complex. To take but two examples, see Jane Roland Martin, "Methodological Essentialism, False Differences and Other Dangerous Traps," *Signs* 19, 3 (Spring 1994): 630–657, and Margaret Homans, "Women of Color" and "Feminist Theory," *New Literary History* 25, 1 (Winter 1994): 73–94. These essays are significant because of their *three*-dimensional structure, which goes beyond the more common dialogic model: in each case the author questions specific feminists about their use or appropriation of other feminists' work.

37. Spillers, "Mama's Baby, Papa's Maybe: An American Grammar Book," *Diacritics* 17, 2 (Summer 1987): 65.

38. Ibid., p. 67.

39. Ibid., p. 80.

40. Martin and Mohanty, "Feminist Politics: What's Home Got to Do with It?" in *Feminist Studies/Critical Studies*, ed. Teresa de Lauretis (Bloomington: Indiana University Press, 1986), p. 193; emphasis original. As I point out in chapter three, too few white feminists have explored the question of racism as it structures *their* lives. Some examples would be Marilyn Frye, "On Being White: Thinking toward a Feminist Understanding of Race and Race Supremacy," in *The Politics of Reality: Essays in Feminist Theory* (New York: The Crossing Press, 1983), pp. 110–127; Adrienne Rich, "Disloyal to Civilization: Feminism, Racism, Gynephobia," in *On Lies, Secrets and Silence: Selected Prose 1966–78* (New York and London: W. W. Norton and Company), pp. 275–310; and Ruth Frankenberg *White Women, Race Matters: The Social Construction of Whiteness* (Minneapolis: University of Minnesota Press, 1993). For a critical response to Rich, see doris davenport, "The Pathology of Racism: A Conversation with Third World Wimmin," in *This Bridge Called My Back*, pp. 85–90.

41. Pratt, "Identity: Skin Blood Heart," in *Yours in Struggle, Three Feminist Perspectives on Anti-Semitism and Racism*, eds. Bulkin, Pratt, and Smith, p. 39.

42. Martin and Mohanty, "Feminist Politics: What's Home Got to Do with It?" p. 202.

43. Pratt, "Identity: Skin Blood Heart," p. 19.

44. This phrase comes from the title of Richard Rodriguez's book *Hunger of Memory: The Education of Richard Rodriguez, An Autobiography* (New York: Bantam Books, 1983).

45. Trinh, "Difference: 'A Special Third World Women Issue,'" in *Feminist Review* 25 (March 1987): 14; emphasis original.

46. For a recent account of its history see Henrietta Moore, *Feminism and Anthropology* (Minneapolis: University of Minnesota Press, 1988).

47. Mohanty, "Under Western Eyes: Feminist Scholarship and Colonial Discourses," *Boundary 2* (Spring/Fall 1984): 337.

48. See her fine essay, "Who Claims Alterity?" in *Remaking History*, eds. Barbara Kruger and Phil Mariani, Discussions in Contemporary Culture 4, Dia Art Foundation (Seattle: Bay Press, 1989), pp. 269–292, and "Can the Subaltern Speak?"

49. There are many instances where Spivak, for example, has done more than any other theorist to hold on to necessary distinctions between "the investigator" and "the woman at the other end." Her contrast between the *paradigmatic* colonial and neocolonial subject, however, has also effected the kind of elision and transparency I am concerned with. In "the Political Economy of Women as Seen by a Literary Critic," she demarcates "the old colonial subject" under territorial imperialism in terms of his (and occasionally her) violent production through the imposition of "a new code of law, a new system of education, and a new perception of needs" (in *Coming to Terms: Feminism, Theory, Politics*, ed. Elizabeth Weed [New York: Routledge, 1989], p. 224). Today, instead, there are "hordes of women [in Asia's export-processing zones] who, because of the patriarchal structures of parental and conjugal power are the new army of 'permanently casual' labor working below the minimum wage—these women represent the international neo-colonial subject paradigmatically" (Ibid., p. 223). It is not clear to me why these two subjects should so singularly and exclusively stand in for the colonial and postcolonial periods, respectively. Although territorial imperialism did see the emergence of a new middle class transformed by the epistemic violence of law, education, and desire, the establishment of empire depended much more, if anything, on the production and exploitation of working classes and subalterns located otherwise in the colonial formation. Again, the elaborate "ideological" constitution of subjects continues to be invented and reproduced internationally and across various classes today. I am trying to suggest that postcolonial feminists like ourselves are not an insignificant strand in the webs of international neocolonialism and should not, therefore, be rendered invisible between such depictions of "the investigator," the "old" and the "new" colonial subjects.

50. Mohanty, "Under Western Eyes," p. 336; emphasis added.

51. Said, *Orientalism* (New York: Vintage Books, 1978), pp. 323–324.

52. Chatterjee, *Nationalist Thought and the Colonial World—A Derivative Discourse* (London: Zed Press, 1986), p. 17.

53. Ibid., p. 17.

54. Johnson, "Introduction" to *A World Of Difference* (Baltimore and London: Johns Hopkins University Press, 1987), p. 4.

55. Omvedt, *We Will Smash this Prison: Indian Women in Struggle* (London: Zed Press, 1980), p. 18.

56. Chow, *Women and Chinese Modernity: Reading Between East and West*, (Minneapolis: University of Minnesota Press, 1991), p. xi.

Chapter Two: Partial Theories/ Composite Theories

1. Wherever it has seemed necessary to distinguish this contemporary body of "theory" from modes of theorizing in general, I have placed it in quotes.

2. Bhabha, "The Commitment to Theory," *New Formations* 5 (Summer 1988): 6–7.

3. Ibid., p. 16.

4. Dhareshwar, "The Predicament of Theory," in Martin Kreiswirth and Mark A. Cheetham, eds., *Theory Between the Disciplines: Authority, Vision, Politics* (Ann Arbor: University of Michigan Press, 1990), p. 235.

5. Bhabha, "The Commitment to Theory," p. 16.

6. Dhareshwar, "The Predicament of Theory," p. 242.

7. Harari, "Nostalgia and Critical Theory," in Thomas M. Kavenagh ed., *The Limits of Theory* (Stanford, Calif.: Stanford University Press, 1989), p. 169.

8. Skinner, introduction to *The Return of Grand Theory in the Human Sciences* (London: Cambridge University Press, 1985), p. 12.

9. Only Lévi-Strauss and the Annales historians have obvious affiliations outside philosophy. But their inclusion remains just as obvious, given the centrality of structuralism in their work, a "grand theory" of philosophical proportions in its cross-cultural and historical reach. Indeed, as Judith Butler has incisively pointed out in Lévi-Strauss's case, "[a]lthough Lévi-Strauss reports in *Tristes Tropiques* that he left philosophy because anthropology provided a more concrete texture to the analysis of human life, he nevertheless assimilates that cultural texture to a totalizing logical structure that effectively returns his analyses to the decontextualized philosophical structures he purported to leave." See Judith Butler, *Gender Trouble* (New York and London: Routledge, 1990), p. 39.

10. Johnson, "Introduction," *A World of Difference* (Baltimore and London: Johns Hopkins University Press, 1987), p. 2. Cited hereafter as *WD*. See also *The Critical Difference* (Baltimore: The Johns Hopkins University Press), 1980.

11. One reason the practice of deconstruction in particular has been able to resist its partial and composite structure has something to do with Derrida's professional affiliations, his predilection for those texts that constitute the canon of Western metaphysics. Even with a different subject, such as "woman" or "Geschlecht," the authors chosen for scrutiny are Heidegger and Nietzsche. How do matters stand, then, in an essay such as "The Laws of Reflection: Nelson Mandela, In Admiration"? (reproduced in Jacques Derrida and Mustapha Tlili eds., *For Nelson Mandela*, [New York: Seaver Books, 1987], pp. 11–42). Derrida analyzes one of Mandela's early speeches from 1962, "Black Man in a White Court: First Court Statement," to show us the reasons behind our admiration for this figure, still in prison at the time of his writing. It is Mandela's "force of reflection," he says, the reflectiveness with which he admires the spirit of the Enlightenment and its proclamation of respect for a universal Law, that we in turn admire so intensely. With someone as reflective as Mandela, and in the face of the monstrosity of South Africa's state racism, this respect gains a phenomenality perhaps for the first time. On the one hand, Derrida is very aware that it is questionable to depict "the struggle against apartheid, wherever it takes place and such as Mandela carries it on and reflects it, . . . [as] a sort of specular opposition, a domestic war that the West carried on with itself . . . [a]n internal contradiction which would not put up with either a radical otherness or a true dissymmetry" (Ibid., p. 16). He also does not forget that Mandela's admiration stems as much from a collective memory of the democratic structure of early African societies as from the existence of the Magna Carta or the Universal Declaration of the Rights of Man. On the other hand, however, Derrida seems content to place Mandela's respect for a Law he himself has never seen enacted in a quasi-Kantian conscience—namely, that groundless place without ontological basis—because such a conscience can provide no reasons for its existence. Why does Derrida foreclose on Mandela's own response to a similar question in court, a response that took the form of an account of his own life (Ibid., pp. 33–34)?

For a related and extremely provocative analysis, counterposing the aporetic claims of the Enlightenment with the paradoxes of a postcolonial identity politics, see Simon During, "Waiting for the Post: Some relations between modernity, colonization and writing," in *Ariel* 20, 4 (October 1989): 31–61.)

12. Mies, "Towards a Methodology for Feminist Research," in Gloria

Bowles and Renate Duelli Klein, *Theories of Women's Studies* (London and Boston: Routledge and Kegan Paul, 1983), p. 125.

13. Clifford, "Introduction," *Writing Culture: The Poetics and Politics of Ethnography,* eds. James Clifford and George E. Marcus (Berkeley: University of California Press, 1986), p. 123.

14. Haraway, "Situated Knowledges: The Science Question in Feminism and the Privilege of Partial Perspective," *Feminist Studies* 14, 3 (Fall 1988): 582–583.

15. Haraway borrows this phrase from Nancy Hartsock.

16. I borrow this term from Katie King. See especially her essay "Audre Lorde's Lacquered Layerings: The Lesbian Bar as a Site of Literary Production," in *Cultural Studies* 2 (1988): 321–342.

17. Said, "Traveling Theory," *The World, the Text and the Critic,* (Cambridge: Harvard University Press, 1983), p. 226–247.

18. Bhabha, "The Commitment to Theory," p. 8.

19. Said, "Traveling Theory," p. 226.

20. Both these essays have been reprinted in Gayatri Chakravorty Spivak, *In Other Worlds: Essays in Cultural Politics* (New York and London: Methuen, 1987), which is where they are most likely to be read by Western audiences. Cited hereafter as *OW.*

21. The *Subaltern Studies* series, brought out by Oxford University Press in Delhi, initially edited by Ranajit Guha and subsequently by different members of the Subaltern Studies collective, now runs into eight volumes. Other texts of interest would be Ranajit Guha, *A Rule of Property for Bengal: An Essay on the Idea of Permanent Settlement* (Paris: Mouton and Co., 1963); Ranajit Guha, *Elementary Aspects of Peasant Insurgency in Colonial India* (Delhi: Oxford University Press, 1983); Partha Chatterjee, *The Nation and Its Fragments: Colonial and Postcolonial Histories* (Princeton, N.J.: Princeton University Press, 1993); and Dipesh Chakrabarty, *Rethinking Working-Class History: Bengal, 1890–1940* (Princeton, N.J.: Princeton University Press, 1989), among others.

22. Given the general context of this discussion, it should not be forgotten that among all the theories one might consider, Marxism has undeniably traveled the most. (That Said's own examples of "traveling theory" came from within Marxist literary criticism is surely no accident.) Indeed, one could go on to speculate whether at this historical juncture, Marxism hasn't evolved into a third-world theory more than a first-world one.

23. Guha, "On Some Aspects of the Historiography of Colonial India," in *Subaltern Studies I: Writings on South Asian History and Society,* ed. Ranajit Guha (Dehli: Oxford University Press, 1982), p. 4; emphasis original.

24. Some examples are "Subaltern Studies II: A Review Article," *Social Scientist* 12, 10 (1984): 3–41; Ranajit Das Gupta, "Significance of Subaltern Mediation," and B. B. Chaudhuri, "Subaltern Autonomy and the Nationalist Movement," both in *The Indian Historical Review* 12, 1–2 (July 1985–January 1986); and Rosalind O'Hanlon, "Recovering the Subject: *Subaltern Studies* and Histories of Resistance in Colonial South Asia," *Modern Asian Studies* 22, 1 (1988): 189–224.

25. Derrida, "Positions," interview with Jean-Louis Houdebine and Guy Scarpetta, in *Positions*, trans. and ann. Alan Bass (Chicago: University of Chicago Press, 1981), pp. 41–43; emphases original.

26. As Spivak points out in the foreword to her recent collection of essays, *Outside in the Teaching Machine* (New York and London: Routledge, 1993), the notion of a "strategic use of essentialism" was first explicitly named as such in an interview with Elizabeth Grosz (Spivak, "Criticism, Feminism and the Institution," *Thesis Eleven* 10/11 (November/March 1984–1985): 175–187). She now sees a shift in her work from such a position to "considerations of institutional agency" (*Outside in the Teaching Machine*, p. ix) My own attempt to broaden the scope of the notion of strategy by prying it loose from the issue of essentialism is perhaps another way of taking up questions of agency. (The importance of essentialism and anti-essentialism is addressed more fully in chapter three.)

27. Spivak, "In a Word," interview with Ellen Rooney, in *differences* 1, 2 (1989): 127.

28. The essays I am drawing from here are "Double Displacement and the Discourse of Woman," in *Displacement: Derrida and After*, ed. Mark Krupnick (Bloomington: Indiana University Press, 1986), pp. 169–195; and "Feminism and Deconstruction, Again: Negotiating with Unacknowledged Masculinism," in *Between Feminism and Psychoanalysis*, ed. Teresa Brennan (London and New York: Routledge, 1989, pp. 206–223).

29. Spivak, "Feminism and Deconstruction, Again," p. 215.

30. Here I depart from Spivak's invitation to treat philosophy as "our" "other," as though we were bound in a symmetrical relation. "We" are rather our own "others"—and in the most complex and uneven ways, as subsequent chapters will continue to attest. She subsequently concludes this essay by invoking a very different figure for her discussion of "catachresis"—the "disenfranchised" woman in third-world nations like India whom she feels her Western feminist audience cannot imagine and who is persistently erased within the world of feminist theory. Just how central such women have been within the emergence of Indian feminist theory is discussed in chapter four.

31. Guha, "The Prose of Counter-Insurgency," in *Subaltern Studies* II, 1983, p. 1–42.

32. Ibid., p. 39.

33. Ibid., p. 33.

34. In the collection *In Other Worlds*, the contrapuntal potential of both essays is emphasized through their location under the section "Entering the Third World," separated by her translation of "Breast-Giver." The initial essay in this section, Mahasweta Devi's "Draupadi," was translated and introduced in 1981 and possibly represents Spivak's first attempt to have the third and first worlds question each other through a negotiation between theory and fiction.

35. What changes are inaugurated when the text being analyzed belongs to the field of literature and not the historical archive? In her introductory remarks, Spivak highlights the degree to which differences (such as the contrasting effects of the "imagined" versus the "real") are not easily come by: the historian must imaginatively subscribe to processes of narrativization not provided by her material, whereas Mahasweta Devi, for one, is engaged in writing historical fiction, creating plausible characters backed up by extensive research. Spivak insists that literature and history do not therefore become identical; she also refuses to privilege any one. Tucked away in the footnote of another article, however, she has this to say: "[T]he figure of the gendered subaltern . . . stands unnoticed and implicit in the cracks of much carefully written documentation in the social sciences. . . . Fiction can make her visible." See "Who Claims Alterity?" in *Remaking History*, eds. Kruger and Mariani, p. 273 and 290, footnote 10.

36. It is important to notice which feminist theories Spivak valorizes here, how they are named, and which ones are excluded. All the theories are white, for one thing, even as white remains an unmarked category throughout the essay. No "radical" feminisms are considered. I will examine the unevenness among different strands of U.S. feminisms, and discuss how this gets highlighted in their unequal travel, in chapter three.

37. Cited in *In Other Worlds*, pp. 258–259. The quotations come from two translated essays of Lacan, "A Love Letter," and "God and the *Jouissance* of The Woman," reproduced in *Feminine Sexuality: Jacques Lacan and the école freudienne*, eds. Juliet Mitchell and Jacqueline Rose (New York: W. W. Norton and Co., 1985), pp. 137–161.

38. Although such composite theory is clearly what is needed, the obstacles are many. One set of difficulties cluster around methods for recovering "Hindu" epistemologies that do not get caught in Orientalist or nativist binds. Also, there are clearly problems in referring to a given concept or worldview as "Hindu" without further qualification—whose Hinduism is being referred to, and which castes are being assumed within its fold?

39. Elizabeth Abel, "Race, Class, and Psychoanalysis? Opening Ques-

tions," in *Conflicts in Feminism*, eds. Marianne Hirsch and Evelyn Fox-Keller (New York and London: Routledge, 1990), p. 184.

40. Ibid., p. 185.

41. Freud, *Jokes and Their Relation to the Unconscious*, ed. and trans. James Strachey, The Pelican Freud Library, Volume 6 (London: Pelican Books, 1976 [1904]); Freud, *The Interpretation of Dreams*, ed. and trans. James Strachey, The Pelican Freud Library, Volume 4 (London: Pelican Books, 1976 [1900]).

42. Freud, *Jokes and Their Relation to the Unconscious*, p. 236. Cited hereafter as *J*.

43. Freud is in some danger of collapsing the social/psychic distinction here; it sounds as if repression could be directly measured from the strength of cultural taboos, with the less educated therefore possessing a less developed unconscious rather than a different one. Furthermore, are the so-called lower classes so simply inured from the cultural influences of the dominant middle classes in sexual as much as in other matters?

44. The fact that Freud took his "ethnic" examples from among Jewish jokes is no reason to confine ourselves here. Indeed, this would be an explicit place where the relevance of psychoanalytic methods for questions of race and ethnicity could be productively explored. It has been said once too often by psychoanalytically inclined white theorists that they cannot deal with questions of race because the Freudian corpus is so exclusively structured around sexuality. Not only are there many well-known figures both from the past and present, such as Frantz Fanon and Homi Bhabha, who have creatively psychoanalyzed race relations, but Freud's texts themselves were not as race-blind as one might be led to believe. The problem does not, therefore, appear to lie with psychoanalysis.

45. Silverman, *The Subject of Semiotics* (New York and Oxford: Oxford University Press, 1983), especially chapters 2 and 3.

46. Freud, *Moses and Monotheism*, trans. Katherine Jones (New York: Vintage Books, 1959), p. 14; emphasis added. Cited hereafter as *MM*.

47. Hurston, *Moses, Man of the Mountain* (Urbana and Chicago: University of Illinois Press, 1984 [1939]).

48. This is why I cannot quite assent to aspects of Michel de Certeau's reformulations of Freud's project, when he glosses it as follows:[T]hrough metaphor, a rhetorical means, and through ambivalence, a theoretical instrument, many things are at play in the same spot. . . . Past and present are moving within the same polyvalent plane. And none of the "levels" of the text is the referent for the others. (de Certeau, *The Writing of History*, trans. Tom Conley, (New York: Columbia University Press, 1988) p.312–313). Once again, I am less opposed to de Certeau's extremely masculine, if not misogynous, reading in itself: "The law of the father" must replace all

"territorial identities"—"the matriarchy of the mother tongue (German), the mother country (Israel), or the nurturing tradition (the Mosaic Scriptures)" (ibid., p.317). My disagreement stems rather from his complete acceptance of Freud's analogy as a sufficient structuring device for an understanding of collective memory, and Judaic nationalism.

49. Coward, *Patriarchal Precedents: Sexuality and Social Relations* (London: Routledge, and Kegan Paul, 1983), p. 253.

50. The anthropological literature here is quite vast and well documented, so I will only mention one of its strands. The debate between Branislaw Malinowski and Ernest Jones on Trobriand society, beginning in the 1920s and resulting in Malinowski's *Sex and Repression in Savage Society* (New York: Meridian Books, 1927), has recently been revived: Melford E. Spiro's defense of a psychoanalytical reading, *Oedipus in the Trobriands* (Chicago and London: University of Chicago Press, 1982), was rebuffed by Annette B. Weiner's "Oedipus and Ancestors" (*American Ethnologist* 12, 4 [1985]: 758–762). For a recent detailed use of psychoanalysis within the field of anthropology, see Gananath Obeyesekere, *The Work of Culture: Symbolic Transformations in Psychoanalysis and Anthropology* (Chicago: University of Chicago Press, 1990).

51. Rose, "Femininity and its Discontents," in *Sexuality in the Field of Vision* (London: Verso Press, 1986); and Wilson, "Psychoanalysis: Psychic Law and Order?" in *Hidden Agendas* (London: Tavistock Publications, 1986).

52. Rose, *Sexuality in the Field of Vision*, p. 6.

53. Wilson, "Psychoanalysis: Psychic Law and Order?" p. 166.

54. Rose, *Sexuality in the Field of Vision*, p. 91.

55. Teresa Brennan, "Introduction," *Between Psychoanalysis and Feminism*, ed. Teresa Brennan (London and New York: Routledge, 1989), p. 1. Brennan continues by identifying four such issues—the status of the Lacanian symbolic, sexual difference and knowledge, essentialism and feminist politics, and the relation of psychical reality to the social. The Rose-Wilson debate probably hinges most closely on the last issue. Another collection of essays is *Feminism and Psychoanalysis*, eds. Richard Feldstein and Judith Roof (Ithaca and London: Cornell University Press, 1989).

56. Mitchell, *Psychoanalysis and Feminism: Freud, Reich, Laing and Women* (New York: Vintage, 1974), p. 364–370.

57. Ibid., p. 367.

58. Ibid., p. 378.

59. Irigaray, *Speculum of the Other Woman*, trans. Gillian C. Gill, (Ithaca: Cornell University Press, 1985).

60. See Jonathan Katz, "The Invention of Heterosexuality," in *Socialist*

Review 20, 1 (January–March 1990). As he puts it, "not ancient at all, the idea of heterosexuality is a modern invention, dating to the late nineteenth century. . . . The formulation of the heterosexual idea did not create a heterosexual experience or order; to suggest otherwise would be to ascribe determining power to labels and concepts. But before the wide use of the word heterosexual, I suggest, women and men did not mutually lust with the same profound sense of normalcy that followed the distribution of the 'heterosexual' as universal sanctifier" (Ibid., pp. 7, 28).

61. Poovey, *Uneven Developments: The Ideological Work of Gender in Mid-Victorian England* (Chicago: Chicago University Press, 1988).

62. It is also instructive to see how much the attitudes of some feminist theorists can shift over time. In an unpublished essay circulated in 1988 ("Gender differences: Feminist Theory and Psychoanalytical Narratives," mimeo, pp. 1–29), Judith Butler more or less dismissed psychoanalysis because she took it to be so irretrievably implicated in the legitimation of an interior heterosexist core to gender identity as to preclude an analysis of the political constitution of the gendered subject. By contrast, far from being discounted in her new book, *Bodies that Matter: On the Discursive Limits of 'Sex'* (New York and London: Routledge, 1993), psychoanalysis has evolved into a privileged discourse for an elaboration of lesbian sexuality.

63. Bhabha, "The Commitment to Theory," p. 8.

64. "An Interview with Juliet Mitchell," by Angela McRobbie, *New Left Review* 170 (July/August 1988).

65. Toril Moi, "Psychoanalysis, Feminism and Politics: A Conversation with Juliet Mitchell," *South Atlantic Quarterly* 93, 4 (Fall 1994): 925–949.

66. Hall, "The Toad in the Garden: Thatcherism among the Theorists," in *Marxism and the Interpretation of Culture*, eds. Carl Nelson and Lawrence Grossberg (Chicago: University of Illinois Press, 1988), p. 50.

Chapter Three: Women, Patriarchy, Sex, Gender

1. Susie Tharu and K. Lalita, "Introduction," *Women Writing in India: 600 B.C. to the Present*, Volume I: 600 B.C. to the Early Twentieth Century, eds. Susie Tharu and K. Lalita (New York: The Feminist Press, 1991), p. 13 footnote 23.

2. Alarcón, "The Theoretical Subjects of *This Bridge Called My Back* and Anglo-American Feminism," in *Making Face, Making Soul, Haciendo Caras: Creative and Critical Perspectives by Women of Color*, ed. Gloria Anzaldúa (San Francisco: Aunt Lute Press, 1990), p. 365. Chela Sandoval has called U.S. third-world feminism an "enigma" because it "represent[s]

a form of historical consciousness whose very structure lies outside the conditions of possibility which regulate the oppositional expressions of dominant feminism" (Sandoval, "U.S. Third World Feminism: The Theory and Method of Oppositional Consciousness in the Postmodern World," *Genders* 10 [Spring 1991]: 1).

3. Haraway, "Gender for a Marxist Dictionary: The Sexual Politics of a Word," in *Simians, Cyborgs and Women: Feminism and the Reinvention of Nature* (New York: Routledge, 1991), p. 130.

4. Ibid., p. 130.

5. Scott, *Gender and the Politics of History* (New York: Columbia University Press, 1988); Elaine Showalter, "The Rise of Gender," introduction to *Speaking of Gender*, ed. Elaine Showalter (Routledge: New York and London, 1989), pp. 1–13; Teresa de Lauretis, "Technologies of Gender," in *Technologies of Gender: Essays on Theory, Film, and Fiction*, (Bloomington: Indiana University Press, 1987), pp. 1–31.

6. Derrida, "Geschlecht: Sexual Difference, Ontological Difference," in *Research in Phenomenology* 13 (1989): 65. See also Derrida, "Geschlecht II: Heidegger's Hand," in *Deconstruction and Philosophy: The Texts of Jacques Derrida*, ed. John Sallis (Chicago: University of Chicago, 1987), pp. 161–196.

7. Harding, *The Science Question in Feminism* (Ithaca: Cornell University Press, 1986), p. 17. Cited hereafter as *SF*.

8. Haraway, "Gender for a Marxist Dictionary," p. 136.

9. *Women, Culture and Society*, eds. Michelle Rosaldo and Louise Lamphere (Stanford: Stanford University Press, 1974), and *Toward an Anthropology of Women*, ed. Rayna R. Reiter (New York: Monthly Review Press, 1975).

10. Moore, *Feminism and Anthropology* (Minneapolis: University of Minnesota Press, 1988), p. 6. Michelle Rozaldo, one of the editors of the volume *Women, Culture and Society*, appears to occupy an interesting intermediate position within Moore's account of the different phases of feminist anthropology in an essay she wrote in 1980, "The Use and Abuse of Anthropology: Reflections in Feminism and Cross-Cultural Understanding" (*Signs* 5, 3 [1980]: 389–417). She, too, warns against wrong versions of the difficulty: "Contrary to those anthropologists who have suggested that our problems lie in incomplete reports or, even worse, in inarticulate and 'silent' female voices, I would suggest that we hear women speak in almost all anthropological descriptions" (Ibid., p. 390) Instead, "what is needed . . . is not so much data as questions. . . . [W]e are challenged to find new ways of linking the particularities of women's lives, activities, and goals to inequalities wherever they exist" (Ibid., p. 390, 417). Looking critically at her own earlier research, Rosaldo frames her

doubts in terms of the need for new conceptual frameworks but without explicitly articulating a theory of gender.

11. Moore, however, also points out that if culture has been a major way feminist anthropologists have dealt with questions of difference, this emphasis has been at the expense of others—questions of race, for one, remain largely unexplored.

12. de Lauretis, "Technologies of Gender," p. 2; emphasis original.

13. Ibid., p. 3.

14. Butler, *Gender Trouble: Feminism and the Subversion of Identity* (Routledge: New York and London, 1990), p. 148.

15. Rubin, "The Traffic in Women: Notes on the Political Economy of Sex," in *Toward an Anthropology of Women*, ed. Rayna R. Reiter (New York and London: Monthly Review Press, 1975), pp. 157–210.

16. MacKinnon, "Feminism, Marxism, Method and the State: An Agenda for Theory," in *Feminist Theory: A Critique of Ideology*, eds. Nannerl O. Keohane, Michele Z. Rosaldo, and Barbara C. Gelpi (Chicago: University of Chicago Press, 1981), pp. 1–30.

17. Butler, *Gender Trouble*, p. 7.

18. Joan Scott is not alone in wanting everyone to be quite aware of the dangerous ease with which gender is entering general academic parlance: " 'Gender' seems to fit within the scientific terminology of social science and thus dissociates itself from the (supposedly strident) politics of feminism. In this usage, 'gender' does not carry with it a necessary statement about inequality or power nor does it name the aggrieved (and hitherto invisible) party" (*Gender and the Politics of History*, p. 31).

19. Showalter, *Speaking of Gender*, p. 2–3.

20. See chapter 4, "Women and The Making of the English Working Class," in *Gender and the Politics of History*.

21. de Beauvoir, *The Second Sex: The Manifesto of the Liberated Woman* (New York: Vintage, 1974 [1954]).

22. Berger, "Categories and Contexts: Reflections on the Politics of Identity in South Africa," *Feminist Studies* 18, 2 (Summer 1992): 284.

23. Sargant, *Women and Revolution: A Discussion of the Unhappy Marriage of Marxism and Feminism* (Boston: South End Press, 1981). An equally well-known anthology was *Capitalist Patriarchy and the Case for Socialist Feminism*, ed. Zillah R. Eisenstein (New York: Monthly Review Press, 1979).

24. See Zillah R. Eisenstein's essay "Specifying U.S. Feminism in the 1990s: The Problem of Naming" in *Socialist Review* 20, 2 (April–June 1990: 45–56), where she moves rather uncertainly from a desire to "incorporat[e] many of the earlier concerns of socialist feminism while moving through and beyond them" (ibid., p. 49) to the opinion that socialism is

"stale" (ibid., p. 51). Older political orientations such as "radical," "liberal," and "socialist" have basically become passé in her view and should be replaced by a radically revised "egalitarianism *between* our differences and our sameness" (ibid., p. 55).

25. Going through the entire collection, particularly for the overall effect this has on the reader, is well worth the effort. The text itself is structured around Heidi Hartmann's lead essay, "The Unhappy Marriage of Marxism and Feminism: Towards a More Progressive Union," to which subsequent contributors responded by way of disagreement, qualification, or further extension of her arguments.

26. de Lauretis, "Upping the Anti [*sic*] in Feminist Theory," in *Conflicts in Feminism*, eds. Marianne Hirsch and Evelyn Fox Keller (New York: Routledge, 1990), pp. 255–270.

27. Butler, *Gender Trouble*, p. 143.

28. Apart from Dixon, Harding cites the work of Joseph Needham and Russell Means on third-world peoples, as well as the discussions of Placide Tempels, Abiola Irele, Lancinay Keita, and J. E. Wiredu on African philosophy to show how representative such a worldview is.

29. Hartsock, "The Feminist Standpoint: Developing the Ground for a Specifically Feminist Historical Materialism," in *Discovering Reality*, eds. Sandra Harding and Merrill B. Hintikka (Dordrecht Reidel Co., 1983), pp. 283, 300; emphasis original. Probably the most influential text for Hartsock's study is Nancy Chodorow's *The Reproduction of Mothering: Psychoanalysis and the Sociology of Gender* (Berkeley: University of California Press, 1978), a book that has undoubtedly played a significant role in the intellectual history of U.S. feminism. But, as Hartsock points out, a number of other feminists—Dorothy Dinnerstein, Jane Flax, Hilary Rose, Sara Ruddick, and Carol Gilligan, to name a few—have also come up with similarly structured conceptions of gendered ontologies, epistemologies, and worldviews.

30. Stepan, "Race and Gender: The Role of Analogy in Science," in *Anatomy of Racism*, ed. David Theo Goldberg (Minneapolis: University of Minnesota Press, 1990), p. 40.

31. An example we have already come across would be Gayatri Spivak's more literal reading of Mahasweta Devi's "The Breast-Giver" in chapter 2.

32. White, *Tropics of Discourse: Essays in Cultural Criticism* (Baltimore and London: Johns Hopkins University Press, 1987 (1978)), pp. 1–2; emphases original.

33. Ibid., p. 3; emphasis original.

34. Hurtado, "Relating to Privilege: Seduction and Rejection in the Subordination of White Women and Women of Color," in *Signs* 14, 4 (1989): 840. She cites Elizabeth Cady Stanton, who in her speech before

the New York State Legislature in 1860 said: "The prejudice against Color, of which we hear so much, is no stronger than that against sex. It is produced by the same cause, and manifested very much in the same way. The Negro's skin and the woman's sex are both prima facie evidence that they were intended to be in subjection to the white Saxon man. The few social privileges which the man gives the woman, he makes up to the (free) Negro in civil rights" (Elizabeth Cady Stanton, Susan B. Anthony, and Matilda Joslyn Cage, eds., *History of Woman Suffrage*, 2nd ed. [Rochester: Susan B. Anthony, 1889], cited in Hurtado, p. 840).

35. Howard Winant, "Postmodern Racial Politics in the United States: Difference and Inequality," in *Socialist Review* 20, 1 (January–March 1990): 121.

36. Gloria Yamato, "Something About the Subject Makes it Hard to Name," in *Making Face, Making Soul: Haciendo Caras*, ed. Gloria Anzaldúa (San Francisco: Aunt Lute Press, 1990), pp. 20–24.

37. "The image of *race* as a phantom word came to me after I moved into my late godmother's home. . . . The power of that room, I have thought since, is very like the power of racism as status quo: it is deep, angry, eradicated from view, but strong enough to make everyone who enters the room walk around the bed that isn't there, avoiding the phantom as they did the substance for fear of bodily harm. They do not even know what they are avoiding." Patricia Williams, "And We Are Not Married: A Journal of Musings Upon Legal Language and the Ideology of Style," in *Consequences of Theory*, eds. Jonathan Arac and Barbara Johnson (Baltimore: Johns Hopkins University Press, 1991), pp. 185–186.

38. The notion of articulation comes from Stuart Hall's excellent essay "Signification, Representation, Ideology: Althusser and Post-structuralist Debates," in *Critical Studies in Mass Communication* 2, 2 (1985): 112, n. 2: "By the term, 'articulation,' I mean a connection or link which is not necessarily given in all cases, as a law or a fact of life, but which requires particular conditions of existence to appear at all, which has to be positively sustained by specific processes, which can under some circumstances disappear or be overthrown, leading to old linkages being dissolved and new connections—re-articulations—being forged. It is also important that an articulation between different practices does not mean that they become identical or that the one is dissolved into the other." "Articulation" has also been brought into greater currency by Ernesto Laclau and Chantal Mouffe's *Hegemony and Socialist Strategy: Towards a Radical Democratic Politics* (London: Verso Press, 1985).

39. Harding, *Whose Science? Whose Knowledge?: Thinking from Women's Lives* (Buckingham: Open University Press, 1991), p. 215.

40. Ibid., p. 214.

41. Far more problematic are cases where analogies are effectively at work but never acknowledged. Susie Tharu and K. Lalita have shown how Elaine Showalter's well-known categorization of British women writers in *A Literature of Their Own* (Princeton: Princeton University Press, 1977) into three phases—the feminine (a phase of imitation), the feminist (a phase of protest), and the female (a phase of self-discovery)—has been borrowed from Frantz Fanon. "What is also obscured," they continue, "is her transformation of Fanon's theory, domesticating an idea of revolutionary action to a liberal-conservative one of self-discovery and individual fulfillment as the goal of literary endeavor." Tharu and Lalita, *Women Writing in India*, p. 18.

42. Irigaray, "Women's Exile," *Ideology and Consciousness* 1 (1977), p. 76.

43. Marcus, "Alibis and Legends, The Ethics of Elsewhereness, Gender and Estrangement," in *Women's Writing in Exile*, eds. Mary Lynn Broe and Angela Ingram (Chapel Hill and London: University of North Carolina Press, 1989), p. 273.

44. Ibid., p. 273.

45. Irigaray, *The Speculum of the Other Woman*, trans. Gillian C. Gill (Ithaca, N.Y.: Cornell University Press, 1978), especially p. 71.

46. Since I am expressly considering U.S. feminist theory here, discussing a French feminist calls for some explanation. Luce Irigaray is possibly foremost among non-Americans in terms of her significance in travel into, and effect on, the field of U.S. feminism. The reasons for this, within the overall privileging of "French Theory," and the considerable body of translators who make work such as hers so readily available to American readers, is not something I can go into here. Even before going into the question of the travel of feminist work from other nations, it is worth noting the inequality between the reception of feminists living and writing in France, on the one hand, and who effectively gets to count as a French feminist in the United States, on the other. Going back to the anthology *New French Feminisms*, eds. Elaine Marks and Isabelle de Courtivron (New York: Schocken Books, 1980), a figure like Christine Delphy (C.D.), to take but one example, is barely included. (A collection of her essays *Close to Home: A Materialist Analysis of Women's Oppression*, has been translated and edited in Britain by Diana Leonard [London: Hutchinson, 1984].)

47. I take this phrase from Hayden White's descriptions of the working of metaphors in his essay "The Historical Text as Literary Artifact," reproduced in *Tropics of Discourse*, especially p. 91.

48. Gordon, review of Joan Wallach Scott, *Gender and the Politics of History*, in *Signs* 15, 4 (Summer 1990): 855. Scott, in turn, reviewed

Gordon's *Heroes of Their Own Lives: The Politics and History of Family Violence* (New York: Viking, 1988) in the same issue. Each scholar also responded briefly to the other's review.

49. Gordon, "What's New in Women's History," in *Feminist Studies/Critical Studies*, ed. Teresa de Lauretis (Bloomington: Indiana University Press, 1986), pp. 20–31.

50. In the introductory essay to *Gender and the Politics of History*, namely "Women's History," which does take up questions of history, Scott is more concerned with pointing out the shortcomings in existing historical approaches than with putting forward a conception of history of her own. Thus, she finds feminist versions of "herstory" to have been "uniquely about women" and therefore "too separatist," whereas the approach of social history tends toward integrating gender at the level of socioeconomic relations (p. 22).

51. Lerner, *The Creation of Patriarchy* (New York: Oxford University Press, 1986), p. 3.

52. Mitchell, *Psychoanalysis and Feminism*, pp. 11–12.

53. Johnson, "Metaphor, Metonymy, and Voice in *Their Eyes Were Watching God*," in *A World of Difference*, pp. 155–171, especially pp. 167 and 169.

54. Marxism's influence has extended well beyond its paradigmatic status for socialist and Marxist feminists to its availability as a resource for radical feminists, ranging from Shulamith Firestone (*The Dialectic of Sex*, 1970) to Catherine MacKinnon. "Sexuality is to feminism what work is to marxism: that which is most one's own, yet most taken away. . . . Feminism stands in relation to marxism as marxism does to classical political economy: its final conclusion and ultimate critique" (MacKinnon, "Feminism, Marxism, Method, and the State: An Agenda for Theory," in *Feminist Theory: A Critique of Ideology*, eds. Nannerl O. Keohane, Michelle Z. Rosaldo, and Barbara C. Gelpi [Chicago: Chicago University Press, 1982], pp. 1, 30).

55. Haraway, "Gender for a Marxist Dictionary," p. 134.

56. Sartre, Jean-Paul, *Search for a Method* (New York: Vintage, 1968 [1963]), p. xxxiv.

57. Some examples would be Vicki Ruiz, *Cannery Women Cannery Lives: Mexican Women, Unionization and the California Food Processing Industry, 1930–50* (Albuquerque: University of New Mexico Press, 1987); Jacqueline Jones, *Labor of Love, Labor of Sorrow: Black Women, Work, and the Family from Slavery to the Present* (New York: Basic Books, 1985); Lourdes Benería and Martha Roldán, *The Crossroads of Class and Gender: Industrial Housework, Subcontracting, and Household Dynamics in Mexico City* (Chicago: University of Chicago Press, 1987); and Aihwa Ong,

Spirits of Resistance and Capitalist Discipline: Factory Women in Malaysia (Albany: State University of New York Press, 1987).

58. "Introduction," *Conflicts in Feminism*, Marianne Hirsch and Evelyn Fox-Keller, eds. (New York: Routledge, 1990), p. 1.

59. "A Conversation about Race and Class" by Mary Childers and bell hooks, and "Race, Class, and Psychoanalysis? Opening Questions" by Elizabeth Abel, both in Hirsch and Fox-Keller eds., *Conflicts in Feminism*, pp. 60–81 and pp. 184–204.

60. Ehrenreich, *Fear of Falling: The Inner Life of the Middle Class* (New York: Harper Collins, 1989), p. 5.

61. Michael Omi and Howard Winant, *Racial Formation in the United States: From the 1960s to the 1980s* (New York and London: Routledge and Kegan Paul, 1986), p. 3.

62. Gates, Jr., "Editor's Introduction: Writing 'Race' and the Difference It Makes," *"Race," Writing, and Difference, Critical Inquiry* 12, 1 (1985): 5. More recent examples that suspend race within quotes are *The "Racial" Economy of Science: Towards a Democratic Future*, ed. Sandra Harding (Bloomington and Indianapolis: Indiana University Press, 1993), and *Women, "Race," and Writing in the Early Modern Period*, eds. Margo Hendricks and Patricia Barker (London and New York: Routledge, 1994).

63. Appiah, "The Uncompleted Argument: Du Bois and the Illusion of Race," in *"Race," Writing and Difference*, pp. 21–37.

64. Evelyn Brooks Higginbotham provides an indispensable corrective to positions such as Gates's or Appiah's: " As a fluid set of overlapping discourses, race is perceived as arbitrary and illusionary, on the one hand, while natural and fixed on the other. To argue that race is myth and that it is an ideological rather than a biological fact does not deny that ideology has real effects on people's lives" (Higginbotham, "African-American Women's History and the Metalanguage of Race," *Signs* 17, 2 [1992]: 255).

65. Williams, *The Alchemy of Race and Rights: Diary of a Law Professor* (Cambridge and London: Harvard University Press, 1991), pp. 256–257.

66. Hortense Spillers, "Mama's Baby, Papa's Maybe, An American Grammar Book," *Diacritics* 17, 2 (Summer 1987): 79.

67. Williams, *The Alchemy of Race and Rights*, p. 163. bell hooks insists that "race and sex have always been overlapping discourses in the United States" where black/white relations are concerned. However, "there is no psychosexual history of slavery that explores the meaning of white male exploitation of black women or the politics of sexuality, no work that lays out all the available information." Instead, such narratives have been effectively displaced by the kind of attention the dynamics between black men and white women have historicaly been accorded, ansd espe-

Notes for Chapter Three

cially with "images of black men as rapists, as dangerous menaces to society" (bell hooks, "Reflections on Race and Sex," in *Yearning: Race, Gender and Cultural Politics* (Boston: South End Press, 1990), pp. 57, 61). Nothing could have brought home the divergent trajectories of race and gender, nor their impossible intersections, more directly than the Clarence Thomas and Anita Hill hearings that stunned so many and could only be painfully traced afterwards. (See for example, the collection of essays edited by Toni Morrison, *Race-ing Justice, En-gendering Power: Essays on Anita Hill, Clarence Thomas, and the Construction of Social Reality* (New York: Pantheon Books, 1992); L. A. Grindstaff, "Double Exposure, Double Erasure: On the Frontline with Anita Hill," *Cultural Critique* 27 (Spring 1994): 29–60; and numerous articles in *The Black Scholar.*)

68. Spillers, "Mama's Baby, Papa's Maybe," p. 80.

69. bell hooks, *Ain't I A Woman?* (Boston: South End Press, 1986), and Deborah Gray White, *Ar'n't I a Woman?: Female Slaves in the Plantation South* (New York and London: W. W. Norton and Company, 1985).

70. Carby, *Reconstructing Womanhood: The Emergence of the Afro-American Woman Novelist* (Oxford and New York: Oxford University Press, 1988), p. 18, emphasis added.

71. Hurtado, "Relating to Privilege," p. 844. Questions of history become even more pressing in contemporary efforts to work through the naming of U.S. women of color as a single entity. What are the different historicities among Native Americans, blacks, Chicanas, and Asian Americans, including their varying presence and valorization in U.S. academia, that are sometimes obliterated in over-easy references to such a collectivity? For a study of some of the specific moments in the Hispanic racial formation, see Amy Kaminsky, "Gender, Race, *Raza*," *Feminist Studies* 20, 1 (Spring 1994): 7–31.

72. Hurtado, "Relating to Privilege," p. 847.

73. Kelly, "The Social Relation of the Sexes: Methodological Implications in Women's History," in Joan Kelly, *Women, History and Theory* (Chicago: University of Chicago Press, 1984), p. 1.

74. Fuss, *Essentially Speaking: Feminism, Nature and Difference* (New York: Routledge, 1989), p. xiii. Cited hereafter as *ES*.

75. Brittan and Maynard, *Racism, Sexism and Oppression* (Oxford: Blackwell, 1984), p. 193.

76. An excellent example would be Stuart Hall's call for "the end of the essential black subject" in favor of "the recognition of the extraordinary diversity of subjective positions, social experiences and cultural identities, which compose the identity 'black'; that is, the recognition that 'black' is essentially a politically and culturally *constructed* category, which cannot be grounded in a set of fixed trans-cultural or transcendental racial catego-

ries and which therefore has no guarantees in Nature" (Stuart Hall, "New Ethnicities," *ICA Documents*, 7 [1988]: 28). One could read this passage not only as displacing questions of essence from "Nature" to the work of cultural and political experience but also as multiplying one ostensible essence into many.

77. It is worth counterposing Marx's method in the *Grundrisse* to what has come to count today as sophisticated theory: "The concrete is concrete because it is the concentration of many determinations, hence unity of the diverse. It appears in the process of thinking, therefore, as a process of concentration, as a result, not as a point of departure, even though it is a point of departure in reality and hence also for observation and conception. . . . The method of rising from the abstract to the concrete is the only way in which thought appropriates the concrete, reproduces it as the concrete in the mind" (Karl Marx, *Grundrisse: Foundations for a Critique of Political Economy*, translated with a foreword by Martin Nicolaus [London: Penguin Books, 1973], p. 101). Nowadays, the move from the concrete to the abstract is taken to be the mark of one's theoretical accomplishments, rather than as a provisional stage along the way.

78. Dipesh Chakrabarty appears to have opted for just such a conceptualization where postcolonials are concerned: There is only one History—that of Europe—of which we can only ever be inadequate variations (Chakrabarty, "Postcoloniality and the Artifice of History: Who Speaks for "Indian" Pasts?" *Representations* 37 [Winter 1992]: 1–26). For a very different discussion of history see Tejaswini Niranjana, *Siting Translation: History, Post-structuralism and the Colonial Context* (Berkeley: University of California Press, 1991).It should be obvious that the notion of historicity I am arguing for—dealing with what is possible and necessary in the present—has little in common with the kind of "compulsory historicism" (emanating from a specialised discipline) Jane Roland Martin believes is being unfairly thrust upon all feminists at this time (Martin, "Methodological Essentialism, False Differences and Other Dangerous Traps," *Signs* 19, 3 [Spring 1994]: 641–643).

79. Degler, "What the Women's Movement Has Done to American History," in *A Feminist Perspective in the Academy: The Difference it Makes*, eds. Elizabeth Langland and Walter Gove (Chicago: University of Chicago Press, 1981), p. 67.

80. Foucault, "Nietzsche, Genealogy, History," in *Language, Counter-Memory, Practice: Selected Essays and Interviews by Michel Foucault*, ed. Donald Bouchard (Ithaca: Cornell University Press, 1977), p. 162.

81. Ibid., pp. 162, 163.

82. West, "The Dilemma of the Black Intellectual," in *Cultural Critique* 1, 1 (1981): 109–124. For a significantly different approach to the

question of the relation of black intellectuals to their community, see Hortense Spillers, "The Crisis of the Negro Intellectual: A Post-Date," *Boundary* 2 21, 3 (Fall 1994): 65–116. She describes the cost, as she perceives it, of not having taken one's identity and location as a black scholar seriously enough, which demands rethinking the boundaries of community itself.

83. Collins, *Black Feminist Thought: Knowledge, Consciousness, and the Politics of Empowerment* (Cambridge: Unwin Hyman, 1990), pp. 21–22.

Chapter Four: Closer to Home

1. Dreyfus, "Holism and Hermeneutics," in *Review of Metaphysics* 34 (September 1980): 3–23. Background practices have less to do with beliefs than with "habits and customs, embodied in the sort of subtle skills which we exhibit in our everyday interactions with things and people" (p. 8).

2. Said, *Culture and Imperialism* (New York: Alfred A. Knopf, 1993), especially pp. 3–43.

3. Ibid., p. 32.

4. By some peculiar coincidence, two essays with this title came out around the same time: Judith Stacey's "Can There Be a Feminist Ethnography?" appeared in *Women's Studies International Forum* 11, 1: 21–27 in 1988, and Lila Abu-Lughod delivered a lecture, "Can There Be a Feminist Ethnography?" in the same year. Abu-Lughod's lecture was subsequently published in *Women and Performance* 5, 1 (1990): 7–27. The title to this section is an obvious modification of theirs.

5. Abu-Lughod, "Can There Be a Feminist Ethnography?" p. 7.

6. Asad, "Anthropology and the Colonial Encounter," in *The Politics of Anthropology: From Colonialism and Sexism Toward a View from Below*, eds. Gerrit Huizer and Bruce Mannheim (The Hague and Paris: Mouton, 1979), p. 91.

7. Caulfield, "Culture and Imperialism: Proposing a New Dialectic," in *Reinventing Anthropology*, ed. Dell Hymes (New York: Vintage, 1974), p. 182.

8. According to Partha Chatterjee, the nation is "the one most untheorized concept of the modern world" (Chatterjee, *The Nation and Its Fragments: Colonial and Postcolonial Histories* [Princeton, N.J.: Princeton University Press, 1993], p. xi).

9. Strathern, "An Awkward Relationship: The Case of Feminism and Anthropology," in *Signs* 12, 2 (1987): 284; emphasis original.

10. Ibid., p. 290.

11. Mascia-Lees, Sharpe, and Cohen, "The Postmodernist Turn in

Anthropology: Cautions from a Feminist Perspective," in *Signs* 15, 1 (1989): 20 ff.

12. Strathern, "Out of Context: The Persuasive Fictions of Anthropology," *Current Anthropology* 28, 3 (1987): 269.

13. Mascia-Lees et al., "The Postmodernist Turn in Anthropology," p. 9.

14. Ibid., p. 21.

15. Abu-Lughod, "Can There Be a Feminist Ethnography?" p. 24.

16. Ibid., p. 27.

17. For a fuller discussion of this notion see James Clifford, "On Ethnographic Authority," in *The Predicament of Culture: Twentieth-Century Ethnography, Literature, and Art* (Cambridge: Harvard University Press, 1988, pp. 21–54).

18. Ginsburg and Tsing, eds., *Uncertain Terms: Negotiating Gender in American Culture* (Boston: Beacon Press, 1990), pp. 1–2.

19. I take this very well-known phrase from the title of Benedict Anderson's book *Imagined Communities: Reflections on the Origins and Spread of Nationalism* (London: Verso and New Left Books, 1983).

20. Stacey, "Can There Be a Feminist Ethnography?" p. 22.

21. Ibid.

22. Chabram, "Chicano Studies as Oppositional Ethnography," Special Issue: Chicana/o Cultural Representations: Reframing Alternative Critical Discourses, *Cultural Studies* 4, 3 (1990): 237–238; emphasis original.

23. Ibid., p. 234.

24. Another example that disrupts and reconstitutes innovative ethnography is Kamala Visweswaran's important essay "Defining Feminist Ethnography" (in *Inscriptions, Feminism and the Critique of Colonial Discourse* 3/4 (1988): 27–44). Here, too, the field contracts around U.S. subjects—Zora Neale Hurston and Cherríe Moraga.

25. Feminists have on occasion gone quite far in demanding greater accountability and a politics of location from the "new" ethnographers. In the course of a crucial essay that provides an incisive and nuanced feminist critique of the poststructuralist turn in ethnography, Deborah Gordon questions Paul Rabinow's claim to "critical cosmopolitanism" (in his essay "Representations are Social Facts: Modernity and Post-modernity in Anthropology," *Writing Culture: The Poetics and Politics of Ethnography*, eds. James Clifford and George E. Marcus [Berkeley: University of California Press, 1986], pp. 234–261). But if there is a problem with Rabinow's aspiration to be a citizen of the world, transcending national affiliation, her essay does not take this up. It is the problematic place of feminism in *Writing Culture* that takes precedence. James Clifford's introduction to the book is the other essay Gordon analyzes for its conflictive treatment

of feminism. This is how he brings up the issue: "The book gives relatively little attention to new ethnographic possibilities emerging from non-Western experience and from feminist theory and politics. Let me dwell on this last exclusion, for it concerns an especially strong intellectual and moral influence in the university milieux from which these essays have sprung. *Thus this absence cries out for comment"* ("Introduction: Partial Truths," *Writing Culture,* p. 19; emphasis added). Clifford feels an accountability toward feminists from his own milieu, his own nation; the exclusion of non-Western experiences, by contrast, goes without further comment and is not a problem. Critics like Gordon display a desire to include third-world women and third-world feminists: "Studies of Third World women by Third World women suggest rich possibilities for linking Western and Third World feminist writers who are embedded in and wish to speak to diverse audiences" (Deborah Gordon, "Writing Culture, Writing Feminism: The Poetics and Politics of Experimental Ethnography," *Inscriptions, Feminism and the Critique of Colonial Discourse* 3/4 (1988): 21). But what are these rich possibilities?

26. Donaldson, *Decolonizing Feminism: Race, Gender and Empire-Building* (Chapel Hill: University of North Carolina Press, 1992), pp. 8–11.

27. Andrew Parker, Mary Russo, Doris Summer, and Patricia Yaeger, "Introduction," *Nationalisms and Sexualities* (New York and London: Routledge, 1992), pp. 1–18, especially p. 7.

28. Let me confine myself to a few examples in southern India of what can only be described as an exorbitant and obsessive literature: Rene Dubois' *Hindu Manners, Customs, and Ceremonies* was compiled at the end of the eighteenth century (trans. Henry K. Beauchamp, third edition 1906, reprinted Delhi: Oxford University Press, 1981); Edgar Thurston's *Castes and Tribes of Southern India* runs into seven volumes (Madras: Madras Government Press, 1906); and early-twentieth-century native anthropologists produced almost indistinguishable works, such as A. Krishna Iyer's *Lectures on Ethnography* (Calcutta: Calcutta University Press, 1925) or his *The Cochin Tribes and Castes* (New York; Higginbotham, 1969).

29. This, according to Louis Dumont, is how Indians should conceive of themselves, in contrast to the Western antithesis, *homo equalis* (*Homo Hierarchicus: The Caste System and Its Implications* [Chicago: University of Chicago Press, 1980 (1966)]). Arjun Appadurai has called caste one of the privileged "gatekeeping concepts" in anthropological theory, a metonym for Indian society as a whole. (See Appadurai, "Theory in Anthropology: Center and Periphery," in *Comparative Studies in Society and History* 28 [1986]: 356–361; and Appadurai, "Putting Hierarchy in Its Place," in *Cultural Anthropology* 3 [February 1988]: 36–49).

30. In a rare discussion on the place of subjectivity in fieldwork, Indian researchers came up against built-in methodological models that inculcate the treatment of one's subjects not just as others but as *distant* others, even when they were studying their own society. See V. K. Jairath and Meenakshi Thapan, "Nature and Significance of Subjectivity in Fieldwork," in *Economic and Political Weekly* 23, 9 (February 27 1988): 408–409.

31. Satish Deshpande, "Imagined Economies: Styles of Nation-Building in Twentieth Century India," *Journal of Arts and Ideas*, Special Issue on Careers of Modernity, 25–26 (1993): 5–35.

32. Dube, "Introduction," to *Visibility and Power: Essays on Women in Society and Development*, eds. Leela Dube, Eleanor Leacock, Shirley Ardener (Delhi: Oxford University Press, 1986), pp. xi ff.

33. Das, "Indian Women: Work, Power, Status," in *Indian Women from Purdah to Modernity*, ed. B. R. Nanda (New Delhi: Radiant Publishers, 1976).

34. The literature here is quite vast and diffuse, beginning with the plan documents themselves. A crucial institution that helped carve out the oppositional discourses of the Indian "imagined economy" is the *Economic and Political Weekly*, initially simply called the *Economic Weekly*. Published from Bombay, this journal has been coming out on a weekly basis since 1965.

35. Desai, "From Articulation to Accommodation: Women's Movement in India," in *Visibility and Power: Essays on Women in Society and Development*, eds. Leela Dube et al. (Delhi: Oxford University Press, 1986), pp. 287–299.

36. Neera Desai and Maithreyi Krishnaraj, "Introduction," *Women and Society in India* (Bombay: Ajanta Publications, 1987), p. 7.

37. Ibid., p. 5.

38. *Towards Equality: Report of the Committee on the Status of Women in India* (New Delhi: Department of Social Welfare, Government of India, 1974).

39. Desai and Krishnaraj, *Women and Society in India*, p. 5.

40. Friedan, *The Feminine Mystique* (New York: W. W. Norton, 1963).

41. For a similar juxtaposition of the *Towards Equality Report* and Friedan's *The Feminine Mystique* as "founding texts" in the Indian and U.S. contexts, see Susie Tharu and K. Lalita "The Twentieth Century: Women Writing the Nation," in *Women Writing in India: 600 B.C. to the Present*, Volume II: The 20th Century, eds. Susie Tharu and K. Lalita (New York: The Feminist Press, 1993), p. 101.

42. Kishwar, "Introduction," *In Search of Answers: Indian Women's Voices from Manushi*, eds. Madhu Kishwar and Ruth Vanita (London: Zed Books, 1984), p. 1.

43. Sen, "Introduction," *A Space Within the Struggle: Women's Participation in People's Movements* (New Delhi: Kali for Women Press, 1990).

44. Ibid., p. 3.

45. Desai and Krishnaraj, *Women and Society in India*, pp. 50–148.

46. Here is a sample from the early phase of a now vast literature: Nirmala Banerjee, "Women Workers and Development," *Social Scientist* 6 (March 8, 1978): 3–15; Kamla Bhasin, "Participation of Women in Development," Consultation on Improving Nutrition of the Rural Poor in Asia and Far East, mimeo (Bangkok, 1977); Bina Agarwal, *Agricultural Modernisation and Third World Women* (Geneva: International Labour Organisation, 1981); Leela Gulati, "Female Work Participation—A Study of Inter-State Differences," *Economic and Political Weekly* 10, 1–2 (January 11, 1975): 35–42; Vina Mazumdar, *Role of Rural Women in Development* (New Delhi: Allied Publishers, 1978). For reviews of the literature, see Uma Kalpagam, "Gender in Economics: The Indian Experience," *Economic and Political Weekly* 21, 43 (October 1986): WS-49–66; and Nata Duvvury "Women in Agriculture: A Review of the Indian Literature," *Economic and Political Weekly* 24, 43 (October 1989): WS-96–112.

47. Omvedt, *We Will Smash This Prison: Indian Women in Struggle* (London: Zed Press, 1980), p. 10.

48. Saradamoni, "Changing Land Relations and Women: A Case Study of Palghat District, Kerala," in *Women and Rural Transformation*, eds. R. Mehra and K. Saradamoni (New Delhi: Concept Publishing House, 1983); Stree Shakti Sanghatana, *"We were making history . . . ": Life stories of women in the Telangana People's Struggle* (New Delhi: Kali for Women, 1989).

49. Saradamoni, "Changing Land Relations and Women," p. 124.

50. Ibid., p. 245.

51. Saradamoni, *Changing Land Relations and Women*, p. 73.

52. Ibid., p. 148.

53. Stree Shakti Sanghatana, *We were making history . . .* , pp. 280–281.

54. Ibid., p. 281.

55. Ibid., pp. 57, 74, 87, 73.

56. Ibid., p. 246.

57. See also Vasantha Kannabiran and K. Lalita, "That Magic Time: Women in the Telangana People's Struggle," in *Recasting Women: Essays in Colonial History*, eds. Kumkum Sanghari and Sudesh Vaid (New Delhi: Kali for Women, 1989), pp. 180–203.

58. Stree Shakti Sanghatana, *"We were making history . . . ,"* p. 31.

59. Ibid., p.258.

60. Kumkum Sanghari and Sudesh Vaid, *Recasting Women: Essays in Colonial History*, p. 3.

61. Ibid., p. 2.

62. Ibid., p. 4.

63. Gandhi and Shah, *The Issues at Stake: Theory and Practice in the Contemporary Women's Movement in India* (New Delhi: Kali for Women, 1992), p. 325.

64. Tharu and Niranjana, "Problems for a Contemporary Theory of Gender," *Social Scientist* 22, 3–4 (March–April 1994): 93–117.

65. Sarkar, "The Woman as Communal Subject: Rashtrasevika Samiti and Ram Janmabhoomi Movement," *Economic and Political Weekly* (August 31, 1991): 2057–2062, especially 2061.

66. Ibid., p. 2060.

67. Ibid., p. 2062.

68. Tharu and Niranjana, "Problems for a Contemporary Theory of Gender," p. 107.

69. Sarkar, "The Woman as Communal Subject," p. 2062.

70. Tharu and Niranjana, "Problems for a Contemporary Theory of Gender," p. 96.

71. Ibid., p. 108.

72. Questions of sexuality are no longer confined to privacy or marginalized. At least since the last national conference of autonomous women's organizations in 1993, sexuality and lesbianism are now explicit, if largely unexplored, themes in the Indian women's movement.

73. For an extremely suggestive essay that employs Western feminist debates to pry open the suppressions of caste in the Indian postcolonial context, see Vivek Dhareshwar, "Caste and the Secular Self," *Journal of Arts and Ideas*, special issue on Careers of Modernity, 25–26 (December 1993): 115–126.

74. Trinh T. Minh-ha's discussion "Not you/Like you: Post-Colonial Women and the Interlocking Questions of Identity and Difference," *Inscriptions, Feminism and the Critique of Colonial Discourse* 3/4 (1988): 71–77 reveals how white expectations get disrupted when a U.S. third-world member makes a film about other third-world peoples.

75. It was surprising and not a little disappointing to discover that Marilyn Strathern has effectively reduced the scope of "the awkward relationship" by treating it as a purely epistemological question, with no institutional or political effects. See her *The Gender of the Gift: Problems with Women and Problems with Society in Melanesia* (Berkeley: University of California Press, 1988).

Bibliography

Abel, Elizabeth. "Race, Class and Psychoanalysis? Opening Questions." In *Conflicts in Feminism*, eds. Marriane Hirsch and Evelyn Fox-Keller, pp. 184–204. New York: Routledge, 1990.

Abu-Lughod, Lila. "Can There Be a Feminist Ethnography?" *Women and Performance* 5, 1 (1990): 7–27.

Agarwal, Bina. *Agricultural Modernisation and Third World Women*. Geneva: International Labour Organisation, 1980.

Alarcón, Norma. "The Theoretical Subject(s) of *This Bridge Called My Back* and Anglo-American Feminism." In *Making Face Making Soul: Haciendo Caras, Creative and Critical Perspectives by Women of Color*, ed. Gloria Anzaldúa, pp. 356–369. San Francisco: Aunt Lute Press, 1990.

Anderson, Benedict. *Imagined Communities: Reflections on the Origins and Spread of Nationalism*. London: Verso and New Left Books, 1983.

Appadurai, Arjun. "Theory in Anthropology: Center and Periphery." *Comparative Studies in Society and History* 28, 2 (1986): 356–361.

——. "Putting Hierarchy in its Place." *Cultural Anthropology* 3 (1988): 36–49.

Appiah, Anthony. "The Uncompleted Argument: DuBois and the Illusion of Race." "*Race,*" *Writing and Difference*, special issue, *Critical Inquiry* 12, 1 (Autumn 1985): 21–37.

Asad, Talal. "Anthropology and the Colonial Encounter." In *The Politics of Anthropology: From Colonialism and Sexism Toward a View from Below*, eds. Gerrit Huizer and Bruce Mannheim, pp. 85–94. The Hague and Paris: Mouton, 1979.

Banerjee, Nirmala. "Women Workers and Development." *Social Scientist* 6 (March 8, 1978): 3–15.

Behar, Ruth. *Translated Woman: Crossing the Border with Esperanza's Story.* Boston: Beacon Press, 1993.

Benería, Lourdes, and Martha Roldán. *The Crossroads of Class and Gender: Industrial Housework, Subcontracting, and Household Dynamics in Mexico City.* Chicago: University of Chicago Press, 1987.

Berger, Iris. "Categories and Contexts: Reflections on the Politics of Identity in South Africa." *Feminist Studies* 18, 2 (Summer 1992): 284–294.

Bhabha, Homi. "The Commitment to Theory." *New Formations* 5 (Summer 1988): 5–23.

Bhasin, Kamla. "Participation of Women in Development." Consultation on Improving Nutrition of the Rural Poor in Asia and the Far East, Bangkok, 1977, mimeo.

Borthwick, Meredith, *The Changing Role of women in Bengal 1849–1905.* Princeton, N.J.: Princeton University Press, 1984.

Brennan, Teresa, ed. *Between Feminism and Psychoanalysis.* London and New York: Routledge, 1989.

Brittan, Arthur, and Mary Maynard. *Racism, Sexism and Oppression.* Oxford: Blackwell, 1984.

Bulkin, Elly, Minnie Bruce Pratt, and Barbara Smith. *Yours in Struggle, Three Perspectives on Anti-semitism and Racism.* New York: Long Haul Press, 1984.

Butler, Judith. "Gender Differences: Feminist Theory and Psychoanalytical Narrative," mimeo, 1988: 1–29.

———. *Gender Trouble: Feminism and the Subversion of Identity.* New York and London: Routledge, 1990.

———. *Bodies that Matter: On the Discursive Limits of "Sex."* New York and London: Routledge, 1993.

Carby, Hazel V. *Reconstructing Womanhood: The Emergence of the Afro-American Woman Novelist.* Oxford and New York: Oxford University Press, 1987.

Chakrabarty, Dipesh. *Rethinking Working Class History: Bengal, 1890–1940.* Princeton, N.J.: Princeton University Press, 1989.

———. "Postcoloniality and the Artifice of History: Who Speaks for Indian Pasts?" *Representations* 37 (Winter 1992): 1–26.

Chatterjee, Partha. "Colonialism, Nationalism and Colonised Women: The Contest in India," mimeo, n.d.

———. *Nationalist Thought and the Colonial World—A Derivative Discourse?* London: Zed Press, 1986.

———. "The Nationalist Resolution of the Women's Question." In *Recasting Women: Essays in Colonial History,* eds. Kumkum Sangari and Sudesh Vaid, pp. 233–253. New Delhi: Kali for Women Press, 1989.

———. *The Nation and its Fragments: Colonial and Postcolonial Histories.* Princeton, N.J.: Princeton University Press, 1993.

Chaudhuri, B. B. "Subaltern Autonomy and the Nationalist Movement." *The Indian Historical Review* XII, 1–2 (July 1985–January 1986).

Childers, Mary, and bell hooks. "A Conversation about Race and Class." In *Conflicts in Feminism*, eds. Marianne Hirsch and Evelyn Fox-Keller, pp. 60–81. New York: Routledge, 1990.

Chodorow, Nancy. *The Reproduction of Mothering: Psychoanalysis and the Sociology of Gender.* Berkeley: University of California Press, 1978.

Chow, Rey. *Women and Chinese Modernity: Reading Between West and East.* Minneapolis: University of Minnesota Press, 1991.

Clifford, James. "Introduction: Partial Truths." In *Writing Culture: The Poetics and Politics of Ethnography*, eds. James Clifford and George E. Marcus, 1–26. Berkeley: University of California Press, 1986.

———. "On Ethnographic Authority." In *The Predicament of Culture: Twentieth Century Ethnography, Literature and Art*, pp. 21–54. Cambridge: Harvard University Press, 1988.

Clifford, James, and George E. Marcus, eds. *Writing Culture: The Poetics and Politics of Ethnography.* Berkeley and Los Angeles: University of California Press, 1986.

Collins, Patricia Hill. *Black Feminist Thought: Knowledge, Consciousness and the Politics of Empowerment.* Cambridge: Unwin Hyman, 1990.

Coward, Rosalind. *Patriarchal Precedents, Sexuality and Social Relations.* London: Routledge and Kegan Paul, 1983.

Daly, Mary. *Gyn/Ecology: The Metaethics of Radical Feminism.* Boston: Beacon Press, 1978.

Das, Veena. "Indian Women: Work, Power, Status." In *Indian Women from Purdah to Modernity*, ed. B. R. Nanda. New Delhi: Radiant Publishers, 1976.

Das Gupta, Ranajit. "Significance of Subaltern Mediation." *The Indian Historical Review* XII, 1–2 (July 1985–January 1986).

davenport, doris. "The Pathology of Racism: A Conversation with Third World Wimmin." In *This Bridge Called My Back, Writings by Radical Women of Color*, eds. Cherríe Moraga and Gloria Anzaldúa, pp. 85–90. New York: Kitchen Table, Women of Color Press, 1983.

de Beauvoir, Simone. *The Second Sex.* Trans. and ed. H. M. Parshley. New York: Vintage Books, 1974 (1954).

de Certeau, Michel. *The Writing of History.* New York: University of Columbia Press, 1988.

de Lauretis, Teresa. *Technologies of Gender, Essays on Theory, Film and Fiction.* Bloomington: Indiana University Press, 1986.

——, ed. *Feminist Studies/Critical Studies*. Bloomington: Indiana University Press, 1986.

——. "Upping the Anti [*sic*] in Feminist Theory." In *Conflicts in Feminism*, eds. Marianne Hirsch and Evelyn Fox Keller, pp. 255–270. New York: Routledge, 1990.

Degler, Carl N. "What the Women's Movement Has Done to American History." In *A Feminist Perspective in the Academy: The Difference it Makes*, eds. Elizabeth Langland and Walter Gove, 67–85. Chicago: University of Chicago Press, 1981.

Delphy, Christine. *Close to Home: A Materialist Analysis of Women's Oppression*. Trans. Diana Leonard. London: Hutchinson, 1984.

Derrida, Jacques. "Positions." Interview with Jean-Louis Houdebine and Guy Scarpetta. In *Positions*, pp. 37–96. Trans. Alan Bass. Chicago: University of Chicago Press, 1981.

——. "Geschlecht: sexual difference, ontological difference." *Research in Phenomenology* 13 (1983): 65–83.

——. "Geschlecht II: Heidegger's Hand." In *Deconstruction and Philosophy*, ed. John Sallis, pp. 161–197. Chicago: University of Chicago Press, 1987.

——. "The Laws of Reflection: Nelson Mandela, in Admiration." In *For Nelson Mandela*, eds. Jacques Derrida and Mustapha Tlili, pp. 11–42. New York: Seaver Books, 1987.

Desai, Neera. "From Articulation to Accommodation: Women's Movement in India." In *Visibility and Power: Essays on Women in Society and Development*, eds. Leela Dube, Eleanor Leacock, Shirley Ardener, pp. 287–299. Delhi: Oxford University Press, 1986.

Desai, Neera, and Maithreyi Krishnaraj. *Women and Society in India*. Bombay: Ajanta Publications, 1987.

Deshpande, Satish. "Imagined Economies: Styles of Nation-Building in Twentieth Century India." *Journal of Arts and Ideas*, special issue on Careers of Modernity, 25–26 (1993): 5–35.

Dhareshwar, Vivek. "The Predicament of Theory." In *Theory Between the Disciplines: Authority/Vision/Politics*, eds. Martin Kreiswirth and Mark Cheetham, pp. 231–250. Ann Arbor: University of Michigan Press, 1990.

——. "Caste and the Secular Self." *Journal of Arts and Ideas*, special issue on Careers of Modernity, nos. 25–26 (1993): 115–126.

Donaldson, Laura E. *Decolonizing Feminism: Race, Gender, and Empire-Building*. Chapel Hill and London: University of North Carolina Press, 1992.

Dreyfus, Hubert L. "Holism and Hermeneutics." *Review of Metaphysics* 34 (1980): 3–23.

Dube, Leela. "Introduction." In *Visibility and Power: Essays on Women in Society and Development*, eds. Leela Dube, Eleanor Leacock, Shirley Ardener, pp. xi-xliv. Delhi: Oxford University Press, 1986.

Dubois, Abbé J.A. *Hindu Manners, Customs and Ceremonies*. Trans. Henry K. Beauchamp. Delhi: Oxford University Press, 1981 (1906).

Dumont, Louis. *Homo Hierarchicus: The Caste System and Its Implications*. Revised English edition. Chicago: University of Chicago Press, 1980.

During, Simon. "Waiting for the Post: Some Relations Between Modernity, Colonization and Writing." *Ariel* 20, 4 (October 1989): 31–61.

Duvvury, Nata. "Women in Agriculture: A Review of the Indian Literature." *Economic and Political Weekly* 24, 43 (October 1989): WS-96–112.

Ehrenreich, Barbara. *Fear of Falling: The Inner Life of the Middle Class*. New York: Harper Collins, 1989.

Eisenstein, Zillah R., ed. *Capitalist Patriarchy and the Case for Socialist Feminism*. New York: Monthly Review Press, 1979.

———. "Specifying U.S. Feminism in the 1990s: The Problem of Naming." *Socialist Review* 20, 2 (April–June 1990): 45–56.

Feldstein, Richard, and Judith Roof, eds. *Feminism and Psychoanalysis*. Ithaca, N.Y. and London: Cornell University Press, 1989.

Firestone, Shulamith. *The Dialectic of Sex*. New York: Bantam Books, 1970.

Foucault, Michel. "The Political Function of Intellectuals." Trans. Colin Gordon. *Radical Philosophy* 17 (1977): 12–14.

———. "Intellectuals and Power." In *Language, Counter-Memory, Practice, Selected Essays and Interviews*, ed. Donald F. Bouchard, pp. 205–217. Ithaca, N.Y.: Cornell University Press, 1977.

———. "Nietzsche, Genealogy, History." In *Language, Counter-Memory, Practice: Selected Essays and Interviews by Michel Foucault*, ed. Donald Bouchard, pp. 139–164. Ithaca, N.Y.: Cornell University Press, 1977.

———. *The History of Sexuality, Volume One*. Trans. Robert Hurley. London: Penguin Books, 1978.

———. "Politics and Ethics: An Interview." Trans. Catherine Porter. In *The Foucault Reader*, ed. Paul Rabinow, pp. 373–380. New York: Pantheon Books, 1984.

Frankenberg, Ruth. *White Women, Race Matters: The Social Construction of Whiteness*. Minneapolis: University of Minnesota Press, 1993.

Freud, Sigmund. *Moses and Monotheism*. Trans. Katharine Jones. New York: Vintage Books, 1959.

———. *The Interpretation of Dreams. The Pelican Freud Library*, Volume 4, ed. and trans. James Strachey. London: Pelican Books, 1976 (1900).

——. *Jokes and their Relation to the Unconscious. The Pelican Freud Library*, Volume 6, ed. and trans. James Strachey. London: Pelican Books, 1976 (1904).

Friedan, Betty. *The Feminine Mystique*. New York: W. W. Norton, 1963.

Fuss, Diana. *Essentially Speaking: Feminism, Nature and Difference*. London: Routledge, 1989.

Gates, Henry Louis, Jr. "Editor's Introduction: Writing 'Race' and the Difference It Makes." In *"Race," Writing and Difference*, special issue, *Critical Inquiry* 12, 1 (Autumn 1985): 1–20.

Ginsburg, Faye, and Anna Lowenhaupt Tsing, eds. *Uncertain Terms: Negotiating Gender in American Culture*. Boston: Beacon Press, 1990.

Gordon, Deborah. "Writing Culture, Writing Feminism: The Poetics and Politics of Experimental Ethnography." *Feminism and the Critique of Colonial Discourse, Inscriptions*, nos. 3/4 (1988): 7–24.

Gordon, Linda. "What's New in Women's History." In *Feminist Studies/Critical Studies*, ed. Teresa de Lauretis, pp. 20–30. Bloomington: Indiana University Press, 1986.

——. *Heroes of Their Own Lives: The Politics and History of Family Violence*. New York: Viking, 1988.

——. *"Gender and the Politics of History* by Joan Wallach Scott." Book Review. *Signs* 15, 4 (Summer 1990): 853–858.

Government of India, Department of Social Welfare. *Towards Equality: Report of the Committee on the Status of Women in India*. Delhi: Department of Social Welfare, 1974.

Grindstaff, L. A. "Double Exposure, Double Erasure: On the Frontline with Anita Hill." *Cultural Critique* 27 (Spring 1994): 29–60.

Guha, Ranajit. *A Rule of Property for Bengal: An Essay on the Idea of Permanent Settlement*. Paris and La Haye: Mouton and Co, 1963.

——. "On Some Aspects of the Historiography of Colonial India." In *Subaltern Studies I: Writings on South Asian History and Society*, ed. Ranajit Guha, pp. 1–8. Delhi: Oxford University Press, 1982.

——. "The Prose of Counter-Insurgency." In *Subaltern Studies II: Writings on South Asian History and Society*, ed. Ranajit Guha, pp. 1–42. Delhi: Oxford University Press, 1983.

——. *Elementary Aspects of Peasant Insurgency in Colonial India*. Delhi: Oxford University Press, 1983.

——, ed. *Subaltern Studies: Writings on South Asian History and Society*, Volumes I–VI. Delhi: Oxford University Press, 1982–1989.

Hall, Stuart. "The Toad in the Garden: Thatcherism among the Theorists." In *Marxism and the Interpretation of Culture*, eds. Carl Nelson and Lawrence Grossberg, pp. 35–73. Chicago: University of Illinois Press, 1988.

——. "New Ethnicities." *ICA Documents* 7 (Summer 1988): 27–31.

——. "Signification, Representation, Ideology: Althusser and Post-structuralist Debates." *Critical Studies of Mass Communication* 2, 2 (1985): 91–114.

Harari, Josué. "Nostalgia and Critical Theory." In *The Limits of Theory*, ed. Thomas M. Kavanagh, pp. 168–193. Stanford: Stanford University Press, 1989.

Haraway, Donna. "Gender for a Marxist Dictionary: The Sexual Politics of a Word." In *Simians, Cyborgs and Women: Feminism and the Reinvention of Nature*, pp. 127–149. New York: Routledge, 1991.

——. "Situated Knowledges: The Science Question in Feminism and the Privilege of Partial Perspective." *Feminist Studies* 14, 3 (1988): 575–599.

Harding, Sandra. *The Science Question in Feminism*. Ithaca, N.Y.: Cornell university Press, 1986.

——. *Whose Science? Whose Knowledge?: Thinking from Women's Lives*. Buckingham, U.K.: Open University Press, 1991.

——, ed. *The "Racial" Economy of Science: Towards a Democratic Future*. Bloomington: Indiana University Press, 1993.

Hartsock, Nancy. "The Feminist Stand-point: Developing the Ground for a Specifically Historical Materialism." In *Discovering Reality, Feminist Perspectives on Epistemology, Metaphysics, Methodology, and Philosophy of Science*, eds. Sandra Harding and Merrill B. Hintikka, pp. 283–311. Dordrecht, Holland, Boston and London: Dordrecht Reidel, 1983.

Heath, Stephen. "Male Feminism." *Dalhousie Review* 64, 2 (1986): 270–301.

Hendricks, Margo, and Patricia Parker. *Women, "Race" and Writing in the Early Modern Period*. London and New York: Routledge, 1994.

Higginbotham, Evelyn Brooks. "African-American Women's History and the Metalanguage of Race." *Signs* 17, 2 (1992): 251–274.

Hirsch, Marriane, and Evelyn Fox Keller. "Introduction." In *Conflicts in Feminism*, eds. Marianne Hirsch and Evelyn Fox-Keller, pp. 1–8. New York: Routledge, 1990.

Homans, Margaret. "'Women of Color' Writers and Feminist Theory." *New Literary History* 25, 1 (Winter 1994): 73–94.

hooks, bell. *Ain't I a Woman?* Boston: South End Press, 1981.

——. *talking back: thinking feminist, thinking black*. Boston: South End Press, 1989.

——. *Yearning: Race, Gender and Cultural Politics*. Boston: South End Press, 1990.

hooks, bell, and Mary Childers. "A Conversation about Race and Class."

In *Conflicts in Feminism*, eds. Marianne Hirsch and Evelyn Fox-Keller, pp. 60–81. New York: Routledge, 1990.

Huizer, Gerrit, and Bruce Mannheim eds. *The Politics of Anthropology: From Colonialism and Sexism Toward a View from Below*. The Hague and Paris: Mouton, 1979.

Hurston, Zora Neale. *Moses, Man of the Mountain*. Introduction by Blydon Jackson. Urbana and Chicago: University of Illinois Press, 1984 (1939).

Hurtado, Aida. "Relating to Privilege: Seduction and Rejection in the Subordination of White Women and Women of Color." *Signs* 14, 4 (1989): 833–855.

Hymes, Dell, ed. *Reinventing Anthropology*. New York: Vintage Books, 1974.

Irigaray, Luce. "Women's Exile." *Ideology and Consciousness* 1 (1977): 62–76.

——. *The Speculum of the Other Woman*. Trans. Gillian C. Gill. Ithaca, N.Y.: Cornell University Press, 1978.

Iyer, A. Krishna. *Lectures on Ethnography*. Calcutta: Calcutta University Press, 1925.

——. *The Cochin Tribes and Castes*. New York: Higginbotham, 1969.

Jairath, V. K., and Meenakshi Thapan. "Nature and Significance of Subjectivity in Fieldwork." *Economic and Political Weekly* 23, 9 (February 27, 1988): 408–409.

Jayamanne, Laleen, Geeta Kapur, and Yvonne Rainer. "Discussing Modernity, 'Third World,' and "The Man Who Envied Women". *Art and Text* 23, 4 (1987): 41–51.

Jayawardena, Kumari. *Feminism and Nationalism in the Third World*. India: Kali Press for Women, 1986.

Jensen, Joan M. *Passage from India, Asian Indian Immigrants in North America*. New Haven and London: Yale University Press, 1988.

Johnson, Barbara. *The Critical Difference*. Baltimore: Johns Hopkins University Press, 1980.

——. *A World of Difference*. Baltimore and London: Johns Hopkins University Press, 1987.

Jones, Jacqueline. *Labor of Love, Labor of Sorrow: Black Women, Work, and the Family from Slavery to the Present*. New York: Basic Books, 1985.

Kalpagam, Uma. "Gender in Economics: The Indian Experience." *Economic and Political Weekly* 21, 43 (October 1986): WS-59–66.

Kaminsky, Amy. "Gender, Race, *Raza*." *Feminist Studies* 20, 1 (Spring 1994): 7–31.

Kannabiran, Vasantha, and K. Lalita. "That Magic Time: Women in the

Telangana Struggle." In *Recasting Women: Essays on Colonial History*, eds. Kumkum Sangari and Sudesh Vaid, pp. 180–203. New Delhi: Kali for Women, 1989.

Katz, Jonathan. "The Invention of Heterosexuality." *Socialist Review* 20, 1 (1990).

Kelly, Joan. *Women, History and Theory*. Chicago: University of Chicago Press, 1984.

King, Katie. "Audre Lorde's Lacquered Layerings: The Lesbian Bar as a Site of Literary Production." *Cultural Studies* 2, 3 (1988): 321–342.

Kishwar, Madhu. "Introduction." *In Search of Answers: Indian Women's Voices from Manushi*, eds. Madhu Kishwar and Ruth Vanita, pp. 1–47. London: Zed Books, 1984.

Kumar, Radha. *The History of Doing: An Illustrated Account of the Movements for Women's Rights and Feminism in India, 1800–1900*. New Delhi: Kali for Women, 1993.

Lacan, Jacques. *Écrits, A Selection*. Trans. Alan Sheridan. New York and London: W. W. Norton and Company, 1977.

——. *Jacques Lacan and the école freudienne*. Eds. Juliet Mitchell and Jacqueline Rose. Trans. Jacqueline Rose. New York: W. W. Norton and Co., 1985.

Laclau, Ernesto, and Chantal Mouffe. *Hegemony and Socialist Strategy: Towards a Radical Democratic Politics*. Trans. Winston Moore and Paul Cammack. London: Verso Press, 1985.

Lâm, Maivan Clech. "Feeling Foreign in Feminism." *Signs* 19, 4 (Summer 1994): 865–893.

le Deuff, Michele. "Women and Philosophy." Trans. Debbie Pope. *Radical Philosophy* 17, (Summer 1977): 2–11.

Lerner, Gerda. *The Creation of Patriarchy*. New York: Oxford University Press, 1986.

Liddle, Joanna, and Rama Joshi. *Daughters of Independence, Gender, Caste and Class in India*. London and New Delhi: Zed Press, 1986.

Lorde, Audre. *Sister Outsider: Essays and Speeches*. New York: The Crossing Press, 1984.

Macaulay, Thomas Babington. "Indian Education." (Minute of the 2nd February 1835.) In *Prose and Poetry*, ed. G. M. Young, pp. 719–730. Cambridge, Mass.: Harvard University Press, 1967. Originally published London: Rupert Hart-Davis, 1952.

MacKinnon, Catherine. "Feminism, Marxism, Method and the State: An Agenda for Theory." In *Feminist Theory: A Critique of Ideology*, eds. Nannerl O. Keohane, Michelle Z. Rosaldo, and Barbara C. Gelpi, pp. 1–30. Chicago: University of Chicago Press, 1981.

Malinowski, Branislaw. *Sex and Repression in Savage Society.* New York: Meridian Books, 1927.

Mani, Lata. "The Construction of Women as Tradition in Nineteenth Century Bengal." *Cultural Critique* 2, 7 (Special Issue: "The Nature and Context of Minority Discourse") (Fall 1987): 119–156.

———. "Multiple Mediations: Feminist Scholarship in the Age of Multinational Mediation." *Inscriptions: Traveling Theories, Traveling Theorists* 5 (1989): 1–23.

Marcus, George E., and Michael J. Fischer. *Anthropology as Cultural Critique: An Experimental Moment in the Human Sciences.* Chicago: University of Chicago Press, 1986.

Marcus, Jane. "Alibis and Legends, The Ethics of Elsewhereness, Gender and Estrangement." In *Women's Writing in Exile*, eds. Mary Lynn Broe and Angela Ingram, pp. 269–294. Chapel Hill and London: University of North Carolina Press, 1989.

Marks, Elaine, and Isabelle de Courtivron, eds. *New French Feminisms.* New York: Schocken Books, 1980.

Martin, Biddy, and Chandra Talpade Mohanty. "Feminist Politics: What's Home Got to Do with It?" In *Feminist Studies/Critical Studies*, ed. Teresa de Lauretis, pp. 191–212. Indiana: Bloomington University Press, 1986.

Martin, Jane Roland. "Methodological Essentialism, False Difference and Other Dangerous Traps." *Signs* 19, 3 (Spring 1994): 630–657.

Marx, Karl. *Grundrisse: Foundations for a Critique of Political Economy.* Trans. Martin Nicolaus. London: Penguin Books, 1973.

Mascia-Lees, Frances E., Patricia Sharpe, and Colleen Ballerino Cohen. "The Postmodernist Turn in Anthropology: Cautions from a Feminist Perspective." *Signs* 15, 1 (1989): 3–24.

Mazumdar, Sucheta. "Punjabi Agricultural Workers in California, 1905–1945." In *Labor Immigration under Capitalism*, eds. Edna Bonacich and Lucie Cheng, pp. 316–578. Berkeley: University of California Press, 1984.

Mazumdar, Veena. "The Social Reform Movement in India from Ranade to Nehru." In *Indian Women from Purdah to Modernity*, ed. B. R. Nanda. New Delhi: Radiant Publishers, 1976.

———. *Role of Rural Women in Development.* New Delhi: Allied Publishers, 1978.

McRobbie, Angela. "An Interview with Juliet Mitchell." *New Left Review* 170 (July/August 1988): 80–91.

Mehta, Rama. *The Western Educated Hindu Woman.* New York: Asia Publishing House, 1970.

Mies, Maria. *Patriarchy and Accumulation on a World Scale, Women in the International Division of Labour*. London: Zed Press, 1980.

——. "Towards a Methodology for Feminist Research." In *Theories of Women's Studies*, eds. Gloria Bowles and Renate Duelli Klein, pp. 117–139. London and Boston: Routledge and Kegan Paul, 1983.

Misra, B. B. *The Indian Middle Classes: Their Growth in Modern Times*. London, New York, Bombay: Oxford University Press, 1961.

Mitchell, Juliet. *Psychoanalysis and Feminism: Freud, Reich, Laing and Women*. New York: Vintage, 1974.

Mohanty, Chandra Talpade. "Under Western Eyes: Feminist Scholarship and Colonial Discourses." *Boundary 2* (1985): 333–357.

——. "Feminist Encounters: Locating the Politics of Experience." *Copyright* 1 (Fall 1987): 30–44.

Mohanty, Chandra Talpade, and Biddy Martin. "Feminist Politics: What's Home Got to Do with It?" In *Feminist Studies/Critical Studies*, ed. Teresa de Lauretis, pp. 191–212. Bloomington: Indiana University Press, 1986.

Moi, Toril. "Psychoanalysis, Feminism and Politics: A Conversation with Juliet Mitchell," *South Atlantic Quarterly* 93, 4 (Fall 1994): 925–949.

Moore, Henrietta. *Feminism and Anthropology*. Minneapolis: University of Minnesota Press, 1988.

Moraga, Cherríe, and Gloria Anzaldúa, eds. *This Bridge Called My Back: Writings by Radical Women of Color*. New York: Kitchen Table, Women of Color Press, 1983.

Morgan, Sandra, ed. *Gender and Anthropology: Critical Reviews for Research and Teaching*. Washington, D.C.: American Anthropological Association, 1989.

Morris, Meaghan. *The Pirate's Fiancee: Feminism, Reading, Post-modernism*. London and New York: Verso, 1988.

Morrison, Toni, ed. *Race-ing Justice, En-gendering Power: Essays on Anita Hill, Clarence, and the Construction of Social Reality*. New York: Pantheon Books, 1992.

Nandy, Ashis. *The Intimate Enemy, Loss and Recovery of Self under Colonialism*. Delhi: Oxford University Press, 1983.

Niranjana, Tejaswini. *Siting Translation: History, Poststructuralism, and the Colonial Context*. Berkeley, Los Angeles and Oxford: University of California Press, 1991.

O'Hanlon, Rosalind. "Recovering the Subject: *Subaltern Studies* and Histories of Resistance in Colonial South Asia." *Modern Asian Studies* 22, 1 (1988): 189–224.

Obeyesekere, Gananath. *The Work of Culture: Symbolic Transformations in Psychoanalysis and Anthropology.* Chicago: University of Chicago Press, 1990.

Ogumyemi, Chikwenye Okonjo. "Womanism: The Dynamics of the Contemporary Black Female Novel." *Signs* 11, 1 (Autumn 1985): 63–80.

Omi, Michael, and Howard Winant. *Racial Formation in the United States: From the 1960s to the 1980s.* New York and London: Routledge and Kegan Paul, 1986.

Omvedt, Gail. *We Will Smash this Prison: Indian Women in Struggle.* London: Zed Press, 1980.

Ong, Aihwa. *Spirits of Resistance and Capitalist Discipline: Factory Women in Malaysia.* Albany: State University of New York Press, 1987.

Parker, Andrew, Mary Russo, Doris Summer, and Patricia Yaeger. "Introduction." In *Nationalisms and Sexualities*, pp. 1–18. New York and London: Routledge, 1992.

Poovey, Mary. *Uneven Developments: The Ideological Work of Gender in Mid-Victorian England.* Chicago: University of Chicago Press, 1988.

Pratt, Minnie Bruce. "Identity: Skin Blood Heart." In *Yours in Struggle: Three Perspectives on Feminism, Anti-Semitism and Racism*, eds. Elly Bulkin, Minnie Bruce Pratt, and Barbara Smith. New York: Long Haul Press, 1984.

Quintanales, Mirtha. "I Paid Very Hard for My Immigrant Ignorance." In *This Bridge Called My Back: Writings of Radical Women of Color*, eds. Cherríe Moraga and Gloria Anzaldúa, pp. 150–156. New York: Kitchen Table, Women of Color Press, 1983.

Rabinow, Paul. "Representations are Social Facts: Modernity and Post-Modernity in Anthropology." In *Writing Culture: The Poetics and Politics of Ethnography*, eds. James Clifford and George E. Marcus, pp. 234–261. Berkeley and Los Angeles: University of California Press, 1986.

Rebolledo, Tey Diana. "The Politics of Poetics: Or, What Am I, a Critic, Doing in This Text Anyhow?" In *Making Face, Making Soul: Haciendo Caras, Creative and Critical Perspectives by Women of Color*, ed. Gloria Anzaldúa, pp. 346–355. San Francisco: Aunt Lute Press, 1990.

Reiter, Rayna R., ed. *Toward an Anthropology of Women.* New York and London: Monthly Review Press, 1975.

Rich, Adrienne. "Disloyal to Civilization: Feminism, Racism and Gynephobia." In *On Lies, Secrets and Silence: Selected Prose 1966–1978*, pp. 275–310. New York and London: W. W. Norton and Company, 1979.

——. "Notes toward a Politics of Location." In *Blood, Bread and Poetry, Selected Prose 1979–1985*, pp. 210–231. New York and London: W. W. Norton and Company, 1986.

Rich, B. Ruby. "Feminism and Sexuality in the 1980s, Review Essay." *Feminist Studies* 12, 3 (Fall 1986): 525–561.

Rodriguez, Richard. *Hunger of Memory: The Education of Richard Rodriguez, An Autobiography.* New York: Bantam Books, 1983.

Rosaldo, Michele. "The Use and Abuse of Anthropology: Reflections in Feminism and Cross-Cultural Understanding." *Signs* 5, 3 (1980): 389–417.

Rosaldo, Michele, and Louise Lamphere, eds. *Women, Culture and Society*, Stanford: Stanford University Press, 1974.

Rose, Jacqueline. *Sexuality in the Field of Vision.* London: Verso Press, 1986.

Rubin, Gayle. "The Traffic in Women: Notes on the Political Economy of Sex." In *Toward an Anthropology of Women*, ed. Rayna R. Reiter, pp. 157–210. New York and London: Monthly Review Press, 1975.

Ruiz, Vicki. *Cannery Women Cannery Lives: Mexican Women, Unionization and the California Food Processing Industry, 1930–1950.* Albequerque: University of New Mexico Press, 1987.

Sacks, Karen Brodkin. "Towards a Unified Theory of Race, Class and Gender." *American Ethnologist* 16, 3 (1989): 534–550.

Said, Edward W. *Orientalism.* New York: Vintage Books, 1978.

——. *The World, the Text and the Critic.* Cambridge, Mass.: Harvard University Press, 1983.

——. *Culture and Imperialism.* New York: Alfred Knopf, 1993.

Sandoval, Chela. "U.S. Third World Feminism: The Theory and Method of Oppositional Consciousness in the Postmodern World." *Genders* 10 (Spring 1991): 1–24.

Sangari, Kumkum, and Sudesh Vaid. *Recasting Women: Essays in Colonial History.* New Delhi: Kali for Women Press, 1989.

Saradamoni, K. "Changing Land Relations and Women: A Case Study of Palghat District, Kerala." In *Women and Rural Transformation*, eds. Rekha Mehra and K. Saradamoni. New Delhi: Concept Publishing House, 1983.

Sargant, Lydia, ed. *Women and Revolution: A Discussion of the Unhappy Marriage of Marxism and Feminism.* Boston: South End Press, 1981.

Sarkar, Tanika. "The Woman as Communal Subject: Rashtrasevika Samiti and Ram Janmabhoomi Movement." *Economic and Political Weekly* (August 31 1991): 2057–2062.

Sartre, Jean-Paul. *Search for a Method.* New York: Vintage Books, 1968 (1963).

Scott, David. "Locating the Anthropological Subject: Postcolonial Anthropologists in Other Places." *Inscriptions, Traveling Theories, Traveling Theorists* 5 (1989): 75–84.

Scott, Joan Wallach. *Gender and the Politics of History*. New York: Columbia University Press, 1988.

——. "Heroes of Their Own Lives: The Politics and History of Family Violence" by Linda Gordon. Book Review. *Signs* 15, 4 (Summer 1990): 848–852.

Seller, Maxine Schwartz, ed. *Immigrant Women*. Philadelphia: Temple University Press, 1981.

Sen, Ilina. "Introduction." In *A Space Within the Struggle: Women's Participation in People's Movements*, pp. 1–18. New Delhi: Kali for Women Press, 1990.

Shah, Nandita, and Nandita Gandhi, eds. *The Issues at Stake: Theory and Practice in the Contemporary Women's Movement in India*. New Delhi: Kali for Women Press, 1992.

Showalter, Elaine. *A Literature of Their Own*. Princeton: Princeton University Press, 1977.

——, ed. *Speaking of Gender*. New York and London: Routledge, 1989.

Silverman, Kaja. *The Subject of Semiotics*. New York and Oxford: Oxford University Press, 1983.

Singh, Jane, ed. *South Asians in North America: An Annotated and Selected Bibliography*. Berkeley: University of California Press, 1988.

Singh, Sangeeta, et al. "Subaltern Studies II: A Review Article." *Social Scientist* 12, 10 (1984): 3–41.

Skinner, Quentin, ed. *The Return of Grand Theory in the Human Sciences*. London: Cambridge University Press, 1985.

Spillers, Hortense. "Mama's Baby, Papa's Maybe: An American Grammar Book." *Diacritics* 17, 2 (Summer 1987): 65–81.

——. "The Crisis of the Negro Intellectual: A Post-Date." *Boundary 2* 21, 3 (Fall 1994): 65–116.

Spiro, Melford E. *Oedipus in the Trobriands*. Chicago and London: University of Chicago Press, 1982.

Spivak, Gayatri Chakravorty. "Displacement and the Discourse of Woman." In *Displacement: Derrida and After*, ed. Mark Krupnick, pp. 169–195. Bloomington: Indiana University Press, 1984.

——. "Criticism, Feminism and the Institution." Interview. *Thesis Eleven* 10/11 (November/March 1984–85): 175–187.

——. "Interview." With Rashmi Bhatnagar, Lola Chatterjee, and Rajeswari Sunder Rajan. *The Book Review* 11, 3 (May–June 1987): 16–22. Reprinted as "The Postcolonial Critic" in *The Postcolonial Critic: Interviews, Strategies, Dialogues*, ed. Sarah Harasym, 67–74. New York: Routledge, 1990.

——. *In Other Worlds: Essays in Cultural Politics*. New York: Methuen, 1987.

——. "Can the Subaltern Speak?" In *Marxism and the Interpretation of Culture*, eds. Cary Nelson and Lawrence Grossberg, pp. 271–313. Urbana and Chicago: University of Illinois Press, 1988.

——. "The Political Economy of Women as Seen by a Literary Critic." In *Coming to Terms: Feminism, Theory, Politics*, ed. Elizabeth Weed, pp. 218–229. New York and London: Routledge, 1989.

——. "Who Claims Alterity?" In *Remaking History* (Discussions in Contemporary Culture 4, Dia Art Foundation), eds. Barbara Kruger and Phil Mariani, pp. 269–292. Seattle: Bay Press, 1989.

——. "Feminism and Deconstruction, Again: Negotiating with Unacknowledged Masculinism." In *Between Feminism and Psychoanalysis*, ed. Teresa Brennan, 206–223. London and New York: Routledge, 1989.

——. *The Post-colonial Critic: Interviews, Strategies, Dialogues*, ed. Sarah Harasym. New York: Routledge, 1990.

——. *Outside in the Teaching Machine*. New York and London: Routledge, 1993.

Spivak, Gayatri Chakravorty, and Ellen Rooney. "In a Word: Interview." *differences* 1, 2 (1989).

Stacey, Judith. "Can There Be a Feminist Ethnography?" *Women's Studies International Forum* 10, 1 (1988): 21–27.

Stepan, Nancy Leys. "Race and Gender: The Role of Analogy in Science." In *Anatomy of Racism*, ed. David Theo Goldberg, 38–57. Minneapolis: University of Minnesota Press, 1990.

Strathern, Marilyn. "An Awkward Relationship: The Case of Feminism and Anthropology." *Signs* 12, 2 (1987): 276–292.

——. "Out of Context: The Persuasive Fictions of Anthropology." *Current Anthropology* 28, 3 (June 1987): 251–281.

——. *The Gender of the Gift: Problems with Women and Problems with Society in Melanesia*. Berkeley: University of California Press, 1988.

Stree Shakti Sanghatana. *"We were making history . . .": Life Stories of women in the Telangana People's Struggle*. New Delhi: Kali for Women Press, 1989.

Stricker, Meredith. "Island." In *Looking for Home: Women Writing About Exile*, eds. Deborah Keenan and Roseann Floyd, p. 273. Minneapolis: Milkweed Editions, 1990.

Takagi, Dana Y. *The Retreat from Race: Asian-American Admissions and Racial Politics*. New Brunswick, N.J.: Rutgers University Press, 1992.

Takaki, Ronald. *Strangers from a Different Shore: A History of Asian Americans*. Boston: Little, Brown and Company, 1989.

Taylor, Debbie, ed. *Women: A World Report*. London: Methuen, 1985.

Tharu, Susie. "Tracing Savitri's Pedigree: Victorian Racism and the Image of Women in Indo-Anglian Literature." In *Recasting Women: Essays in*

Colonial History, eds. Kumkum Sangari and Sudesh Vaid, pp. 254–268. New Delhi: Kali for Women Press, 1989.

Tharu, Susie, and Lalita K., eds. *Women Writing in India: 600 B.C. to the Present*, Volume I: 600 B.C. to the Early Twentieth Century. New York: Feminist Press, 1991. Volume II: The Twentieth Century. New York: Feminist Press, 1993.

Tharu, Susie, and Tejaswini Niranjana. "Problems for a Contemporary Theory of Gender." *Social Scientist* 22, 3–4 (March–April 1994): 93–117.

Thurston, Edgar. *Castes and Tribes of Southern India.* 7 volumes. Madras: Madras Government Press, 1906.

Trinh, Minh-ha T. "Difference: 'A Special Third World Women Issue.'" *Feminist Review* 25 (March 1987).

——. "Not You/Like You: Post-colonial Women and the Interlocking Questions of Identity and Difference." *Inscriptions: Feminism and the Critique of Colonial Discourse* 3/4 (1988): 71–77.

Viswanathan, Gauri. *Masks of Conquest: Literary Study and British Rule in India.* New York: Columbia University Press, 1989.

Visweswaran, Kamala. "Defining Feminist Ethnography." *Inscriptions, Feminism and the Critique of Colonial Discourse* 3/4 (1988): 27–44.

——. *Fictions of Feminist Ethnography.* Minneapolis: University of Minnesota Press, 1994.

Weed, Elizabeth, ed. *Coming to Terms: Feminism, Theory, Politics.* New York and London: Routledge, 1989.

Weiner, Annette B. "Oedipus and Ancestors." *American Ethnologist* 12, 4 (1985): 758–762.

West, Cornel. "The Dilemma of the Black Intellectual." *Cultural Critique* 1, 1 (1981): 109–124.

White, Deborah Gray. *Ar'n't I a Woman? Female Slaves in the Plantation South.* New York and London: W. W. Norton and Company, 1985.

White, Hayden. *Tropics of Discourse: Essays in Cultural Criticism.* Baltimore and London: Johns Hopkins University Press, 1987.

Williams, Patricia. "And We Are Not Married: A Journal of Musings Upon Legal Language and the Ideology of Style." In *Consequences of Theory*, eds. Jonathan Arac and Barbara Johnson, pp. 181–208. Baltimore: Johns Hopkins University Press, 1991.

——. *The Alchemy of Race and Rights: Diary of a Law Professor.* Harvard: Harvard University Press, 1991.

Wilson, Elizabeth. *Hidden Agendas.* London: Tavistock Publications, 1986.

Winant, Howard. "Postmodern Racial Politics in the United States: Difference and Inequality." *Socialist Review* 20, 1 (January–March 1990): 121–147.

Yamato, Gloria. "Something About the Subject Makes It Hard to Name." In *Making Face Making Soul: Haciendo Caras, Creative and Critical Perspectives by Women of Color*, ed. Gloria Anzaldúa, pp. 20–24. San Francisco: Aunt Lute Press, 1990.

Index

Abel, Elizabeth, 156n39, 166n59
Abu-Lughod, Lila, 111–112, 116–117, 119, 141, 169n4
Acchamamba, 134
Adivasis, 123
Africa, 84–85, 86–87; African philosophy, 162n28; African women, 86. *See also* Colonialism; Third world
African American, 21, 100; literary theory, 104, 106; women, 13, 21, 101. *See also* Black; Race; Women
Agarwal, Bina, 173n46
Alarcón, Norma, 71, 83
Allegory, 48, 50
Althusser, Louis, 32
Anderson, Benedict, 170n19
Anthropology: and colonialism, 112–117, 122, 123; and feminism, 2, 3, 23, 74–75, 111–121, 122–125, 128–143, 160n10, 170n24, 170n25; in India, 121–123, 124, 125, 143; institution of, 18, 111; as metaphor, 3, 128–143; and native informants, 2, 22–23, 26, 28, 110–121; and poststructuralism, 113–120
Anzaldúa, Gloria, 147n19
Appadurai, Arjun, 171n29
Appiah, Anthony, 99
Aristotle, 106
Articulation, 90, 163n38
Asad, Talal, 112
Asian American, 13, 14, 15, 167n71

Banerjee, Nirmala, 173n46
Barker, Patricia, 166n62
Behar, Ruth, 145n4
Benería, Lourdes, 165n57

Bentham, Jeremy, 147n15
Berger, Iris, 80
Bhabha, Homi K., 30–31, 66, 157n44
Bhadramahila, 9
Bhasin, Kamla, 173n46
Black, 101, 167n71, 167n76; community, 26, 100, 101, 106, 169n82; men, 26, 89, 101, 166n67. *See also* African American; Feminism; Race; Women
Bonacich, Edna, 148n23
Borthwick, Meredith, 198n10
Brahmin, 48, 51, 131. *See also* Caste
Brennan, Teresa, 158n55
Brittan, Arthur, 104
Bulkin, Elly, 149n36
Butler, Judith, 77–78, 82–83, 152n9; and psychoanalysis, 159n62

Capitalism, 7, 24, 81, 97
Carby, Hazel, 102
Caste, 10, 42, 51, 123, 129–131, 137–138, 140, 143, 156n38, 171n29, 174n73; backward, 137; lower, 141, 142; oppression, 138, 140; upper, 138, 141, 142
Caulfield, Mina Davis, 112
Census Report, 123
Chabram, Angie, 119–120, 142
Chakrabarty, Dipesh, 154n21, 168n78
Chatterjee, Partha, 9, 26, 146n10, 154n21, 169n8
Chaudhuri, B. B., 155n24
Cheng, Lucie, 148n23
Chicanas, 13, 119, 142, 167n71; Chicana/o studies, 119–120. *See also* Feminism; Race
Childers, Mary, 166n59

Text:	11/13.5 Caledonia
Display:	Caledonia
Composition:	Keystone Typesetting
Printing and binding:	BookCrafters